FAST COMPANY

60

FARRAR
STRAUS
GIROUX

FAST COMPANY

A MEMOIR OF LIFE, LOVE,

AND MOTORCYCLES IN ITALY

DAVID M. GROSS

FARRAR, STRAUS AND GIROUX --- NEW YORK

Farrar, Straus and Giroux
19 Union Square West, New York 10003

Distributed in Canada by Douglas & McIntyre Ltd.
Printed in the United States of America
First edition, 2007

Library of Congress Cataloging-in-Publication Data
Gross, David M., 1966–
    Fast Company : a memoir of life, love, and motorcycles in Italy /
David M. Gross.
        p.   cm.
    ISBN-13: 978-0-374-28133-5 (pbk. : alk. paper)
    ISBN-10: 0-374-28133-5 (pbk. : alk. paper)
    1. Bologna (Italy)—Social life and customs.   2. Motorcycles—Italy.
I. Title.

DG975.B6 G76 2007
338.7'62922750945—dc22

                                                    2006024540

Designed by Jonathan D. Lippincott

www.fsgbooks.com

1   2   3   4   5   6   7   8   9   10

What follows is a true story. In an effort to safeguard the privacy of certain individuals, I have changed names and, in some cases, disguised identifying characteristics.
                                                                    D.G.

FOR MY PARENTS

At worst, one is in motion; and at best,
Reaching no absolute, in which to rest,
One is always nearer by not keeping still.
—Thom Gunn

PART ONE

1

The porticoes march on like soldiers—columns of pale stone and red plaster over brick. The terrazzo rolls out for miles, a great expanse of sparkling sidewalk, rising and falling like swells in a rough sea. On the ground lie the patterns of antiquity: a Greek key motif in ochre, an intricate bargello of ebony. Overhead, fat angels and a playground Virgin soar—gilded, exalted—restored to polychromatic wonder. Walkers in the city don't much talk about the architectural details. What they care about are the shoes.

Stroll the arcades of the Piazza Maggiore and watch the fancy-dress ladies peering into windows, wearing stenciled ankle straps in bronze-patinated calf. The feet are animated! Shop the oval-shaped Piazza Cavour with the pretty girls in green lizard patchwork pumps. The heels are talking! The moody streets of via Zamboni like it darker: vamps in spike motorcycle boots with nickel-plated hardware that could shift gears at any moment. And stop to smoke a cigarette. Or drink a glass of wine. Soles tip. Soles tap. They shuffle against rough marble. They go clip-clop on smooth mosaic. Soles echo and boom—sound reverberating down the arcades—thundering their arrival in the center of town.

In the fall any businessman with *quattro soldi*—four lire to put together—kicks off the season by slipping into custom brogues with squared-off toes. Fine footwear isn't just a woman's game. Two-tone man leather—toffee and cream, with contrasting stitching—looks right against faded walls. Shoes follow seasons and they're also coordinated with activities. There are morning cappuccino shoes. There are afternoon loafers to buy groceries. Cesare Paciotti makes designer trainers just to work out in at the gym. And because Bologna is a medieval stage set of a town, complete with ancient gates and battle ramparts, doing the *passeggiata*, or stroll, *in centro*, can make you feel like a conqueror—if you're wearing the right footgear.

If it is spring in Riccione, the style capital of the *riviera romagnola* and the Hamptons of Greater Bologna, then we are talking about sandals. But not the crystal-beaded sandals that say skipping across beach sands and flirting with boys. No. Those are saved for August, when feet are tanned, toes are buffed smooth, and a single cord of sparkling leather—on the right *figa*—can make a man's heart leap with desire.

In early May *ragazzi* want something simple. Here is a *figata*—a beautiful thing—that stops traffic: a suede bikini in fringe and feathers. And what is a *figa*, you ask, if you don't speak Italian or haven't spent the better part of a decade, as I have, watching men watching women negotiate cobblestones or race mint green Vespas in short skirts and heels while boys hiss *"fiii . . ."* through their teeth? It's a matter of genitalia. The masculine version of the word, *figo*, is also used and is just as misleading. For what is macho about the breed of musclemen who, at least at the beach club where I go, get their eyebrows waxed as well as their bikini lines?

Long ago, figo and its female equivalent, figa, lost their literal meanings: penis and vagina, respectively. Today they stand for virtually anything that is hip or desirable. A fire-engine-red superbike, made by the company that I help run, is figo. So is a silver Ferrari 360 Modena. Sprinkling your conversation with choice dialect, like *socc'mel*, "blow me" in Bolognese, is considered very cool, very *figo* to the people in this part of the world. The funny thing about *figa*, and the Italian male's obsession with it, is that the term isn't considered vulgar except when hurled at a statuesque beauty who refuses to acknowledge the chorus of compliments that comes her way while wandering the water's edge in a g-string. *"Figa di legno,"* an Italian will mutter under his breath, "wooden pussy," as if the frustrated insult had the power to ignite a failed flirtation into the blaze of erotic possibility.

On the first Saturday of the summer, I am decompressing with a flute of *prosecco* and my best friend, Daniele, a pure-blooded Bolognese with a foot fetish. This isn't Capri, where the fancy Americans congregate. It's not the *costa azzurra*, where the Milanese fashion crowd flocks. This is Italy's eastern, Adriatic coast—a Fellini-esque circus of trendy exaggeration and trashy excess—where *bolognesi* go to embrace modernity without the weight of monuments or masterpieces. On my feet are ninety-nine-cent flip-flops. I'm not obliged to follow *all* of the rules. I'm American.

A serious figa with sky-high Sergio Rossi sandals begins her slow, sensual *giro* from the bar toward the water. She is not made of wood. Her summer cashmere pareo comes on and off again, exposing large natural breasts with dark erect nipples. *"Wow!"* She couldn't be more perfect! Her pareo doubles as a head wrap, halter, and finally a sarong. The garment is flipped and unfurled in a choreographed ballet that moves from chaise to cabana before an admiring audience of beach cognoscenti.

All eyes, men's, women's, and the appraising gaze of Daniele, who knows the product range of Sergio Rossi the way a connoisseur knows dry, dramatic Barbaresco, are upon her. The particular sandal in question, with leather laces that wind halfway to the knee and cork platform heels, is referred to here as *alla schiava*. "I'm a slave to Rossi!" he declares, breathless, "Sai . . ."

"They cost 425 euro for the pair on via Ceccarini," I remind him. "We saw them yesterday."

"For me it's always like the first time," he says dreamily, watching her work the boardwalk. "He is a *master*."

"The man does seem to know what to do with feet," I answer, putting down my *Herald Tribune* for just a second.

"I hope he doesn't ruin it!" pronounces Daniele, suddenly indignant. He is referring to my lunch last week with the CEO of Gucci, who told me he was going to buy the Bologna-based company.

"Have you seen the toes?" I ask.

"Like well-manicured rosebuds."

One has to admire the high sandal in summer. It stretches the calf. Elongates the line of the leg. Gets a pretty girl around town and aficionados—like Daniele—*aroused*. At the beach, Italian men also appreciate the color white and they know a good tan when they see one. The paradox of the very darkest, all-over suntan on the whitest woman creates the perfect backdrop for designer *pelle*—skin longing for skin. The mix is a combustible hormonal cocktail, a shot of summer Viagra for young Italians who can tell the difference between real crocodile and pressed leather at five hundred paces.

A new girl walks by, who we think is our housemate, Nicoletta, incognito. Dark as chocolate, thin as an After-Eight dinner mint, she slides rhinestone-encrusted sunglasses down her nose and looks out at the sea of sleek, oiled, leering *ragazzini*. If you were with us at the beach that summer, you'd know the model name of the wraparound aviators rimmed in brushed gold that I'm talking about ("Dior Flash"). Every girl had them—even a barmaid like Nicoletta.

Nearby, each pyrotechnic gesture is watched, evaluated, priced in the *bagni*—beach clubs with evocative names of mythical personae like Ettore and various states of desire: Paradise, Ecstasy, Hedonism. These beach clubs, even the simple ones like Luca, are never referred to by their names, but rather by their numbers. To further complicate matters, each *bagno* has its own restaurant, which has yet another name, and usually a different owner. You eat skewers of fresh local shrimp or calamari and delicate tortilla-like *piadine* "*da Nello*" or "*da Carlo*" . . . at Nicky's, at Charlie's. The menus are standard. The addition of cherry tomatoes to a plate of spaghetti with baby clams makes for news.

On Nicoletta's feet is something truly noteworthy: a pair of the latest Gucci slides, box-fresh, with the gold horse bits and house pattern. "*Minchia!*" Daniele has no idea where she found the money to buy them.

2

When I came to Italy in the mid-1990s I knew nothing about shoes. I moved here to escape the consequences of the last American economic boom, which in my case meant endless nights and most weekends at a Wall Street law firm churning out vast amounts of paper to finance corporate mergers and acquisitions. I fled the Greatest City in the World—at a time when the Dow Jones Industrial Average hovered near 6,500, when investors were rushing into mutual funds in a great stampede of available capital, and a loft apartment in Tribeca could still be had for less than a million dollars. I didn't feel the opportunity of a boom economy, though. The city seemed small to me—and suffocating. My life was a prison of routine: black coffee and a bagel, the number 6 train to Grand Central, skipping lunch for the treadmill at the gym, document review late, late into the night. Consolation was deciding where to order out—sushi from Sushisay or strip sirloin from Sparks—compliments of the client.

After dinner, I would retreat in a Carmel "limousine," racing down Second Avenue, watching the chain stores encroach on my neighborhood, the East Village, once the refuge of punks and skateboarders, now home to K-Mart. The remaining artists and rebels, skulking around the Cube, seemed to accept their anachronism more easily than I, content to become extras in a film, providing color for a cinematographer's frame—the acid green of a Mohawk, the pallor of blue Goth skin.

I lived at One Astor Place, a grand address—in reality just a Quonset hut of prefabricated concrete panels erected on the roof of a building gut-renovated in the 1970s. The place had once been a sweatshop. Occasionally, old horn buttons popped up from the baseboards, skittering across the floor like mice, to wake me up in the middle of the night. Disoriented, I would sink back into office-induced exhaustion, dreading morning. My particular unit had previously been home to Evan Dando, lead singer of The Lemonheads—a band still remembered by women of a certain age. Dando had once been something of a sex symbol, the definition of pretty-boy guitar. Love letters in fancifully colored inks arrived occasionally at my doorstep. To gain some privacy, the singer had blackened out the windows of the apartment with photographic film that my roommate (another lawyer) and I spent hours scratching off. But since we spent most of our waking hours at the firm—Latin American telecommunications IPOs were the craze—our efforts at making light mattered little.

Billable hours were what counted. Young associates competed to see how many they could amass. For about a year it was tolerable. My client, a money center bank, wanted due diligence done in exotic places like Santiago de Chile. I charged them for travel time and racked up American Express air miles, traveling all over South America largely unsupervised. Then I found out why. The deals were unsecured. No collateral backed the credit. If a company reneged on its loans, the bank had no recourse to any asset. The bank called it loss lending—"building a brand" in Latin America. The bankers were even younger than I—mostly dumb frat boys right out of college. We lawyers did the work. They drank the beer. It was a decent gig that lasted until the Mexican peso crisis, which dried up deals south of the border and forced me to reinvent my practice. ·

My first Italian project was the initial public offering of one of the great Italian retail banks; I was representing the American underwriter. I was so junior on the transaction that all I remember was couriering documents back and forth between New York and Milan—and having a suit made to measure at Davide Cenci on via Manzoni. I organized my trips to Europe based on the fitting schedule of the master tailor, Giuseppe. I wanted something as far away from a Brooks Brothers' sack as possible. Giuseppe directed me to a double-breasted number—in iridescent olive—with two racy back vents, slash pockets, and multiple pleats. When I got back to New York my senior partner—his name was Hopewell Hyatt (no relation to the hotel chain, nothing hopeful about him)—took one look at the flashy tropical wool and my time sheets and wrinkled his fine aquiline nose. The man was from Georgia and had gone to a second-rate law school. He had nothing to wrinkle about.

I caught his bulbous blue eyes peering through the steam at the New York Health & Racquet Club on Fifty-sixth Street one lazy afternoon, scrutinizing my navel, which at the time was pierced with a tiger's eye that my friend Amir had given me as a twenty-sixth birthday present. I was naked. He was naked. Thankfully, we didn't exchange a single word or gesture. I was hoping he hadn't recognized me. But the next morning, when I arrived at my desk, I glanced over at my phone and—dread, *loathing*—his name was flashing insistently on the screen. "Hyatt!" "Hyatt!" in bright green LED. I picked up the receiver. Did I have a moment to come to his office, he asked sweetly. I couldn't refuse.

"The firm has decided," he drawled, sucking on his sticky mustache, "that you, Mr. *Gross*, had better start investing more time in your career." I considered the prim decor of his unimaginatively appointed partner's suite—repro Chippendale furniture, framed horse prints on the wall, Persian carpet—and knew that

European trips were a thing of the past. Layovers in Miami Beach on the way back from Montevideo were history. "The firm is going to challenge you like you've never been challenged." He never spoke in the first person. No one did at Powers, Plimpton and Profitt. The *firm* considered. The *firm* recommended. *They*— not *he*—had now decided to stick me with a real project, an important deal that would either make or break my career: the merger of two pharmaceutical giants. "It isn't the glamorous part," he warned, using his poor-wasp-stuck-in-the-jelly-jar accent, "the negotiation of the purchase and sale." My eyes had glazed over, waiting for the final blow. "It's the credit agreement."

Translation: the mind-numbing task of putting together a multibillion-dollar term loan and revolving credit—the largest ever at the time—and the syndicating out of that megaborrowing to a consortium of regional banks, terrified that if they didn't pony up the bucks without asking too many questions or demanding revisions, they'd be frozen out of future business by the powerful institution leading the deal.

"And in case you don't realize it," Hopewell was now lecturing, tapping his Montblanc pen on a desktop littered with Lucite deal toys representing billions in previously transacted paydays, "the bank is the firm's bread-and-butter client. Don't fuck it up." His syrupy Southern accent had plain done up and disappeared.

It was the fall of 1996. Leaves were swirling gold on the streets of Manhattan. The firm was raking in "the big bucks" from the merger of the drug companies. I needed Zoloft. Round-the-clock revisions to a document fast becoming the size of a phone book were killing my spirit. Depressed, I dreamed of escape— anywhere, anyhow—to walk out of those bronze revolving doors and never return, leaving all of those pages of documents unrevised, in need of blacklining, stacked high in some paralegal's cubicle. I pressed my face flat against the corporate glass, looking out over a midtown deserted on a Saturday. "God, get me out of here." A gust of Atlantic wind sent flowering pear and plane leaves from the oasis at Bryant Park toward Lexington. It was a sign. When I was lucky, an updraft would carry nature's castaways up the side of the building, and for a moment the colors of fall would hang dreamily in the air, calling cards to a great adventure. No matter how long I looked though, those autumn leaves never reached my perch on the twenty-third floor.

People at the law firm talked about how they hated the work but loved the people. That was the mantra: "Love the people." I knew better. There would be no hope or love among lawyers. Hopewell guaranteed that. The phone rang. A friend from Harvard, an oversized investment banker at a Texas-based buyout shop, was calling on an early-model global satellite phone from Mexico. Did I have a minute to talk? Most of what we did was talk—about entrepreneurial ventures, about billionaire corporate raiders on Wall Street. Once, years ago, we had actually *done* something, founding an indie label—Warped Records—that specialized in obscure garage bands from Boston. We pressed five thousand copies of our first single—it just happened to be his sister's grunge band—and spent two weeks hawking "Incinerator" at local rock dives before we realized that there were no big bucks in vinyl and found proper corporate jobs.

"You're not going to believe this," his voice now crackled over the phone, worlds away. "I think my two-wheel deal is actually going to close." Months earlier, he had begun work on a real longshot of a transaction—a troubled Italian motorcycle company that was looking for financing. Would his fund be interested in making a loan? Through a series of intermediaries, he said that his firm didn't make loans, but that they would consider buying the company outright. After months of tortuous negotiations with the family that owned the company, its banks, its lawyers, and even its spiritual advisers, the deal was almost ready to sign. Now, he wanted me to meet the future CEO and help him turn around the legendary manufacturer. "Are you ready to fly without a parachute?" I took a big gulp.

3

I met my future boss in the marble lobby of the Lipstick Building—"anything but Italian food," he had requested—and as we shook hands on the way to Vong, he began complaining about his arch nemeses, bankers. "I just can't *stand* asking them for money," he said. "It makes me feel like a circus bear dancing for its dinner. You're not a banker are you?"

"No," I said, "a corporate lawyer."

"Even worse. You guys just eat cash." He had just flown in from a meeting in Dallas where he had raised the last of the financing needed to restart motorcycle production and was dressed in a blue serge suit for the occasion. "Do you mind if I sit with my back to the wall?" He had already unbuttoned his collar and removed his tie by the time we reached the table. "Otherwise I just don't feel comfortable." I gave him the banquette seat—and a dead-on view of a platinum-haired Cher, planning her latest comeback. Now, with his rear covered, he was happy.

"Max"—he never went by his real name, Massimo—was a tall man in his forties, fattish, still boyish, brilliant in his ability to suss out a situation, to size up any person. With the diva in earshot and a plate loaded with crunchy noodles to dip in peanut sauce, he began to talk—in English. (His wife was Canadian and he was proud of his subtle command of the idiom.) About his upbringing in a rich suburb of Milan where people lived in self-imposed poverty—sitting around in their underwear, eating boiled rice—even though they owned factories and ornate villas in Como. About relatives who lied about Caribbean cruises when all they really did was slip across the border and go discount shopping in Switzerland.

Every so often, his hands would rise up from the table, involuntarily taking flight, to punctuate a salient point. The gesture came naturally—he was, after all, Italian. But every time he shot those eagles down. An international businessman who worked for institutional investors, Max didn't want to be perceived as too colorful, too Latin. He forced himself to communicate with language, not hand gestures.

"The lake must be gorgeous," I said, trying to break into the conversation.

"I prefer the view from my house on Chestnut Hill."

Shifting gears, I asked about his experience as a turnaround manager. "What's the key to success?"

"There are no secrets," Max said, pouring a glass of water, "it's always touch and go." He took a sip—he rarely drank wine—warming to the old war story, the sound of his own voice, and a listener with fresh ears. "I once did a project for a glass factory—legendary Murano name, product in museums. The only problem was they weren't making any money." He stole a glance at Cher to see if she was listening. She wasn't. "By the way, consultants *only* work for companies that lose money. No one pays you for advice on how to spend profits." I was entranced by his utter frankness, his cynical wit. "Speaking of money, I was doing consulting for the city of Venice . . . Do you love Venice?"

I nodded. "Who doesn't? It's a dream."

"Millions of Chinese think so too. The problem with Venice is that everyone wants to go but there's nowhere to stay. So they walk around Piazza San Marco, buy an ice cream cone, and go home. The city doesn't get much out of it." The waiter took our order: Thai beef salad and spicy tuna rolls. "As a consultant, I once commissioned a market study about the travel desires of the Chinese. Do you know the number one place they want to see?"

"Venice?" I ventured.

"So I said to the city commisioners, 'Forget about new hotels and all the expensive infrastructure for the Chinese tourists of the future. We're *Italian*! We'll never get it right anyway. Just put up a big gate and charge admission to the city.' "

"Like Vegas!"

"*David!*" he sounded shocked, almost disappointed in me, "I'm talking Disneyworld."

"And the glass blowers?" I asked, curious about their fate.

"Don't worry, they're still blowing."

"So you turned that company around, right?"

His eyes darted around the room looking for a place to land. He settled on me for just a moment. "Not exactly." He studied the dessert menu, then ordered for both of us. "The glass people were difficult," he said, in between spoonfuls of crème brûlée with coconut sorbet and the molten chocolate soufflé that was ostensibly mine. "We just didn't hit it off." He described weeks in a damp factory interrogating the master blower—about the pieces he made each day, the number he broke—desperately trying to figure out ways to boost productivity. "Now this craftsman isn't thinking about profitability. He's musing about eating a plate of linguine with baby clams or screwing his mistress on the Lido . . ."

"Or maybe even blowing the glass," I suggested.

"How the hell would I know?" He didn't appreciate a mid-story interruption. Not while he was on a roll. "Now, everything this guy does involves some special time-consuming technique: like dipping the blowpipe into a basin of molten color or breathing tiny bubbles between glass layers or grinding the surface to produce the right pattern of pitting." His green eyes glittered with each recollection. "Well, here I am, this number-crunching, chart-making consultant—trying my hardest—but the more I talk, the more pissed off the blower gets. 'Can't you cut any corners?' I prod him. 'Can't you possibly work faster?' Exasperated, he lowers his pipe and looks at me with a cold fish-eye. 'I can speed up the process any time I want,' he says. He takes the bowl he's working on—a complicated mosaic of individual discs fused into a singular form—and lets it drop to the floor. 'Where's your efficiency now, smart man?' he wonders over the sound of fine silicate carbon—ten thousand dollars' worth—shattering on cement. 'I guess I'll just have to start all over again.'

"Sometimes you just can't fix the business," the boss said conclusively, wiping the last of the chocolate sauce off my plate with an index finger. "It has to die on its own. But the secret usually lies in mixing the new and old. The team has to come together around the product. If that happens, it's *magic*."

I was spellbound.

He never wanted to know if I spoke Italian. "If you don't, you'll learn fast enough." He never asked me about my riding skills. "We have enough real bikers already." This was what was on his mind: "How many journalists do you know?"

"Most of them," I bragged, drunk on red wine and his not insubstantial charisma. (I had formerly been a reporter at a newsmagazine.)

"Good. The project requires lots of media."

I had one question: What would I actually do at the company?

"*Whatever you want*," he winked, "the factory is practically bankrupt. If they knew what they were doing they wouldn't need us. Now *would* they?" And without thinking much more, I signed up for six months in Bologna, trading wing tips for motorcycle boots. I departed not knowing much about the place, except that it was a left-leaning university town that had invented the luncheon meat that Americans refer to as "baloney" but was actually called mortadella.

Real mortadella hasn't been available in America for a generation, because the USDA prohibits the importation of pork products that have not been heated internally to 158 degrees Fahrenheit for at least thirty minutes to kill things like hoof-and-mouth disease. Hoofs and mouths are why my parents, intermittently observant Jews, never let me eat baloney in the first place. For them (my father's family owned supermarkets in the Bronx), baloney, in addition to not being kosher, was a food strictly reserved (along with peanut butter) for poor people. They prided themselves on eating first-cut brisket.

Mortadella, a guidebook said, far from being the pig of poverty, was the food of celebration in Bologna. It marked the moments of every day—shavings at breakfast, slices on sandwiches at lunch, cubes with a Negroni cocktail before dinner—and the high points of the life cycle: birthdays, weddings, wakes. Its origins went back to the Middle Ages and it took its name from the Bolognese monks who would mince pork in a *mortaio* (a giant mortar) with spices, adding pearly squares of *lardetti*, fat taken from the pig's throat or back, to enhance flavor. The porky mixture was then poached, cooled, stuffed into a casing, and allowed to age.

By the seventeenth century, mortadella from Bologna was traded extensively for silk, velvet, hemp, and linen. Two hundred years later, the English and the Americans were calling any type of pork sausage made in Bologna "bologna." If pig was scarce or too expensive, cow, horse, or even donkey meat was added to the mix. Bolognesi remain flexible to this day about the making and marketing of mortadella. Dozens of varieties are sold, leading to fantastic debates at deli counters as to which version is the most authentic. Black peppercorns? Studded with pistachios? Even offal can be added to the gelatinous stew: intestines, hearts, kidneys, and/or tongues. The line is thankfully drawn at spleen and liver, because they turn mortadella from its desired shade of pink to a muddy brown.

What was I expecting of the bolognesi? I had been told that their city was the only place in the Western world besides Havana where Che Guevara still ruled as a sex symbol, where Noam Chomsky reigned as a media personality, and where there was a street called Stalingrado and a piazza named Granma. The bolognesi were self-proclaimed lefties. They knew the words to the "Internazionale" by heart. Everything was done up in shades of *rosso*. The houses were glazed in red stucco. The rooftops were terra-cotta. The mayor was a Communist. When the setting sun cast copper shadows under the porticoes and the ancient walls of the city shimmered in fiery blazes of garnet and vermilion, you understood why Enzo Ferrari painted all of his sports cars red in the first place.

I thought "La Rossa" would be a quiet, intellectual town, far from the theatrical excesses of Rome, the fashion frenzy of Milan, and the American girls who study art history in Florence. Since the city was Marxist and, therefore, presumably unproductive, I imagined lazy hours drinking espresso, browsing a newspaper, deciphering thick novels by Umberto Eco, who taught semiotics at the local university (the oldest in Europe)—all of the things my frantic lawyer's life had denied me. I had no idea that I would be swapping my law grind for a set of social obligations every bit as grueling.

Before I left for Italy, I thought I had better learn to actually ride a motorcycle. I applied for a license at the Department of Motor Vehicles and took a written test. While waiting for the results, I overheard an administrator talking about a safety course given near Kennedy Airport by a man named, rather inauspiciously, Gasper Trama. She assured me he had a sterling reputation. There were two parts to the program, a classroom lecture about rules of the road and then a day of practice. A week later, I took the number 7 subway out to Woodhaven, Queens, to begin life all over again—this time as a biker.

I arrived at Trama's Auto School on Jamaica Avenue and sat down in a drab classroom filled with unshaven guys in concert T-shirts, a sprinkling of (presumably) Wall Street bankers with fat bonuses to spend, and the odd female cop, intimidating in black leather and jack boots. Everyone was wearing some element of biker gear—a logoed cap from a gas station, a bandana—in antic-ipation of becoming the real thing. Each had an attitude. While we were waiting for the master of ceremonies to arrive, a middle-aged man with muscles entered the room. He took off his leather jacket—a supple designer model—and walked up to the lectern. "There are . . . *only* . . . two types of motorcyclists," he blew like a big band trumpeter, puffing out an impressive physique. "Those

. . . who have *been down* . . . ," he paused for a moment, surveying students who were now hanging on his every syncopated word, "and those . . . who are *going down!*"

It was a dramatic line, perfect in pitch, delivered during his many years of teaching actors—Alan Alda, Liam Neeson, Scott Baio, and Matthew Broderick (to name just a few)—how to ride. "That is *fact!*" He shrugged his shoulders, suddenly deflated, as if to say, "What else can I say?" and then sat down. We had arrived at the crux of the matter.

A transit cop trembled, breaking the silence with "Is there anything we can do to be safe?" Trama came alive. Jumping up from his folding chair, he moved around the classroom like a cat sprung from a cage. "Survival is possible!" He leaped onto a desk. A number of steps, ruthlessly followed, could reduce the risk of injury. Rule number one. He wrote it on the blackboard for emphasis: *Always ride with a full-face helmet!* "Otherwise, when you crash, you may survive, but you won't be chewing bubble gum." And body protection. "Wear *leathers!* Not denim, which just gets caught up in the debris on the road." Never drink and drive. "If you're caught drunk and not wearing protection, emergency room nurses will make mincemeat of you." I thought of my sister, a gentle physician's assistant. He talked of legions of Nurse Ratcheds with scrub brushes and squirt bottles of alcohol—itching to scrape road rash from wounds without anesthesia. Learn the rules of the road. "Know that most accidents happen just a few miles from your house." And finally, "Take a safety course once in a while to brush up on your riding skills. Just being here enhances your mathematical odds of survival." His eyes were flashing, searching our damned faces. Who would live? Who would die? Who would finish life as a donor-cycle? He made sure that we could read his mind.

The next day, petrified, we went riding. There were no pretty fields of flowers to look at, no panoramic vistas to embrace. Dressed like warriors—first time in boots and leather armor—we went off to battle, to ride a square mile of abandoned asphalt near Kennedy Airport on a cold but sunny day in late November. Low-flying planes soared overhead, sending plumes of smoke in limpid skies. Engine thunder—every ten minutes like clockwork—drowned out words. I was riding a tiny Honda Nighthawk, a 250cc trainer machine—magenta, the color of blood. Looking back on it now, that trusty little bike was oh so easy to ride, so forgiving. But I was nervous as hell that first day, praying that I just wouldn't fall.

Orange cones had been set up in the parking lot in rows. Swerving around them, we learned how to turn, how to shift, how to stabilize the bike at low speeds by working the throttle. Then we tested stopping, forcing the bike into full skid, locking front and back drum brakes simultaneously—controlling the bike's trajectory with just handlebars and body weight. One of the Wall Street guys, an ex–managing director, recently fired from his job, was cursing. He couldn't understand the basic principle of counter-steering: the application of pressure by either pushing or pulling the handlebars, causing the bike to change direction. Whenever he stared at the handlebars—figuring out whether he had to push right on the bars to go left or push left to go right—he was mesmerized by the pavement just a few feet below. "Don't look down!" the female instructor yelled at him through a plastic megaphone. "Look down, go down!" The guy crashed every time.

My riding was unsteady but upright. I kept my eyes high on the horizon, determined to avoid the demons of asphalt. Head up—fresh and alert—I looked through the cones in their soldierly lineup toward the Bay of Jamaica, where seagulls were swooping and soaring. Above them, a British Airways Concorde was leaving its holding pattern, preparing for landing. Wheels unfolded from a hatch in its underbelly, and guided by the blue lights on the runway, the supersonic jet touched down, first on its haunches, rear wheels spinning and smoking, absorbing impact, then easing over on its nose cone. The elegant plane glided into the gate without a tow.

Less gracefully, I weaved in and out of the cones. The instructor, an Italian-American firefighter from the Bronx, waved me on. I had passed the test, knocking over just one pylon. "Thank you! Thank you! My flight to Bologna is next week," I gushed. "If you ever want to buy an Italian sport bike, look me up!"

She asked just one thing in return: "Make sure you support women riders in your new job. It's not all dykes on bikes, ya know."

As soon as my license arrived, I called the local dealer in Manhattan to arrange a test ride. With an icy wind whipping off the river, I walked into the dealership on Forty-second Street and Eleventh Avenue and watched as two salesmen carried out the last Softail, bedecked in so much custom chrome and black-fringed leather, I thought of pallbearers carrying the Don in the funeral scene that opens Scorsese's *Mean Streets*. Eric, the owner of the dealership, had heard I was coming. Out went the custom Harleys and used Jap bikes! Away with the inexpensive Triumph Speed Triples that made up the bulk of his business! What was left was Italian, which meant just a few machines, because our own production had skidded to a virtual halt. A bright red race bike sat on a platform. In the corner of the shop, there was an exotic Bimota Tesi 1D and some leftover Moto Guzzi Californias in burgundy and black.

"Pardon us, we were just, uh, cleaning up a bit," said a bearded Eric, showing a set of bright but crooked teeth. "The new season and all." (Moving out competitor bikes was a stunt he would deploy often in the years ahead—in fact anytime one of our executives paid him a visit.) He shook hands with me in the hip-hop manner, then gave me a "man hug"—knocking my chest with his shoulders. Now, he dragged me over to the glassed-in workshop where mechanics were working. There, right in front of me, freshly polished—for Eric wanted to make a bella figura in front of a future manager—was the Beast itself.

Just two wheels, a silver-painted fuel tank, a trellis frame cradling an exposed engine, and a big round headlight, the Beast was a brute of a motorcycle—as unfinished as it was done. Its allure was immediate—seeming to preexist in my imagination— two wheels of desire that any boy would *die* to throw his leg over and *ride*. On the road! In the open air! More than a vehicle, the Beast was like a character in an adventure tale—not the hero, the scoundrel. A cult sensation from the moment it was launched, the bike had invented a new niche in motorcycling: the "naked."

For a bike that started a revolution—most motorcycles back in the day were fully faired, that is, their engines were clothed in fiberglass—the Beast had been a parts-bin job. I learned this later. Its designer, a South American of Italian origin, took a steel frame from an existing race bike, a fork from the Japanese Showa catalog, and a shock absorber by Boge. Into this chassis, he dropped a 900cc air-cooled powerplant, styled a simple gas tank, and bang: the Beast was born. Bike enthusiasts went nuts. "Finally, a designer who thought like they did, a man interested only in engine and chassis!" The style was no styling at all.

"May I ride the Beast?" I asked Eric, eager to try it.

"Only if you *can* . . ."

It is a thrilling thing to hear a V-twin engine roar for the first time. A mixture of fuel and air enters sealed twin cylinders. Pistons compress the gas. A spark ignites the volatile carbon cocktail and *boom*—combustion! Crankshafts convert energy into circularity. Gears turn. The sequence repeats itself: induction, compression, transferring power through the transmission to the rear wheel, producing speed and exhaust fumes.[1] In the case of our engine, "Cosmodromics" meant that the opening and closing of the engine valves—allowing the air-gas mixture to enter the cylinder head—was achieved mechanically, not with the conventional springs but with camshafts.

A small technical detail, not even patented, the Cosmo system was developed by a German automobile company in the 1930s. A Bolognese engineer applied it to motorcycle engines after the war when Italy supposedly "lacked the high-grade steel to make springs." That, at any rate, was the story we told. True or not, the result was pure engine music. Not the *whee-whee* of Japanese crotch rockets, not the *potato-potato* of Harley relics, but a deeply satisfying *vroom-vroom*—the heavy thunder of what a motorcycle is supposed to sound like and why man is attracted to motors in the first place. Engines shake your bones. Motors rattle your brain. They transmit not the sense of power, but the raw thing itself—the low-down grunt and grumble of fire tamed to produce speed.

I threw a leg over the saddle, revved the engine, and, in a squeal of rubber on asphalt, took the Beast out for a spin. Eric followed. The first few blocks on the bike were all bucking and bronc-ing as I got acquainted with low-down Italian torque. Vibrations crept up and down my legs. I felt a not unpleasant buzzing in my groin, the warming of the tank against my balls. No longer trapped inside the safety glass of a Lincoln Town Car, buffeted by reams of legal documents, I saw the street from a different perspective. Fumes entered my lungs. Noise pounded in my ears. I felt alive. The colors of a great city became tangible: the neon glow of a lonely Irish bar, the silver sparkle of headlights on the Hudson. A taxicab drove right next to me bright and shining like a small yellow sun. I wanted to reach out and caress that cab, to touch it, to feel the liquid texture of its painted coat of arms, its proud fiery medallion.

Is it this irresistible impulse—this refusal to be bound by mortal limitations—that begs the biker to test fate? The urge to jump off a building after having climbed it! The desire to crash an exotic sportscar after having acquired it! The need to go ever faster, farther! I was flirting with danger. I knew it. My riding skills were not good enough to guarantee finding neutral at a stoplight (the gearbox was famously tricky), but already I was dreaming of chasing furies.

A black bike messenger weaved in and out of traffic, backpack slung over his shoulder, swaying in his slipstream. He pulled alongside me, wanting to race or just humiliate me? I couldn't say. How smooth he was, how sleek! How properly muscled, darting and rushing among vehicles much larger, much faster than his. He swiveled his head around as he passed me in a streak of purple dreads, and then just smiled, showing teeth and the tip of a pink tongue. What arrogance! What smug satisfaction! I knew the taunt well enough: *You* may be rich; *you* may have all the fancy toys in the world. But I am young! I am beautiful! Catch me if you can!

I charged ahead, accepting the dare. I had to give some chase. The engine was lively low down and my hand heavy on the handlebars. I dipped the clutch while opening the throttle and the front tire reared up off the pavement, spinning like a pinwheel at a country fair. It was on this contested piece of pockmarked asphalt, bordered on one side by a dark churning river and on the other by seedy hotels with hourly rates, that I popped my first wheelie. Indifferent taxicabs looked on, hunting customers. Out on the river, tugboats blinked like Christmas lights, inching in the direction of the bridge linking the city to the Palisades. It wasn't one of the long, slow wheelies for which the Beast is admired—"easier to lay than Polish girls."[2] It was more like a fluke, a flounder—an immature cowboy bested by his bronco.

Eric pulled over at the Cupcake Café on Ninth Avenue and Thirty-ninth Street. I struggled out of my gear, ordered a cupcake with iced flowers, then thought better of it. "On second thought, just gimme a doughnut." Ever the gentleman, Eric never once mentioned how close I had been to disaster. It was just backslaps and raunchy jokes. He pretended that I knew what I was doing—"Riding the Beast is *pussy* business"—even though he had to show me where the electric starter was and how to work the choke when we took off again.

The transformation had begun. The David in me—that soft, sensitive person—began to recede. I thought about it over the cup of coffee. How many Davids were there in New York? How many striving lawyers? Doctors? Accountants? In my "tracked" high school class there were five Davids alone. I was referred to as "David Two." There were David Goldbergs, David Steinbergs, David Levines (all sons of a Hebrew king), and also David Orlandos and David Russos (heirs to a great Renaissance sculpture). They were all *good* boys. In Manhattan, the name "David Gross" placed me squarely in time and space: Ivy League, white-shoe lawyer, suburbanite gone city, a young man in his mid-twenties trapped in a corporate job, desperately not wanting to be a tool. *"Davide!"* the Italian biker would have no such associations.

How do fantasies form? Where does a little boy get the idea of becoming a fireman, a policeman, or a cowboy? As a teenager I fooled around on stolen dirt bikes, secretly, in the abandoned drainage sumps and decommissioned schoolyards of Long Island. But I never became a *rider*. We did not have bikers in my North Shore neighborhood. We did not discuss cars, let alone super-bikes, while I was growing up. My parents did not know about torque ratios or tire widths, nor did they wait with bated breath for the latest model with more horsepower and a slipper clutch. My father is a graphic designer, my mother a self-styled phobic turned group therapist. We never woke up at God's hour to haul ass in a camper hooked to a flatbed rig just to see some cracker-jack put a 250cc rice burner through its paces on a racetrack in the middle of nowhere.

The vision stuck in my imagination though—images looping

on a silver screen of consciousness. Of adolescent knights in armor, of rebel bikers riding custom chrome, of intrepid explorers carving trails deep into woods moonlit with Mohicans. I remember dreaming about Indians. Squeezing through a trap door under my mattress, climbing down vines that crept up the faux columns of our imposing new colonial. Brushing my face with war paint, adorning my hair with a clutch of bright feathers, and slipping into the birch canoe that was waiting to whisk me silently away. Away to adventure! Away to a secret world of boys! And in that recurring dreamscape, I paddled across the Sound to meet up with warriors on other shores, the heroic place of deeds.

I decided then and there on Eleventh Avenue: I would become a boy racer. Clad in a multicolored leather suit with well-worn knee pucks, willing and able to scrape asphalt. I would become a modern centurion, Kevlar-reinforced, free to explore roads—black ribbons of satin tarmac, cobblestone paths fit only for a mule, streets that were sandy, soft, or eroding away at the edges—brave enough to negotiate mechanical risk and not just the finer points of a bank credit agreement.

Eric had to return to work for a couple of hours and sell some bikes. "Practice!" he told me. "Every day till you get on that plane. Till your fingers are numb! The West Side Highway will be your training wheels." In those days it was still an edgy, off-limits place, where the streets ran red from actual meatpacking—the carving and chopping of steaks and chops from Western slaughterhouses—and the nightlife was transgressive. Streetwalkers were not Jeffrey's shoppers back then, but professional dominatrixes, trannie hookers, and leathermen who haunted The Vault and The Lure, places whose very names sent shivers of pleasure and shame through the bodies of patrons.

"Meet me at Hogs N Heifers after closing time," said Eric before barreling off, Chinese pigtail flying in the wild. And three hours later, hands buzzing from miles of clutch work on cobblestone, we drank Maker's Mark on the rocks, pounded beers, and watched as impossibly tall, big-titted girls—dressed in little more than heels and g-strings—bumped and grinded above our heads, serving drinks to favorite patrons like Eric, whose tongue was now hanging out like a dog's.

The first time I saw the factory was from the air. I was flying Lufthansa to Bologna via Frankfurt when, while in the middle of eating my fish ball, the pilot announced that, in a few moments, on the right side of the plane, we would be seeing "the monarch of mountains," Mont Blanc, five thousand feet below us. I looked out my window. The great crag was covered in snow pack, a stole of cloud draped around its summit. Flying southeast, we were now entering Italian airspace. Below was the glorious green Valle d'Aosta, famous for its mineral waters, lush river valleys, and crenellated mountain peaks. Beginning our descent, we flew across the Piedmont and into the industrial heart of northern Italy. Ten minutes later, we were hovering over the Pianura Padana, the flat checkerboard of rich farmland that stretches south and east from Milan to Bologna and grows the bulk of the country's produce, waiting for air traffic control approval to land.

A campanile rose in the hazy sky to define a square mile of civilization. Power lines limned the frank horizontality of the plains. The last thing I saw before passing through a cloudbank was a white factory built in the functionalist style with great clerestory windows like curved sails at sea. Below the clouds, the landscape darkened considerably. Fog, thick as a down coat, was rolling down from the hills to wrap farmhouses in smokiness.

The airport of Guglielmo Marconi, lit by floodlamps, came into misty orange view. Beyond was the smudge of hills, then the Apennines rising in the east, and farther yet, out of sight, the Mediterranean. It all seemed quite tranquil from the air.

With no bags to claim—I had brought nothing but a backpack from New York—I hailed a cab that took me racing along Via Emilia, the old Roman road. Choking streets crammed with scooters and diesel smoke, the G. Fabbri distillery that made sour cherries in syrup, the bridge across the green ribbon of still water called the Reno—those first images still remain fresh in memory as if I were seeing them for the first time. In minutes I was approaching Borgo Panigale, a small suburb on the outskirts of town, lost in the gray fog that is called *nebbia*.

The factory occupies a full city block on a triangular site. On the northwestern side of the property, adjoining the motorcycle test track, is a modern shopping center called the Centro Borgo. Fronting the Via Emilia is a local church parish, an excellent southern Italian restaurant called La Luna, and the Vivaldi Hotel, where I lived for those first few months in Bologna. Beyond are blocks and blocks of worker housing. The southern point of the property faces the hills, the mountains, and just to the east, the city itself, with its elegant miles of porticoed streets, its medieval Jewish ghetto, and its great piazzas and brick churches.

I checked in with the guard at the gatehouse, got a visitor pass, and began wandering the plant. Though hundreds of people had been furloughed during the company's long liquidity crisis, the place was buzzing again. Everywhere there were young workers: drinking coffee from the ubiquitous machines, eating *cornetti* at the bar, playing pinochle on folding tables—or just standing outside in the parking lot, smoking cigarettes in the cold. At the loading bays, workers were sorting components:

steel trellis frames and exhaust pipes. The factory was preparing to start manufacturing. New workers were learning assembly techniques from old hands on the line. They, like me, had been hired upon the closure of a deal that put the company squarely in American hands—able, with an infusion of fresh capital, to finally pay its bills.

I climbed the stairs to the executive offices and presented myself at reception. A bottle blonde with pinned sausage curls— she was the switchboard operator—showed me to what was to be my temporary office: a shoebox of a space with a view of San Luca, the basilica that looks over the city from the hills to the west. I sat down among the sacks of mail and began to unpack my books—titles about engines, about racing—that I had bought at Rizzoli in New York just days before. I read the words of Filippo Tommaso Marinetti, the poet who invented Futurism at the dawn of the twentieth century with a strident manifesto in the Paris newspaper *Le Figaro*. He wrote that the Italian love for engines was visible, "flaming on the cheeks of mechanics scorched and smeared with coal." Nearly one hundred years later, at a nearly bankrupt company, that passion for speed and motors smoldered. I could feel it everywhere.

A tiny ferret of a man popped his head in. I had never seen someone with such dark olive skin and pomaded hair the color of a Tahitian pearl. He took one look at me, his yellow eyes jumping up and down in surprise, and said in broken English, "Socc'mel! You're the American here to save us!" And then he disappeared. I couldn't tell if he was joking or afraid of me, but he ran off before I could ask any questions. It turned out that he was the postman and this was his office. Since no formal greetings were forthcoming, I decided to introduce myself around.

I wandered down the linoleum-tiled hallways—the real stuff, made with plant resin and marble dust—hoping to find the boss's office, when I bumped into a bearlike man wearing deck shoes and dark aviators. It was the chief executive himself, almost unrecognizable from the Vong dinner, now in Gap clothes and floppy hair. A phalanx of anxious subordinates trailed him, vying for attention. He was listening simultaneously to changes in his travel itinerary, chatting on multiple cell phones, *and* rushing to catch the last flight out to London. He was at the peak of pleasure. "Hey, wanna go for a ride sometime?" I asked, reaching out to shake Max's meaty hand.

"We'll talk motorcycles when I get back," he said when he saw me. "Enjoy the chaos!"

"Twenty minutes till boarding," a pink whippet of a girl announced. It was his English secretary, Elizabeth, daughter of an ex–colonial official just out of Hong Kong. She handed him tickets and promptly got down on her hands and knees.

"I just wanted to ask him a few questions before he leaves," I tried.

"Get in line, sweetie, so does everybody." She wrestled his luggage to the ground, using the full force of her thinness to shut it. "There!" she said triumphantly. "Now you're good to go."

But he wasn't biting. He was delaying his departure to the last possible minute, playing beat-the-clock with the boarding time. The man lived to business-travel. He *hated* wasting time at the airport. I got a first taste of his penchant when he had me accompany him to JFK after our dinner in New York— ostensibly to continue talking about the turnaround. Instead he spent most of the ride bragging about how he actually *liked* being late. "Efficiency," he yelled over his shoulder, guards whisking him through the security check, "is never wasting a moment!"

Like many executives of his ilk, he found tranquillity mostly above thirty thousand feet. Coddled by flight attendants armed with boxes of chocolate and fluffy blankets, he passed the hours blissfully, memorizing entire route systems and studying competing frequent flyer programs in exhaustive detail. In a personal leather log (kept just for this purpose), he recorded each plane's carrier number for future reference.

During moments of extreme stress on the ground—as I would soon discover—too many rival appointments in places such as Tokyo or San Francisco, he would retreat to his office and take a secret file down from the shelf. Oh, the convenience of not waiting for an "equipment change" in Frankfurt! Ah, the thrills of watching a big city grow small from an oversized picture window! The only perk that interested this turnaround king was a corporate jet. But no matter how many times he crunched the numbers—buying, leasing, even with the advent of fractional ownership—a Gulfstream 4 just didn't make economic sense. Elizabeth lorded it over him: "There are two options here: fly commercial or get more successful."

Now she was getting increasingly anxious about his impending departure. "I used to consult for a brassiere company in Boston," he mused, considering her hardening nipples beneath the thin layer of lilac cashmere. "The psychographic marketing was so accurate I could just look at a girl and tell you what type of bra she was wearing."

"That won't work with me, love," she said, neutralizing him with a nanny tone. "I always go bare. Now, move along!"

"Have you met David?" he asked, changing tack. "I just rescued him from the legal profession—"

"I'm not calling security for a waiver this time!"

I shook her cold hand. It was bony and businesslike.

"He has a lot of buzz to create around here. Sign him up for back-to-back meetings."

She glared at me, then softened. "Cheers. If you buy me some Maltesers the next time you come through Heathrow, love, I'll be sure to put you into the agenda. *He*"—she pointed at the boss—"never brings me anything!" So she had some cockney charm after all.

The CEO opened a closet door, then flicked on a switch. A warehouse of broken-down race bikes came into dim view. "What do you think?" he asked, gnawing at a ragged cuticle.

"I think your car is waiting," she pressed, but he was ignoring her.

"David, I want to build the museum right here in the middle of the plant." The room smelled of must and motor oil, but nothing could kill his good mood. "Let's show our engineers that the future is in the brand, not technology!"

"I think you need to invest money in design." It was a rangy man with thick hair, blond as winter wheat. He was chewing gum, sucking a breath mint, gulping coffee from a cup, *and* talking. "Give me some proper resources and I'll done do you a show bike that'll make everyone's jaw drop!" The accent was heavy, Australian. "Man, look at that single-cylinder beauty in the corner there! All made by one person—the frame, the tank, the engine!"

"Build me something beautiful like that!" Max dared him.

"You can't do it anymore," the designer snorted.

"Why not? That's why I hired you."

"Today, it's all style by committee. One guy does the tank. Somebody else does the motor—then everyone from the technical director on down to his pet dog fights like hell to change the details." His mood had changed completely. He was now twitching as he talked, plucking at his overgrown eyebrows. "You can see the results for yourself. Most of it fucking sucks."

"Then make it better."

The designer looked around in disgust, boiling with anger and ambition. "*Right.* Like trying to turn an ugly bird into a supermodel. You can dye her hair, fix her nose, and buy the bitch the most expensive implants for Christmas, and still she'll look like a dog!" Our laughing didn't appease him. "Do you know that the best designer in the industry is a plumber?" He was addressing me directly. "*Do you?*" I shook my head, sheepishly. No, I didn't know that. "A fucking plumber! There's no respect for professionalism in this business—none at all!" And he stomped off.

The boss wasn't offended. Turmoil at the company was exactly what he wanted. "If Jacques can't build me something gorgeous, tell him I'm going to hire that fucking plumber!" He grabbed his flight bag. "What are you people waiting for?" he barked. "Call the architects! I want to see a feasibility study by the time I get back." His secretary looked at her watch. The flight was just about to board. She edged him into the hallway— *softly, softly, catchy monkey*—then down the stairs. "And by the way, lose the banker suit," he stage-whispered to me before slipping into the chauferred BMW station wagon. "You're better dressed than I am!" And he sped off into the fumes and fog of Bologna.

9

Everyone was young at the company, with the exaggerated good looks of soap opera stars, and despite Marinetti's charge—to action, to industry—no one seemed to be actually working. They were mostly posing at the water fountain trading gossip, in front of the coffee machine evaluating style. Sprawled out in a chair pretending to be reading *Motociclismo* was a slick-haired marketing Romeo. He was staring at me from a large orb whose damaged lids opened and closed like the wings of a butterfly. The other socket was almost sealed shut—just a sliver of pupil and dark lashes. When he caught me looking at him, he stamped out his cigarette, slipped a patch over the emerald eye, and walked over to introduce himself. "Your suit she's from Milano?" So he spoke a little English.

"How could you tell?"

"The buttons speak loudly for themselves." And he smiled. His teeth were greenish black from a childhood lack of iron. "I'm Alessandro. Would you like a coffee?"

"I'd love one." He put out his hand—it was a warm and wet thing—and took me down to the bar, a steaming Arabica island in a sea of gilt trophies, medals, and pennants from the 1950s. The walk through the factory—past the shouts and hurled objects of the graphics department, past the slammed doors and vicious threats of Jacques's design studio—was a trip back in time, a journey across culture. I saw secretaries tapping out Telexes with French-manicured nails. I passed bathrooms equipped with Turkish toilets, the mechanics of which—cantilevering my legs over the gaping ceramic hole—took weeks to master.

Though he was junior in the department, Alessandro walked like he owned the place. With each step, the stacked heels of his boots clicked. By the time we got downstairs to the damp manufacturing part of the plant, he had twisted a red silk square into an ascot—stylish protection against the cold—and draped his arm around my neck. We had become the best of friends. We wandered down the production line, cut across a sea of work-in-progress motorcycles, and came under the cloud of coffee exhaust mixed with cleaning fluids that signaled arrival at the company bar.

"How do you take it?" Alè wanted to know, squinting. A scintilla of fine wrinkles shot across his scarred skin. "Your coffee?"

"Black," I said, "nothing added." We sat down at a folding card table. He lit a Camel and took a long contemplative drag. Drinking a cup of coffee was ceremony in Bologna. It required more personalization than a simple pour. How did one take it?

"Cappuccino senza schiuma in vetro." Alessandro took his in a glass cup—instead of ceramic—with a tiny metal spoon. Upon his heavy suggestion, I ordered a cappuccino without foam, drank it, then rinsed my mouth with a thimble of fizzy water to cleanse the palate.

My education had begun.

"I have to get back to work," I pleaded with him after two more rounds.

He stuck his tongue in the cup to lick out the last grains of sugar. "Too late," he grinned, showing those mottled teeth again. "It's already lunch time." He called over the barman and ordered us some grappa. After downing the clear liquid, one fiery shot after another, he began tapping out drum and bass beats on the tabletop with his assorted rings and silver Ibiza bracelets. Work occupied the hours. It did not engage his fantasies.

Alessandro became my first Bolognese friend, very *culo a camicia*, slang for close—literally, how shirttails cling to buttocks. During the week, he took me on rounds of appointments: manicures, pedicures, body waxings, gym workouts with a trainer, and *lampade* (tanning sessions under a sunlamp). He did the minimum of real work—the marketing of sport bikes—preferring to spend his few "dead" office hours organizing raves in the hills. He instructed me on the more important aspects of Italian life: how to fast-roll a cigarette, how to mix flat and fizzy water, how to cut one's hair in an acceptable office style, something that could be easily transformed, with heat and hair wax, into something much cooler, like a *cresta*.

We were always in motion. "Never stop," he warned. "Move without thinking! Don't even *try* to feel!" He said these things as if they required no explanation at all—not even to a foreigner like me. And then: "Thank God for my accident! It taught me how to live every moment."

On the weekends, it was nothing for him to sprint two hundred kilometers on the autostrada, at breakneck pace, hit the discos, dance for a few hours, and then rush back to Bo by morning. His life was lived close to the edge, between destinations, flashing headlights to pass some dim-witted *scemo*, because his *giro* was not fast enough. He only stopped for coffee: espresso at the machine, cappuccino at the company bar, and one night near Rome, while he was racing down the exit ramp to get a shot of Joe at the Autogrill, some fool cut him off. The driver—drunk on cheap *fragolino* wine—cut across lanes, without signaling, just as Alè was rolling down his window to gesticulate and shout, "*Figlio di puttana!* Son of a whore! *Testa di cazzo!* Head of a prick!" revving his engine so loud that thunder could be heard in the hills and forests outside the Eternal City.

Alessandro drove like that and crashed like that—hard—in a great spectacle of color and light and a radio station set to Tricky. The accident didn't slow him down though—not at all. After months of reconstruction and rehabilitation, he was more determined than ever to race through life, quick as rhythm.

Every morning he would pick me up at the hotel in his Fiat Panda and we would zoom over to his personal haven, a small bar in the old Jewish ghetto. We rushed up via Ugo Bassi past the crooked Asinelli towers, survivors of the necklace of sentinels that had once ringed the city center. We crossed Piazza Aldrovandi, then barreled back down San Vitale with its stone then brick then stucco-painted porticoes—butter pale, burning copper—capped with elaborate terra-cotta capitals that glowed in the eastern light. We turned onto via Oberdan and watched its *caffès*—Soverini, lit in ghostly blue neon, Bar Oberdan with its gleaming cherrywood and 1960s aluminum fittings—open for business. We passed *gastronomie* and saw the purple flash of octopus salad, the green of whole zucchinis stuffed with pork. We saw uniformed ladies laying out semolina-dusted trays of Bologna-famous *tortelloni*—perfect pasta, peaks reaching toward the heavens.

One of Alè's hands worked the steering wheel. The other played "clutch." As with most Italians, driving fast still felt modern to him, as if the motorcar had been invented yesterday and not at the turn of the last century. To ride a sport motorcycle was to become a superhero: a comic character bursting out of its frame, with all of the smoke, flash of light, and destruction of perspective that the graphic artist could conjure. In between sucking a cigarette and dialing up radio stations, he sang Giorgia: "Vorrei illuminarti l'anima . . ." The only discordant element—I exclude the scars on his face, which he wore like medals of honor—was his tiny nose. It was as fine and as elegant as a doll's.

10

The sky was thick with fog. The stones were washed in shades of gray. The clear colors of my suburban childhood—the green of manicured lawn, the white of weathered clapboard, the blue of Atlantic sky—were an ocean away. Rising out of the mists, oak beam and stone porticoes that had originally been built as shelter for an expanding medieval populace gave shape to a city rich in earth tones. A pink neon sign flickered in the dark. We dropped the car in the middle of the sidewalk and walked toward the Caffè dell' Arlecchino to down the reductive coffee and brioche that Italians call breakfast.

Inside the bar, a girl with sleep still in her eyes was opening the place. She rolled up the iron gates. She unlocked the plastic tables and chairs and arranged them in the patio facing Piazza San Martino even though it was bone cold outside. That was bella figura. Then she went inside to lay croissants on long metal trays and prepare the first coffees of the day on the Cimbali M21 Premium, which brewed six cups simultaneously, with two steam nozzles to foam milk, because someone, inevitably, the moment she turned on the lights, would come in wanting his fix.

"*Che freddo boia!*" Alè said upon entering the bar. That's what people said in the morning: "It's cold. It's dog cold out."

"*Che palle!*" Balls!

"*Che palle fredde!*" Cold balls!

Or when it was hot, everyone said: "It's hot! It's hell hot. Worse than Africa hot." What could one do but shake one's head in agreement, which was what the girl did. Her profession required her to agree with almost anything customers said. She was hidden behind a big jar of bell peppers in oil, slicing salami for sandwiches when Alè introduced us for the first time. "Nico, I have someone for you to meet." All I could see was the flash of unusual yellow eyes and a curly mass of hair—the color of eggplant—untamed by a red bandana.

"Is he an executive?" she asked. She rearranged her turban and stood up a little bit straighter.

"Yes!"

She came out from behind the counter and offered me her hand. It was cold and greasy from handling luncheon meats. After the requisite niceties, she showed us to a table on the terrace, then went back inside to prepare coffees. Her first customers of the day were arriving—painters, electricians, carpenters—men gruff and assertive, all wanting to flirt with the pretty girl who had no time for the working class. "Are you still with Elena?" Nicoletta called from behind the counter, cutting a piece of *torta della nonna*—grandmother's cake.

"No," Alè answered smiling. "You're thinking of Anna."

"Oh, Anna the Russian?"

"Not that Anna. The other one, the dancer from Rimini."

Nicoletta wrinkled her nose and squished her lips, "*Alè, dai!* You're like parsley. You go with everything!" She brought us our cake and coffee, then disappeared.

I watched the crowd change. Businessmen were arriving on scooters. They came on big-bore motorcycles customized with carbon fiber. Sometimes they pulled up in late-model Porsches with bespoke suits and all the trimmings. When Nicoletta heard the roar of a twin-turbo Targa—and her ears were always tuned for this—she interrupted her duties to check her makeup in the Coca-Cola mirror near the cash wrap and dab some gloss on her lips.

A student still on last night's bender interrupted any potential flirting. He vomited all over the terrace, then stumbled across the street to disappear into the basilica of San Martino, refuge of the Carmelites. "I can't drink coffee with the stink of vomit in the air, bella," said a boy in mufti, stepping deftly around the mess and taking a seat at the bar. He wore layers of sweaters, a duffel coat, and a long striped scarf. He adjusted a too tight neckerchief and belched.

"You shouldn't be drinking anyway, Daniele," she said, kissing him on the forehead. "It's bad for your stomach." She set a plate of doughnuts down in front of him and went to get the mop. "Don't!" she warned. "They're filled with pastry cream. You can't digest it." He took two bites anyway, rolling a hand upward from his waist, bobbing his head up and down, letting out this low-pitched sound: *"ehhrr."* Such an utterance, unheard of in English, is called a glottal stop. A moan more than a meaning, in this case it signified one thing: gluttony.

When he finished chewing, he stuck out his hand to meet me. "Now, who is this *bono* the color of mozzarella?" he asked, cheeks flushing apple red. He still had a rich tan, even late in November. I looked closer and saw the light-reflecting radiance of foundation makeup. "I had a terrible date with a dockworker from Ravenna last night—all the sex appeal of a dead mosquito. I need to meet someone new." Alessandro introduced us and I went to shake. The hand went limp in mine. "My name is Daniel," he said in English, eyes downcast. They were almond-shaped, kohl-dark, and staring at my feet, which were shod in black lawyer's Churches. "American taste is just impossible to understand," he said, wincing. "Someday you'll have to explain it to me."

He went behind the bar to make his own *orzo*—barley coffee—*in tazza grande*—in a large cup. He took a sip, then opened his valise. "Now, look at this Spanish beauty!" He held the slick Nappa loafer to the light. "So fine and textured." I nodded. "And cheap too! Or if you like boots," he pulled out khaki-colored ones, "look at the grain of this lizard. Ciao! Chicissimo! Already sold out. Done! Talk to me next spring!"

Alessandro drank rounds of shotgun espresso while Daniele showed us his new collection of men's spectator pumps and monkstraps in antiqued calfskin. He tried to engage us in a conversation about the travails of a traveling salesman—"The Chinese are always undercutting me . . ." and "If I see one more businessman in designer sneakers, I'm going to shoot myself . . ."—but there was no time. At 8:45 the bells of the basilica started to ring, clang of centuries, forcing everyone to their work. We said our goodbyes and Alessandro got on the gas. In moments we were hurling down the Via Emilia toward the factory. We had spent exactly ten minutes at the bar.

Alè parked the car at the back of the factory—the front was now reserved for motorcycles—and, after a second round of coffee at the company bar, we walked the plant floor looking for inspiration. I started in the receiving area, where trucks delivered components from all over northern Italy. Workers in blue jumpsuits were unpacking crates, sorting the parts to feed the production lines. These boys didn't look like factory workers to me—not with their dark tans, manicured nails, and designer stubble. But then again, we *made* nothing in Bologna. We washed. We cleaned. We polished all manner of holes—sanding seams, perfecting edges. And then we dried things. Using industrial fans and handheld hair blowers, our workers removed every last drop of moisture from a part. And then, only when everything was clean and smooth and dry, did we assemble.

My mission was a rescue operation—to stop the bleeding and help turn the company around. Our American owners expected to make money on the spread between what they paid for the company and what they'd get when, one day, they flipped it to a competitor or took it public. To do that they had to change perception of the place from a traditional manufacturer, what the Italians call *metal-mecchanica*, to an entertainment brand. Entertainment brands traded at higher valuation multiples on

Wall Street. At the company no one knew about the value of brands. The unions fought for jobs. The engineers longed to go racing. Superbike was competition in this part of the world, not market capitalism.

Though the financial world assigned great value to the power of the brand and my job was to burnish it, I was in awe of the plant itself. The brute gigantism of the heavy machinery! The heady buzz from evaporating cleaning solvents! I watched in amazement as forklift operators rushed fuel tanks wrapped in protective paper to the mechanical sorting machine that controlled inventory, as young drivers speeded steel trellis frames—painted bronze or black—to the lines. Who could *not* appreciate the brawn of a finely muscled worker operating equipment with such grace, with such balletic precision? This was excitement for a lawyer looking to dirty his white shoes!

If I spent too much time looking at a crankshaft—one piece of solid steel, drop-forged, tempered outside the factory then rough-lathed, balanced, and precision-cleaned inside—or a camshaft—surface-hardened, heat-treated, tested repeatedly for oil channel conductivity—I was sure to lose Alessandro to some seductress in a miniskirt, lying in wait behind a crate of engine blocks or tower of Pirelli tires. The minutes before the morning whistle blow was prime time, factory workers looking for lust.

I came to a big green monster, the size of a small house. The extruding machine was sending out a slow gurgle of green sludge and silver shavings. It was roped off with a plastic link fence and a sign that read "Destined for Museum." I thought it was the boss's idea of a joke. I asked the nearest operator for an explanation. "We've tried to have this dinosaur taken away," he shook his head. "More than once."

"And?"

"The boss won't allow it. He says it is a reminder." And he

went back to packing defective cylinder heads in boxes to be sent back to the supplier. "A reminder of what?" he mumbled under his breath.

I wasn't the only one walking the plant during those cold days of fall. The general manager of the plant was also marching around—architectural plans in hand—dreaming of all the good things, new things that American money could buy. He was an impossibly elegant man in Brioni suits and shoe-polish black hair. He rode horses every morning, not motorcycles. Though he hated new management, he feigned a degree of enthusiasm because he intended to spend our capital. He wanted to expand the technical department! Build a high-tech paint shop above the production lines! Bring the forging of critical aluminum components in-house!

"Forget about fixing holes in the factory roof," the boss warned him. "Eighty-five percent of our cost of goods comes from outside. We're assemblers, not manufacturers. Think modern! Think Nike!"

"But the plant is outdated!" he objected. "It needs investment. Certain technologies must be kept in-house or we risk losing control of production." There were a thousand buts, but the boss, newly minted as company CEO, prevailed. We were spending that money to build a museum.

A myth arose, nurtured by the boss, of course, that there actually was a hole in the roof that needed fixing. It became one of the "dramatizing moments" in the turnaround—Max was always on the lookout for these—something not necessarily true, but real enough in spirit. It permitted the telling of a story. During an early question-and-answer session with prospective bankers, an automotive analyst asked to actually see the hole. He wanted to inspect it, to gauge the potential damage a storm could inflict on future motorcycle production. The boss went silent for a second, I thought at a momentary loss for words.

"The plant *is* in a general state of disrepair," I improvised, searching for a suitable answer to the analyst's inquiry. "But really, the hole is a metaphor for the kind of challenges we're confronting."

Which later earned me a rare rebuke from my superior: "Never interrupt the telling of a story," Max warned, "especially one that's going well."

And things were starting to go well. With money borrowed from the banks, we had paid off our suppliers and restarted the production of motorcycles. Sales were taking off. Exuberance was the order of the day. How many back orders did we have? "Demand is virtually endless!" Max crowed. Who was our real competition? "We have none! The Japanese aren't brands and Harley makes no race bikes!" Was the business recession-proof? "Of course it is! In the early 1990s, when European gross domestic product declined, we kept growing!"

"So would you *really* like to see that hole?" the boss asked the impertinent young banker. "Maybe you can give us some advice about whether it is worth patching." The guy nodded his head. Max went to the closet and pulled out a bunch of construction helmets. "Better put these on," he warned the group. "It's a battlefield out there." And he took us downstairs to a never-before-seen section of the plant, originally a kindergarten for the children of the thousands of workers who had once toiled building radios, intercoms, and electric razors in the years before World War II.

The space was a sprawling warehouse with no lights, no heating. Not only were there gaping holes in the original brick walls, there was no roof at all. We looked up at the colorless Emilian skies and it began to drizzle. "Look around," suggested Max cheerfully. Raindrops had put an ethereal gloss on his face. Old saddles, broken headlights, rusted tailpipes, and the signage of long-dead motorcycle dealerships were heaped in a corner of the crumbling room. "Old management was throwing away our history!" An audible hush came over the bankers. "But don't worry! I put a stop to all that. I have a team of young students—I pay them nothing, of course, the company's turnaround is their university thesis— and they're recuperating our past from the dumpsters." He went to retrieve a chrome gas tank from the pile, its logo still visible in red-and-black enamel. "Now, look at this little piece of sculpted wonder!" The tank shined like a candy apple in the dying light. "Do you have any idea of its value to a collector?"

Any discussion of holes in roofs was immediately put to bed. Dusk neared and the warehouse turned a moody blue. "I think we had better continue this discussion over a coffee at the bar."

Wet helmets nodded in agreement. The analyst had one last question. "So if I understand correctly, there's no limit to the number of bikes you can make at this plant?"

The boss smiled broadly. "All I have to do is call suppliers and order more parts."

If I had any further doubts about his oratory talents, he would goad me on with even greater tales. "All we care about is that they are talking, David. If they stop talking about us, now *that* would be a problem." He was quite consistent on this point. When Wall Street bankers asked what might happen if we stopped winning races, "Would it adversely affect the business?" Max turned on significant charm, though he was terrified of losing, to say: "Ferrari hasn't won a championship in twenty-five years and it hasn't hurt their sales. All we need to be is competitive." When Michael Schumacher finally took home the Formula One trophy, a few years later, the first in a string of consecutive victories, he adjusted the message accordingly. "It's not how often you win," he said, "but whether the fans are entertained." Boredom was our mortal enemy, not Honda.

After my morning tour of the plant, I would go to the boss's office to plot grand strategy. I had just begun its architectural transformation from banal workspace to slick motorcycle dealership of the future. On one wall was an engineering "wire" drawing of the company's top-of-the-line superbike. Another had mounted graphic panels recounting our race history. There were numerous blond wood shelves, glass vitrines, and aluminum helmet hooks to display memorabilia. On a low, red-lacquered commode, just arrived from Cassina, was arranged his personal collection of die-cast toy motorcycles, signed racing fairings, and logo baseball caps.

Max was at his desk sketching on graph paper, trying to represent his main thesis: that we were the other great brand in motorcycling. I sat down next to him. He drew a vertical line. At the top of the Y axis he wrote the word "Performance." At the bottom he put "Comfort." On the X axis was "Functionality." To the right was "Fashion." His big idea was that there were basic trade-offs in the bike market. The more performance a motorcycle offered, the less comfortable it was. The better its functionality, the less fashionable it was.

In the upper left quadrant was our high-performance Italian brand, the maker of uncompromised race machines. Down in the lower right was Harley-Davidson, builder of expensive chrome clunkers, perfectly adapted for endless American highways. In the middle he drew a Japanese flag. It was a small banner, but not to be ignored. The Japanese controlled 80 percent of the global market—in every segment, in every category. Satisfied at last with his chart, he wound the gears of the Cosmodromic engine mounted on a Lucite base and watched pistons fire. He called out to Elizabeth to bring him a lemon soda. His left foot was racing.

In our corporate presentations, he dismissed the makers of "rice burners" with a flourish of rhetorical genius: "They *are* excellent manufacturers, no doubt," he admitted. "No one can compete with them." He would never dare criticize the product. "But they aren't *brands*. Slap a Honda sticker on a Suzuki bike or a Kawasaki plate on a Yamaha and you can't tell the difference." On another chart he drew a big circle. In it he wrote the word "motorcycles." Around this orb he sketched a solar system of future activities: a museum, rider clubs, Web site, advertising, and enhanced racing activities.

Now he took a pencil and began drawing lines furiously, connecting the heavenly bodies. This web of activity existed for one reason only: to sell T-shirts. In the middle of that great sun, under the word "motorcycles," he wrote "accessories and apparel," related products that had higher gross margins than bikes, merchandise that could be made under license with no labor headaches and almost no working capital. "No one pays fifty dollars for a T-shirt if the brand stinks," he told me. "Make ours cool." My marching orders were clear.

And as if to punctuate his command, he passed wind. He didn't excuse himself when that bugle blasted. And he didn't seem particularly embarrassed by the smell of baked beans. I thought of Lyndon B. Johnson. The great arrogance and/or utter laziness of power! Being boss meant not just having subordinates, but being able to subject them to your habits.

13

After work he always wanted to keep talking. "What about Bolognese for dinner?"

I would suggest, *"Tagliatelle al tartuffo?"* when white truffles were in season, or *"Tortelloni di zucca*—pumpkin-stuffed pasta?" when the weather turned cold and the only color left on the trees was the orange of persimmons.

"No, no. My stomach can't take it," Max said. "I need simple." After the third night at a pizzeria on the outskirts of town that had only good parking to recommend it, I was begging for some culinary excitement. Slices I had grown up eating on Long Island. "Okay, tell you what. Why don't you come to the house tonight? My wife doesn't mind cooking and you can finally meet the kids." He speed-dialed her with the news. "She only shops at the Baita," he said with pride, "the most expensive prosciutto in town and mozzarella *di bufala* shipped in fresh every day from Naples. You'll love it."

He drove me home in his new Five-series station wagon, ignoring traffic lights, talking nonstop on his headset. "Now how many bikes have you sold?" he harangued each manager who called. "Don't bother me with details! I just want the number!" We careened around the ring road toward the *gabelle* leading to Santo Stefano, the Romanesque square built by medieval monks dreaming of Jerusalem.

"Like a fairy tale," I whispered, almost to myself, when I saw it. A pile of diversely styled churches rose from a field of black-and-white stones set in geometric patterns. In the piazza kids were playing Frisbee. Rastafarians strummed lazy guitars.

"The most expensive house in Bologna and I can't sleep at night. The riff-raff is always singing."

I thought he was joking. "Have you called the police?"

"And you know what they told me? 'Sleep in the attic. It has no windows and doesn't face the square.'"

"How do they know what your house is like?"

"Everyone knows everything in Italy."

We parked the car in the courtyard and climbed the elliptical stairway of the Palazzo Isolani, noted for its Florentine-influenced grace, all the way to the baronial apartment facing the friezes, medallions, and terra-cotta busts of once important, long forgotten nobles decorating the Palazzo Bolognini across the square. I was expecting traditional Italian elegance—fifteenth-century mahogany. Or its opposite: all white Milanese minimalism with low tables and overstuffed sofas by B&B Italia. I hoped the disappointment didn't register on my face when he opened the great wooden door. Everything was rigorously IKEA. "I put together each piece myself," he announced, beaming with parsimoniousness. "It took hours."

I recognized many of the models: the white Klippan loveseats with brushed metal legs, the Tullsta armchair with Lack sidetables in plastic laminate, the Poäng recliner that I had once owned in my student apartment in Cambridge. Beyond the decor was the splendor of the piazza itself, from the seven churches of Saint Stephen, once the site of a pagan temple, to the leaning towers. Streetlamps flickered on as evening descended, gilding the medieval architecture with light.

Before I could step one foot on the rag rug to take in the view, the boss blocked my entrance to the living room. "Wait! You have to take your shoes off! Otherwise my wife will just go crazy!"

Alice was a Vassar girl, still dressed for school. Though it was freezing cold, she wore hip-hugging jeans, a ribbed college tank-top that exposed her flat stomach, and no socks. She dismissed me with a weak smile and a wave of the hand, too tired to get up from the couch. "Hello my love," he said, bending over to give her a long tongue kiss.

Alice barely took her eyes off the book she was reading. "Look, you guys are going to have to make your own dinner. I'm just too exhausted to cook."

"Where are the kids?"

"In the playroom."

I took off my sneakers and we walked into their realm. Every inch of the place was covered in toys. The little girl was sketching with crayons. "Hello, pumpkin," the boss said to her. "Come, give daddy a kiss."

Tears welled up in her eyes. When they spilled over, she started to bawl, "Go back to your office! I want my mommy!"

The boy ignored him completely. When pressed about his plans for building a giant new Thomas the Train station, he whispered, "I'd rather not talk about it now."

"He isn't much of a conversationalist," the boss explained, "but very brilliant. Michael knows the name of every major airport in the world." We retreated to the kitchen. He opened the refrigerator. It was blazingly white, empty. On the countertop sat a sack of rice, a block of parmigiano cheese, and some fresh beans soaking in water. "Could be worse," he shrugged. "At least it's *carnaroli*, which makes a good risotto, not *arborio*, which is just marketing." The boss shelled the beans of their pink wrinkled husks, revealing speckled ivory legumes. They reminded me of the cranberry beans that I had once seen at the greenmarket at Union Square but never eaten. "They're called *borlotti*, if you're wondering. Poor people's food."

He rinsed the beans once or twice, then set them in a pot

with fresh water. He added a spoonful of olive oil, salt and pepper, and a sage leaf. When they turned brown, he began adding their broth to the risotto cooking in the other pot. I tried to talk business, but he just gave me a wooden spoon and suggested that I stir continuously. "Don't stop mixing or it congeals and becomes inedible," he said, ladling broth into the rice until the grains could absorb no more liquid. His wife had gone across town to watch an episode of *Sex and the City* that her American friend had shipped in weekly from New York. We ate alone.

After dinner he washed the dishes and I played with his kid. The boy pulled a soccer ball out of the toy chest and started kicking it back and forth to me. He was good with the ball. When the boss saw us playing, his face went pale. "No, Michael! Stop!" He was almost livid. "Every boy in Italy wants to be the next Paolo Maldini. My son has better things to do." He snatched the forbidden ball from him and asked, "Now, tell me, what's your favorite national stamp? Malaysia or the Seychelles?"

"Madagascar!"

"Then that's where we'll go on our next vacation. Go get your stamp collection. I want you to show it to David." The boy refused.

14

Walking the factory floor every morning had given me an idea.
Unlike the Japanese, who make everything from lawn mowers to
outboard engines, we built only one thing in Bologna: sport motorcycles. What was more exciting than seeing hot metal, shiny
paint, or hearing a Cosmodromic engine roar? Only the faces of
our workers—young, charismatic Italians. They were as stunning
as the bikes they assembled. I thought they should be the center
of our marketing. With no real money to invest, supermodels
and name fashion photographers were out of the question. I
bought a Polaroid camera and started taking snapshots of our
workers on the line.

A few weeks earlier, I had hired an icy blonde from Green-
wich, Connecticut, who had been living in Milan since college.
Even though Krystle looked like a Hemingway sister and had
been discovered not once but twice by Helmut Newton, she
chose a career on the business side rather than on the runway.
Valkyrie tall, with excellent bones, Krystle would have looked
perfect poured into a rubber dress stamping out cigarettes in
some businessman's mouth. Instead, she became my glamorous
assistant.

One day, while reading a women's fashion magazine, _Io
Donna_, she came across a photo-essay about the forgotten piazzas

of Italy, shot by a former Magnum photographer skilled at capturing the intensity of ordinary people walking around cobblestones in bright light and deep shadow. She thought he could celebrate our workers in their greasy glory.

I showed the photographer's portfolio and my test Polaroids to the boss. "Everyone else in the industry uses color . . . ," I explained.

"Then we should consider black-and-white."

"The Japanese shoot action shots on racetracks . . ."

"I love artistic portraits."

"We have no money," I reminded him.

Max smiled. "Your set is Bologna and our workers cost nothing." What was so stimulating about him was that he finished your thoughts for you. Naturally, his understanding of his own strategy was exhaustive. But if your ideas fit comfortably into his, there was nothing he wouldn't let you do. "Good luck," he said, dismissing me with a wave of the hand. There was a long lineup of other managers looking for his yea or nay on various projects. As I turned to leave the office, he added: "Everyone will hate it, of course." My stomach dropped. "But don't let that stop you. They don't understand anything anyway."

A few weeks later, Krystle and I dressed muscular line operators in wifebeaters and ripped jeans and positioned them in front of San Domenico, the great church where the ascetic founder of the order was entombed, on custom Beasts. We shot hard-boiled testers on the hills of San Luca, silhouetted against porticoes leading to the basilica. Krystle did the styling—mostly rubbing Vaseline on faces to give some summer sparkle in the cold. I artfully ripped T-shirts and lent out my silver jewelry. Bologna supplied the atmospheric mists and fogs.

The star of the campaign was a shy redhead from the accounting office. Her name was Maddalena. She had a great nose—a downward sloping hook—hooded Madonna eyes, and a large inviting bust. The photographer could not get enough of her. He shot pictures at point-blank range—of her face, her profile. "Maddalena, Maddalena," his lips mouthed to the metronomic shutter of his Canon. "My Maddalena!"

With me he played the artiste: "A photograph is born by looking, staring at something to the point you have the impression of actually having seen it, and only then snapping." To Maddalena he was much more direct. "Yes!" he encouraged her, "YES! Give me more of that face! I don't give a goddamn about Dominican brothers or sister saints! I want the sexy Maddalena! Pout some more! Show me the *whore!*"

She had a subtle show of power on her lips. "Better! Now, improve the posture. Hold your head higher. *Higher!* There, almost regal!" He put the camera on a tripod and used it like a walking stick, pivoting on one leg until a shot came into focus. He clicked and clicked. "Madonna! Che bella!" And clicked some more. "You're really beautiful!" He shot rolls of film. He moved around her like a wolf, approaching, retreating, then coming back in again for the kill. He leaned all the way over and shot straight up from under her cleavage. "Breasts!" he started to howl. "I see big beautiful breasts!"

The photographer, a rather diminutive, almost elderly man, was slithering on his belly, shooting up from her patent leather boots, when I suggested: "Maybe we should add men to the picture?" and "Remember, I need to get a bike in the frame. It's an ad campaign for motorcycles." He resisted at first, but when I positioned the two musclemen like bookends, with Maddie in between, astride the Beast, something clicked in his mind's eye.

"Yes!" he said, in hushed tones, "I'm seeing it. *Now I'm really seeing it.*" He photographed the no longer timid redhead with two testers whose baldness glowed like streetlamps. He photographed the trio in the piazza, along the arcades of the city, in light, in shadow, in grainy black-and-white neorealism. We posed the group at the base of the two leaning stone-and-brick towers, next to the statue of San Petronio. The testers, faces chapped by years of exposure to the elements, had the scorched gaze of soldiers. In between was Maddalena on her Beast, wearing high boots and black leather.

Oh, praise the petrol princess, the lady rider who knows how to pop a proper wheelie! All hail the humble girl who can change a broken chain drive! In the 1990s, biker babes rarely twisted the throttle themselves. They were birds on the poop deck of a boyfriend's wheels, cheesecake to ogle at motor shows. Harley had female wrestlers who competed in vats of mud and oil for HOG members at Daytona Bike Week. We had the brolly girls—pit candy who made shade for racers on the grid with umbrellas at the start of every Superbike race.

But Maddalena! Such a rare and helmeted beauty was the future of a sleek and sexy motorcycling, a sport that enthusiasts wet-dreamed about. To see such a girl riding in the hills outside Bologna—that narrow-waisted *ragazza* with masses of chestnut-colored hair billowing out from under her helmet, silhouetted against the white skies—was something to take your breath away. To watch her downshift and brake—the back brake, not the front—keeping the front end steady, engine engaged, right before entering the twisty, sparked a moment of motorcycle reverie. It was a signal that times were changing, even in the conservative world of motorcycling.

In front of the camera's lens, Maddalena became this ragazza. Beneath the gloss of the photographs, one could imagine the grime under her fingernails, the nostrils rimmed with dust after a day of hard riding. With every click of the shutter, she seemed to grow in stature. She became regal, haughty—even dictatorial. At her side were two henchmen, ready to kill for their leather-clad biker mistress.

The photographs of Maddalena scandalized the company.

"Fascist pornography!" people cried. "Two Nazi SS guards and their moll!"

"How can these workers look German to you?" I questioned my irate colleagues. "They're the same Italians who work right here with you on the line!" But there was no reasoning with them. The boss, always searching for logs to toss on the bonfire he wanted roaring at the company, gave the green light. The "Bologna Biker" campaign was born.

The motorcycle world, accustomed to seeing bikes hauled over on corkscrews or barreling down straightaways in streaks of color, was shocked when we published the first ads. Die-hards cried: you can smell the stink of Madison Avenue from miles away. The fashion world cheered: hot biker boys and their babe. And whether riders loved or hated it, everyone wanted copies of the charged images. We printed posters of Maddalena that started to appear in adolescent boys' bedrooms. Requests for her cell phone number and e-mail address became common. Fans came from everywhere looking for the mythical goddess of Bologna, an Etruscan princess who could perform burnouts.

The strange thing was that no one could find her. Even when she was standing right next to them, taking her double coffees at the bar, smoking her long cigarettes near the women's lounge. Two months after the campaign wrapped, Maddalena took two weeks of medical leave and slipped away to see the local surgeon. She had her face remodeled. The regal nose that had entranced an artist became a stub. The cleft chin was erased. Even her big breasts seemed to go down a bra size. She was still a pretty girl, but she had become generic, without character. The mystical Madonna of motorcycling would ride no more.

A couple of weeks later I went down to the assembly lines to find another employee we had photographed. She was an *operaia*—a line worker—with cream-colored skin and the enormous eyes of Anna Magnani—or so said the photographer. She also looked like a natural on a motorcycle—a real, live biker girl—kitted out in head-to-toe leathers. In some of the shots though, dark circles had appeared under her eyes and a troubling leer twisted across her lips. She'd looked less motorcycle princess and more like an extra from *Caged Heat II*. The photos were shadowy—even sinister—and a shade too provocative for our clean-cut racer image. We needed to do additional shooting.

I made my way downstairs to the area in the factory where Beasts were made. The bike was 50 percent of our overall sales and the key to future volume growth. The line was run by one of our top floor managers, a well-known prima donna. From high atop a wooden stool, megaphone bandied about like a bullwhip, he barked orders, struck poses, and oversaw his minions on the line. Now, a female factory worker in Italy—even an ordinary one—does not look like her American counterpart. It is not uncommon, for example, to see a young girl working the line in a push-up bra, false eyelashes, and a dark tan. In America, she would have a modeling contract. Here, in industrial northern

Italy, she sweated it out with the other workers, under the strict, or lazy, as the case may be, supervision of her padrone.

As I wandered among the latter-day Gina Lollobrigidas and young Sofia Lorens, I didn't see my model manquée, Cinzia. Other girls were toiling with four-valve race engines or attaching front forks to wheels—listening to deep house music on Walkmans, text-messaging on cell phones, applying lipstick, or all of the above. Many of them had been hired when La Perla, the manufacturer of high-end lace bras and panties, laid off hundreds of workers. We made a gamble that the same fingers that had the dexterity to do piecework—applying pearls, fastening sequins— could handle the inner workings—pistons, rocker arms, and cylinder heads—of our race-bred engines. When the girls succeeded fabulously, even outperforming the men, we desegregated the engine production line in one fell swoop. It was a great day for feminism and proof that not only Russian prostitutes wore daytime Versace.

Walking down the assembly line to where the motorcycles exited for "wet testing" on diagnostic machines, I asked a couple of workers where Cinzia was. "How would we know?" they said, mindful of their overseer. I tried to catch his eye. He swiveled immediately in the opposite direction. When I waved, he became absorbed in smoothing wrinkles in his royal blue shirt. I passed the stations where the engine was bolted onto the chassis, where the front forks were attached to the frame. I took a few more steps and there he was: all sartorial splendor and polished shoes. Face to face with his mirrored Gucci sunglasses, I started to say something.

"No she can't!" he barked through his megaphone.

"But I need her."

"*Impossibile.*"

"But why?"

"There is no 'why'—because *I* said so." And he turned his attention to picking lint from his linen suit, dull with the sheen of a recent pressing.

What one wears on the line has nothing to do with what one actually does for a living. A line supervisor is better dressed than the executive who manages him because he has something to prove and (usually) the physique with which to prove it. This supervisor—I called him "Eagle Beak" because of his sharp nose and predatory nature—was preening. Like any good *fighetto*, he had the uniform down pat. Status was counted in buttons. How many could be sewn onto a collar? The calculation was not obvious. At a minimum, two were needed to keep the collar tacked down. But sometimes, four were used. An accent button, purely decorative, brightly colored, was often sewn in the center of each collar. Cuffs were another story. Eagle Beak's sported enameled links, buttons, *and* monograms.

I examined his magnificence for a moment longer, then approached. "Come on then. Where is Cinzia? *Dimmelo.*"

"She's not around."

"Where is not around?"

"Studying lean production this week. *Kaizen.*"

We had hired Porsche Consulting, an arm of the Stuttgart automobile company, to help us improve efficiency. We went to the Germans because they were European. They went to the Japanese because they weren't. Porsche had learned to be efficient from Toyota, who had reorganized their Zuffhausen factory in the late 1980s. Kaizen was more mentality than methodology. To stay competitive a business required continuous improvement. Nothing was too small to escape consideration. We boiled down the principle to its minimum: instead of maintaining lots of components in inventory, we stocked only the material that was needed for that week's production. Those parts were packed into supermarket carts and carefully positioned at critical points on the assembly line.

The supermarket cart idea worked well in Japan. But an Italian supermarket was not like its Japanese counterpart. To begin with, supermarkets were not at all popular. A recent phenomenon, they were mostly relegated to the outskirts of big cities and the lesser suburbs. The inside of an Ipercoop or the local Standa was never neat or logical. Ropes of salamis were draped over countertops. Dripping legs of prosciutto hung from the ceiling. In America, the supermarket wars meant that the most powerful consumer product companies controlled the prime real estate— sight-level shelving at the grocer's. Italy maintained bella figura whatever the cost. So, while toilet paper and toothpaste were essentials in the ordinary Italian home, they were always impossible to find at the supermarket. Choice space was given to pretty little cockles in extra-virgin olive oil or the olives in sweet rather than salty brine.

The factory worked on a similar rationale. No matter how much we invested in efficiency and quality, no matter how many supermarket carts we placed in the aisles, our motorcycles stayed pretty much the same, which was to say: charmingly handmade.

"But Cinzia is a natural," I pleaded. "Salt of the earth, *buono come pane*"—as good as bread, as the Italians say.

"Nothing natural there. And she's not going out again on another photo shoot. *Figurati!* She has real work to do." There was something about his tone, the way he said the word *figurati*, that reminded me of someone. It took me a minute. Yes! It was that other hawk-nosed prima donna. Al Pacino: He pronounced *figurati* just like Pacino's trademark response in *Donnie Brasco*: "Fuhgeddaboudit."

"But I need her as a model." I was now begging.

"*Non me ne frega niente*. She's not a model," he said, unbuttoning the cuffs of his shirt and letting them hang free, Gianni Agnelli style.

"But it's for the company's *corporate image!*" At the time I had the mysterious job title of "Corporate Image Director," which had little weight with anyone, let alone this line manager.

The man waited a beat and then said deadpan: "I don't give a shit about the company image. She has hands that build cylinder heads and I have a quota to make." And he walked off to smoke a cigarette.

In Italy, no doesn't necessarily mean *no*. And even yes is up for interpretation. Contracts aren't worth the paper they are written on because they're constantly renegotiated even before the ink dries. Multimillion-euro deals are done with a wink and a handshake, but that doesn't mean that there isn't room for haggling with the supplier for juicy kickbacks—like a swimming pool installed in your backyard. I hoped that Cinzia's fate was not sealed.

Eagle Beak had come back from his nicotine break in a better mood. Satisfaction rolled across his face like clouds on a summer day. He sighed. He breathed. He even hummed a cheesy Andrea Boccelli tune. He was that relaxed. "You're crazy, David, you know that?" he laughed over the manufacturing din.

"Why do you say that?" I tried to keep the tone light and breezy.

"Because Cinzia is not even the prettiest. There are many other faces around. Much nicer than hers."

"*Really?*" He had my interest piqued. "I haven't seen them."

"Ah . . . that is the true talent," he said, getting down from his stool, slipping his arm conspiratorially into mine. "The art of selection. You know I have a little theory . . ." He was a different person now, almost avuncular. "Let's go for a little stroll and I'll tell you about it."

"Sorry, but I have to finish this casting." I tried to squirm away, but he held me in a vise grip—elbows locked together—so close that I could smell his underarms, which were, thankfully, well deodorized.

"You've been in Italy long enough already to know that there's always time for a little espresso," he said, and twaddled my nipples. He actually did that—like it was the most normal thing in the world for a man to do.

After we had quick *caffè* at the machine, he told me his theory. He believed that the critic was as important as the artist and that the best creative work came out of an intense dialectic between talented creator and educated audience. "These are relationships of a profound symbiosis in which the one could not exist without the other."

"Yes, I agree!" At least I thought I did. I needed to get back to my selection process. Eagle Beak was not finished philosophizing.

"Would Michelangelo have been a master if Vasari had not written about him? Have you read his work?" he asked, as if it were required reading in the industry.

"Have *you*?" I snapped back.

"David, *please*, I am Italian! I've lived Renaissance aesthetics since birth." I had heard that Eagle Beak lived in a cement housing project down the road, but knew enough to keep my mouth shut. "You know what?" he went on. "Without Vasari, Michelangelo would have remained one of a handful of Florentine sculptors—a real *finocchio*—long ago forgotten by history." I was pretty shocked. It wasn't every day that you got a Vasari lecture from a line manager. He even said "fag" in a sensitive way, caressing his own large package. (In Italian, *finocchio* also means fennel, a feathery plant with a licorice smell.)

"What I want to say is that when I look at my workers I see them with the eye of the true connoisseur. I scrutinize every detail." I bet he did. "I even know where their beauty marks are located." He raised an eyebrow that I refused to acknowledge. He went on: "I know exactly what they want and what they dream about. With Italians it's in our blood, this attention to detail. It's like . . ."—he was struggling for the metaphor—"like pearl buttons on a shirt!" He was pleased with himself indeed. "It must be hard for an American like you. What tradition can you look back on?"

"Actually, we never look back," I said, staring straight at him, "only forward. That's why we're so successful."

"You're right there, Davidino. Listen, I may decide to help you after all. You just have to know where to look."

"And where is that?" I asked.

"Not so far away after all. Sometimes, you don't realize that right in front of your eyes is that someone who could be perfect. You don't realize it because this person might look very different on film. You just need to give him a chance to shine."

I asked him about the tiny *pugliese* with the dramatic Egyptian eyeliner and three perfectly placed beauty marks above her left upper lip. "No, no, moles make me think of spiders, which are unlucky and not beautiful at all." I asked him about a Monica Bellucci lookalike with black hair and a skull-and-bones tattoo in the small of her back. "I'm surprised at you. Don't you think that she's a bit passé, too Harley-Davidson?" I was trying to be flexible, but he shot me down every time.

"I don't think anyone here works," I said, frustrated.

"There must be someone!" He looked worried now. "We're the best-looking people in the factory!" He brushed the hair away from his brow, jutting out a prominent chin. He had fallen right into the trap set for him.

"Wait a minute!" I said. "Actually, you're right." He was still pursing his lips and sneering royally.

"I *usually* am."

"There is someone else I can use."

"Who?" he asked, stroking the stubble of his beard, immaculately clipped in a permanent five o'clock shadow.

"Why, *you*!"

"*Me?*"

"Yes. I was thinking of putting you in the shoot."

"I am shocked, Davidino." It was the second time he had called me that.

"The idea crossed my mind this morning." He was beaming. His large teeth, expensively capped, were wet with the saliva of anticipation. "Now that I can really *see* you, I know you could do it. You'd be perfect on film."

"I would?"

"Yes, of course. You're *radiant*."

"What a great idea, Davidone!" His hands swooped upward in excitement. "This changes things. *Everything*." He was now gesturing grandly, using his full arms and muscled upper body. Then he hugged me. A sweaty, cologne-infused bear hug. I was just hoping that his Man Tan wouldn't rub off on me. It wasn't so much the celebratory dance, the parading around as if he had won the lottery that signaled his mood change. Italians were capable of changing body language as quickly as they switched cell phone from buzz tone to vibrate and back again.

It was the lingual progression from *Davide* to *Davidino* to *Davidone* that mattered. Word endings have significance in Italian. Changing the suffix is one of the exciting things that you can do in the Italian language that is not possible in English. *Davidaccio* is the bad, dastardly David. *Daviduccio* is the sweet, sexy David. *Davidino* is little David. And *Davidone* is the towering powerful David. Eagle Beak's progression from the insignificance of *Davide* to the cute diminutive and on through to the greatness of *Davidone* was an impressive journey in the span of twenty minutes. It meant that he was warming up to me at last.

"The shoot would be with Cinzia, of course." I reminded him.

"Of course." Nothing could kill his good mood now. "She is just right over there in the conference room. I can get her whenever I want."

"I'd like to capture the feeling of you as a couple," I said, "as if you were lovers who always rode together."

And with a sly wink and the gesture that signaled "perfect"—closing his index finger with the thumb—he smiled and said, "Why, we practically *are*." And with that he went to go get her.

It wasn't that he was an unattractive man, quite the contrary. But on film, he looked too good in the wrong ways. He was a fifty-year-old man who seemed preternaturally young, over-groomed. His muscles were too big, his thick hair too glossy. You knew that he waxed his chest. His nipples popped through the Egyptian cotton of his made-to-measure shirt. He plucked his eyebrows. His prominent nose, proud and predatory, dominated the page. The bulge in his pants looked like socks, but wasn't. His body language dominated Cinzia. It wasn't exactly the image that we wanted to project. The pictures weren't a waste of time though—Photoshop saw to that. Cinzia looked great. This time, she had no circles under her eyes. It didn't matter that I edited Eagle Beak out of the campaign. And, in the end, he didn't care much either. He had made his point. He had won his game. He was one of the great ones.

In Italy, the whole country is a theatre and the worst actors are on the stage.

—*George Bernard Shaw*

The "spectacularization" of the company, as my boss called it, had dramatic effects on our workers. They blossomed. Italians are accustomed to walking around the office like divas in a melodrama. Now, our employees played to a wider audience. Hats, wraps, muffs, furs, shawls, and scarves (and motorcycle jackets, biker boots, and bandanas for the men) proliferated and were paraded around the hallways and corridors of the factory like props in a staged production of *Rigoletto*. In the executive offices, designer sunglasses were fingered, removed, sucked on during meetings, and then reset with rhythm. Cell phones were switched on, switched off, set to mute during conference calls, and placed on the table to mark territory. Star-struck, our employees could hear the call of the casting agent. Women line workers applied eye makeup like supermodels. Maintenance men trained their muscles to look like bodybuilders. They glistened under their coveralls. They had taken the message of the boss to heart: play it to the hilt, go over the top.

The head guard at the *portineria* (gatehouse), Pasquale, a *cal-*

abrese, picked out a conservative blue suit from Milan and matched it with flame-colored monk straps from Ferragamo. He became almost gentlemanly. I started calling him *consigliere*, the Italian honorific for esquire. His colleague, a female guard named Godeberta, put her brown hair up in braids, dyed them blond, and began swimming laps at the country club. Poolside at the indoor club, she applied moisturizer to a taut, almost nude body and slowly opened and closed surprisingly blue eyes. She watched us watch her breasts rise and fall with the weight of her humid breathing.

Every once in a while, a plane from Guglielmo Marconi Airport roared into view through the dome, flashing a silvery underbelly before disappearing in the white skies of the Pianura Padana. Godeberta roasted. She radiated. She glowed. The sunlamps broiled her skin the color of Parma ham. The chlorine turned her cornrows the chrome yellow of cheese doodles. Watching her relax made *us* sweat. Poised on her beach chair in the middle of winter, basting in creams and lotions, she was no longer a watch guard in police uniform but a voluptuous night porter, a seductress who could steal you away from the routine of industrial work at a metal-meccanica company and tempt you down a titillating path of vice and personal degradation.

She stroked her finely muscled thighs suggestively (*how far would she go?*), fingered a flat navel (*she had great tone for forty*), and, every once in a while for good measure, sprayed herself down with Bilboa coconut-almond water (*she was nothing if not equipped*). We stared in mock horror at such displays of brazenness. Once Alessandro turned to me and asked, "Do you think that Godeberta is her Christian name?"

"Is Godeberta *anyone's* Christian name?"

In the *carnevale* atmosphere of the turnaround, the production chief at the plant felt free to flaunt a darker tan, wear tighter muscle T-shirts, and further develop his passion for facial hair:

goatees, Vandykes, soul spots. His beard and mustache transitioned from style to style, trend to trend, like the phases of the moon. He was fifty. The head of procurement, a short, shy genius of logistics and information technology, quietly acquired a brand-new wig. He wore it like a fedora, cocked to one side. Sex lives improved and multiplied. Marriages deteriorated. An engineer in the racing division was frequently seen in the company of a Brazilian transvestite. It was not always the same one.

People took tango lessons. The chief financial officer—a pint-sized Roman—went skydiving in Umbria. Alessandro learned capoeira, the Brazilian martial art of self-defense. The dress code was abolished. No more charcoal suits, pale shirts, and subtle-printed neckties for the men or conservative blouse/skirt combos for the girls. The CEO came to work in Topsiders with no socks and preached "creative chaos." Secretaries wore black thongs underneath sheer miniskirts and were encouraged by their bosses to do filing in the lower reaches of the file cabinets.

Dino, the chubby head of the museum project and a long-suffering virgin, began the Italian version of the Zone diet: no pasta after dark, one small gelato a day, and white rice with Parmesan cheese. He gave up mortadella and various other pink meats. He stopped smoking Toscano cigars—the ones shaped like fat torpedoes—and forswore syrupy digestives like Montenegro after his nightly pot of *panna cotta*. He began working out—which mostly involved walking on a treadmill while wearing an elasticized girdle—and let everyone know he was looking for a girlfriend. Above his right ankle, he tattooed "917" (after the Porsche driven by Steve McQueen in *Le Mans*).

"Do you notice any change?" he would ask colleagues at the coffee machine. "I mean with regard to myself." On the scale, he was twenty kilograms lighter. He now wore cargo pants, Timberland boots, tight tank tops with baggy overshirts, and a red glass choker. He practically skipped through the hallways. After living in Borgo Panigale for the last forty years and never venturing north of Modena or south of Sasso Marconi, he now flew regularly to visit "his good friends" in London. Even so, good Bolognese to the core, he refused to see Rome. "When I want to go to Africa, it will be on safari." Dino was *un mito*, "a myth," as they say, and he loved the company with all of his old, Bolognese soul.

The turnaround changed me too. Each month, despite a diet rich in lasagna with béchamel, mortadella, and parmigiano reggiano, I lost a pound. My stomach flattened out. My cheekbones grew more prominent. I stopped going to the gym and became leaner, more Italian. I changed my way of holding myself. I learned how to pose at the bar, how to smoke a hand-rolled cigarette, how to talk on a cell phone—looking equally animated *and* bored. I stopped shaving so often. I buzzed my head and washed the fuzz only once a week. I began to chew with my mouth tightly closed. Italians prefer lips to be pouting—never flapping—always waiting to be kissed. All manner of lip goo was kept in pockets, in purses—in hope of such providence.

In a country without much of a birthrate, I became younger. There was no next generation nipping at one's heels. Middle-aged people acted like teenagers. Children listened to the same bad pop music as their parents. Everyone went to the disco on a Saturday night to unwind. My friends were a decade younger than I, but thought I was their contemporary. *I* hadn't spent the lasty twenty years in the sun, under sunlamps, and had no wrinkles or sunspots to speak of.

Alè (along with everyone else at the factory) would laugh at the lawyers, the analysts, the consultants, and the moneymen who descended on the company during the turnaround, people with no particular commitment to the industry perhaps, but skilled professionals nonetheless who were turning ours into an extremely profitable motorcycle company, second only to Harley-Davidson. "Look at the fools working overtime!" he cackled, trying to persuade me to take off early on a Friday afternoon and go for a ride. "Bald, fat, white men! No life, no style!" Unlike him, they couldn't manage a tryst at lunchtime and a handful of girls after dinner.

I—ex-suit myself—learned to adapt. At first I thought it was humiliating when I was trotted out to describe, in great detail, the images of an advertising campaign that people inside the company had taken to calling "Calvin Klein with Bikes." It took months, even years, for me to understand that I too was expected to play the *divo*. I was supposed to be outrageous. My ideas should be preposterous, fantastical, expensive to execute, impossible to understand—never rational or backed up by data. And as for implementation, well, that was other people's business. My secretary rebelled if I tried to do my own dirty work: to send a fax, to make my own photocopy. "That's what an assistant is for! If you do it," Alè warned, "she won't thank you. She'll hate you."

"But she doesn't want to do the work anyway."

"It's not about *work*, David. The question is *role*. She deserves hers, just as you do yours. And right now your role is to party! Let's go for a ride!" And we rushed to get our gear on.

Alessandro did one thing slowly. I wasn't there when he made love to his girlfriends, though he came to the bar so exhausted some mornings he could barely open his damaged eyes. "David . . . ," he would sigh wearily, "she was twenty-two years old . . ." I would shake my head in disbelief. "*Twenty-two!* And Brazilian!" He was a leisurely shopper when it came to clothes. On Saturday mornings we would motorcycle down the block to the chic haberdashery Winchester's on via San Felice, and together with the manager, Stefano, and Daniele, take inventory of new arrivals. As Alessandro's fingers (they too were reconstructed) flipped expertly through the racks, stopping to consider a pair of leather pants or a velvet jacket, Stefano and Daniele would nod or shudder, accordingly.

Unlike the mincing Sal Mineos who worked at Barneys, Stefano was bold and beautiful, a master clotheshorse with a shining cranium that was magnificently bald. His voice rang out like church bells: "The most exquisite Ballantyne cashmere has just arrived! Seashell pink!" He had an oiled chest and deep-set blue eyes capped by crescent moons of perfectly tweezed brow. Haircuts come and go like the *nebbie* that blow in and out of the city in fall and winter. A mini-Mohawk currently reigned. Stefano's baldness endured.

In any other culture he could only be homosexual, with his encyclopedic knowledge of clothes and acid humor. Here in the land of Mussolini, where sexuality was as indeterminate as his hairless torso and as bombastic as the rectangularity of his abdominal wall—gym-worked into an extraordinary flatness—what he did in bed was anyone's guess. His body was like Fascist architecture—noted for an absence of sensuality, a lack of texture. His calling card was a starched white shirt—perfectly pressed, open to the waist—showing off lots of sunned skin. All of Bologna was in his thrall. Men and women, boys and girls of all ages lingered in front of his storefront, as calculated and artful as a Cornell box, just to catch his eye, to be part of his *giro*.

One Saturday morning I walked into the store wearing a cherry red tracksuit and a silver chain necklace with Roman heads that Gregg Wolf, my silversmith friend on East Ninth Street, had made for me when he heard I was moving to Italy. Shocked at East Village casual, the Italians turned on me like wolves. "Never wear a sweatsuit outside of the house," Daniele stammered, looking for the right word. "It's . . ."

"It's *Sicilian!*" Stefano said definitively. He was poking his fingers around my midsection, considering a diagnosis. "What do you think about icy blues, pale pinks?"

"He's too pale for pastel," Alè said, "and he refuses sunlamps."

"The new elegance for spring?" Stefano said in English, holding up a waxed linen suit for perusal. "You can wear it with sneakers." My beard growth was days old and I was itching to get back on my Beast parked outside, humming like a chain saw. "Try these on," he ordered, hurling a lollipop-colored cashmere sweater and slim flannel pants across the store as an athlete throws a discus.

"*Bravo!*" chimed in Daniele. "He'll eat less with tight clothes."

We settled on a Napoli shirt with a huge collar, mother-of-pearl buttons, and an all-purpose crocodile belt, items without which, they insisted, no true figo could survive. I drew the line at a pair of monkstrap shoes in mustard yellow with spiral stitching on the soles. I didn't want to look like a clown.

17

Life at the factory was never boring. On a crisp January day when the skies were a robin's-egg blue instead of cotton, the head of communications, a woman named Marzipane, came to work dressed up as a cowgirl. It was the highlight of the winter. Born in Bolzano, a town in the German-speaking region of the Alto Adige, where farmers tend animals and apple strüdel, Maria was a polyglot bombshell who spoke fluent German, Italian, English, and French—all with the same Heidi-like accent. She said she loved "the American country." That day she wore a spangled shirt, suede miniskirt, fringed jacket, fishnets, and cowboy boots. When I saw her marching down the hallway, I said, "Howdy."

She stood straight up and saluted: "Yahoo!"

The boss was less cheerful. When he heard her clip-clopping around in the hallway during a conference call with bankers, he got up from his desk and confronted her. "What the hell are you dressed up as?"

"Why, myself, of course," she answered automatically.

"But aren't you giving an interview today to *Motociclismo*?" he asked. She didn't quite follow his logic. "We do work in the motorcycle industry, right?" he prompted, as if to jog her memory.

"Why, yes . . . we do work *there*." She seemed uncertain, but kept beaming.

"I just thought you might be on your way to a rodeo."

Now Maria, it should be said, took tremendous care with her appearance. Her hair was permanently permed and dyed a deep, dark red. Her face was plastered with Kabuki-like makeup. "Are you suggesting that I look like a cow, sir?" she asked, flushing under her matte-white foundation. If pressed, he would have said that what she most resembled was a horse's ass, but he was too smart to risk a charge of sexual harassment—a popular claim at a company fast becoming hip to American legal mores.

"I just think you should go home and change," he stammered at last, embarrassed by the situation. "If you want to look sporty, that's no problem at all. Put on a motorcycle-racing suit. *That* would be appropriate."

Expressions of indignation now crackled across her face like snapdragons. She couldn't believe he had anything against cowgirls. "Let me ask you just one thing," she began in earnest, examining his deck shoes and scruffy chinos. "Do you own a boat?" Max looked down at his feet. He had bought the Topsiders years ago and worn them so often that the leather had become colorless like Nantucket wood. He inspected the threadbare chinos, stained here and there. His Polo shirt was missing a button. He shook his head slowly, smelling defeat. He didn't own a boat.

Maria didn't miss a beat. "Then I won't ask you whether you are a fisherman." She brightened underneath the armor of her pallor. "I dress the way I do," she continued, licking her lips, "because it cheers me up." The boss wasn't so much humbled as caught off guard. "You say you want happy, productive workers at your plant?" She wasn't waiting for his answer. "Well, you have one." And with that, she clicked her heels, smiled bravely, and sauntered off to the refuge of the coffee machine for a double espresso. She was a great PR woman—brilliantly charming. She never sweated, had lots of teeth, and never stopped smiling. Six months later she was gone.

18

There was always kinetic energy in the company. You could feel it. It was an enchantingly frantic place, full of life, full of chaos; what Italians call *casino*—a whorehouse, but in a good sense. The previous owners would turn away fans when they came to glimpse the holy grail of sport motorcycling. We instituted an open door policy. Everyone was welcome to come inside and take a look. And they did. Bikers came in small groups at first. Then they came in caravans. They motored into town in campers and chartered tour buses. And if for some reason they couldn't make it in person, a barrage of letters, faxes, and e-mails was sent in their stead, making sure that new management wasn't messing up their adored sport bikes.

Old motorcycle racers, sunburned and battle-scarred, came to walk the company's hallways in worn leathers, searching for traces of their own glorious past in the trophies and championship pennants that we hauled out of storage or rescued from the trash bin to put in places of honor. These pilgrimages, often unannounced, sometimes at great personal cost and physical effort, poignantly connected the new company to the old, and made us aware of the great responsibility we had taken up when we decided to burnish a rough jewel of a motorcycle maker and return it to glory.

During the early stages of the turnaround, we hired more than five hundred workers. Many were young and charismatic. Others were cranky and charismatic. Giorgio, the new head of the art department, was an old-school leftist. His face was red and mottled. His body was radically round. He strutted around the studio—clown ball of a nose, double chin, and a barrel chest—laughing diabolically and thundering, *"Ma va cagare!"* (Go take a shit for yourself!) to anyone who crossed his path and suggested that there might be work that he needed to do. In more professional moments he chatted with suppliers on the phone and ordered pots of black coffee and croissants from the bar, "Well-toasted and extra-hot," all the while stroking a handsome potbelly (his body seemed to be missing angles and evidence of bones) with the tenderness that most adults reserve for children. Giorgio had none.

His staff was a cast of misfit art directors and illustrators—all self-styled young anarchists. Though ostensibly left-wing, Giorgio never talked politics. He preferred eating. His staff spent an inordinate amount of time—company time, naturally—organizing trips to the countryside to taste sparkling lambrusco (it has nothing in common with American "cold duck") and gorge on *crescentine* (fried pasta dough) stuffed with prosciutto, salami, pickled onions, and *scquaquerone* (a soupy cheese made from cow's milk). Dessert he ate twice: once cooked, crème caramel or panna cotta at the meal's start, and once cold, ice cream or *semifreddo* to help him digest afterward.

His dream was to build a gelato stand in Zanzibar and serve the best homemade flavors—like *nocciola* and *cioccolato fondente*—that the Dark Continent had ever tasted. He even went to school to learn how to make ice cream in a tropical climate and optioned a piece of coastline not far from Stone Town, on which he used to go camping and dock his rented dhow. "It's a simple project," he told me on numerous occasions. "Success is *assured.*" And as if to prove it, he would take out the stack of photographs he was carrying around, to show me in blazing color the patch of white sand and red-painted sailboat anchored to a stand of mangroves. "There is where I am going to build," he would say, and then sketch on a napkin the holiday villages and scuba diving centers he imagined in the Zanzibar of the future.

"You think those tourists want to eat ice cream?" I dared to ask. "They are coming to visit Zanzibar after all, not Rome."

Giorgio looked at me as if I was certifiably crazy. "Are you kidding, David?" he said, rolling his eyes in disbelief. "They're *dying* for it."

When it came to actual motorcycle work, though there was little enough of that, Giorgio exercised an unerring policy of realpolitik. He allied himself with only one person, cunningly choosing the chief executive officer. The boss assigned certain key tasks to Giorgio, none of which, of course, had anything to do with his titular role as head of the art department. This work included glad-handing the police chief, procuring parade permits for motorcycle rallies, and setting up the occasional off-site secret meeting. There were never any delays for these projects. "Don't worry," Giorgio would say, the picture of professional responsibility, "I'll take care of everything." And he usually did.

If an ordinary manager, like myself, brought him a project that didn't have the boss's imprimatur or wasn't sexy enough, Giorgio would not deign to work on it. He resisted such assignments. He stalled. He undermined them. He had more glamorous things to do. The boss, maddeningly, gave tacit approval to his divadom. "Work around him," he would tell me, or "Don't let him bother you so much. He's a pussycat if you rub him the right way." But if you didn't pet him properly, claws came out.

One of the few graphic jobs that interested Giorgio was overseeing the implementation of our new corporate identity. We had hired Leonardo Leonardi, the renowned designer responsible for several department store and airline logos, to revamp ours. A lifelong minimalist, Leonardi served up a classic, commercial typeface straight out of the sans serif 1960s: "univers" italic. He matched the typeface with a dynamic -o- symbol—a simple red circle with a slash through it—that people in the company immediately derided as a *gettone* (a token), a *chicco* (a coffee bean), or a *cagata* (a piece of crap).

I was there when Leonardi sketched the logo for the first time on a napkin one night after rounds of red wine, *moscato*, grappa, and the small almond cookies called *cantucci* that are served with *vin santo*. The company had rejected an earlier version of the dynamic -o- because it looked too much like the Dunlop arrow. So I nervously asked Leonardi to give it another go, which seemed to be no big hassle for the designer, who, it must be said, was almost as famous for his client relations as for his graphics. "There's your new logo," he said, after five minutes of fast doodling. "Let's finish our drinks."

I was nervous. I knew the stark design would cause trouble among motorcyclists better known for outrageousness than elegance. How did I tell this to the towering figure of late-twentieth-century graphic design, a man who had built his reputation on eloquent minimalism? I said, "Simple is always best."

"That is what good taste is all about," answered Leonardi, settling the matter once and for all, "and you have it. Now pass me one of those chocolate truffles. They are very good *too*." Months later Leonardi gave me a Christmas present, a copy of his book *design: Leonardi*, reinforcing his belief in my belief in him. In a penciled dedication he wrote: "To David Gross, because he knows what is good and what is not!"

It was my job to sell Leonardi's corporate identity project internally, and I expected attitude problems from Giorgio, who had wanted a crack at the work himself. But when I showed him the new logo, he was inexplicably delighted. It turned out that Giorgio had been hunting at the Grand Elite Hotel, where the great designer had been holed up. In the lobby near the bar, Giorgio bagged a bronze ashtray that looked a lot like the dynamic -o- and hung it immediately in his studio like a big-game trophy. He told anyone who would listen that the great designer had taken the logo idea from the Elite Hotel on the old Via Emilia, which had also been designed circa 1965. The corporate identity project cost the company half a million dollars. A night at the Elite—globe lamps, shag rugs, built-in Formica—ran about seventy-five euro. The ashtray was free.

The incident did not preclude Giorgio from attending numerous dinners with Leonardi, where the two discussed travel and girlfriends and ate large quantities of fritto misto, green lasagna, and steamed meats with *mostarda*. They got on famously—the best of friends. When the time came to complete the project, Giorgio, who spoke no English, dispatched an emaciated young art director to New York, where something entirely unexpected happened. After a few weeks at the great man's temple of stone severity, Piero, previously an anarchosyndicalist with a tongue piercing, became a disciple. He started preaching the virtues of white space. "Graphics need space to breathe," he declared with the zeal of the convert. "Otherwise they die!" He spruced himself up, trimmed his goatee, and started dressing like the maestro himself—in black-and-gray Mao suits, originally designed in the mid-1980s for Charivari.

Giorgio could not abide Piero's conversion. "The kid is becoming a kook," he said, making the Italian gesture for *matto*— crazy—waving his right hand in front of his nose as if to shoo away a noxious odor.

"Maybe Manhattan has overwhelmed him," I offered, careful of Giorgio's fiery temper.

"Obviously, not enough," he said, licking his thick lips. "Piero needs to stop looking at fonts all day and get fucking *laid*. He's at risk of becoming the court eunuch."

"The guy is just trying to do a good job," I said, trying to appease. But Giorgio wasn't paying any attention. He was flirting with a new intern, stroking her delicate hands with his hammy ones.

The graphics tension was just beginning. As the corporate identity project wore on, and it went on for months, Giorgio and Piero's relationship deteriorated into long-distance shouting matches. They battled over the application of our Pantone color to materials. They fought about whether a white logo on a gray background was within the rules. Giorgio was pragmatic. Piero was as rigid as a dictator. "No. You can't use gray. It's not allowed."

"Fuck off!" Giorgio bellowed, veins throbbing in his temples. "I'm the boss around here."

"But the manual says—" Piero protested.

"The corporate identity is a guidebook, you idiot, not the Ten Commandments."

"I'll talk to the Signore and see what he says."

"*You'll* talk to *him*? *Porca puttana!*" Giorgio shot back. "Who the fuck are you?" His face contorted into a gargoyle. There was no longer anything Italian about him. He became a fat burgher in a Hieronymous Bosch painting—eyes wild, skin wet, and angry. He cocked his head toward the receiver, mouth open, ready to spew obscenities.

"I'll ask him nevertheless," Piero was defiant.

Giorgio's nose twitched once or twice. "*Eh . . . ,*" he said, lowering his voice. "Let me tell you something. You do that and I'll take a cleaver and chop your fucking fingers into *tagliatelle al ragù*. Va bene? Hai capito?" His face had turned a color not in the corporate palate: purple—with rage.

When Piero returned to Bologna, Giorgio lost no time in moving from verbal sparring to an actual fistfight. The pretext may have been the graphic panels for a trade show and the "horizontality" of the lettering, but the showdown had been boiling for months. "*Porca miseria*, he was rigid!" Giorgio grinned after slugging him hard. "I should have loosened him up a long time ago." Giorgio was hauled down to the personnel office, where the chief gave him a dressing down and had the incident noted on his record. He was a made man though.

Despite his many outbursts—or maybe because of them—the boss thought Giorgio provided a valuable service to the company. He was polarizing. He unleashed energy. "I think he's undermining the look and feel of the brand," I complained time and again. "He adds his personal touch to everything!"

"Remember the mix of the new and old?" the boss reminded me. "You can't just fire everyone you don't like!"

One summer, Giorgio flew to Zimbabwe to photograph a humanitarian effort, supported by the company, to deliver medicine by motorcycle to remote tribal villages. He gave up vacation time and quite effectively smuggled cameras and equipment into a country then eager to keep Western journalists out. He traveled hundreds of miles, across rugged terrain, by jeep, by bike, and on barnyard animals. He took breathtaking pictures of the physical beauty—and poverty—of the African bush and its people, later to be made into a coffee-table book to benefit the British charity that organized the junket. Gamely, he made sure that some of the children were wearing company T-shirts or holding die-cast toy models of our ten-thousand-dollar bikes in their hands.

When the boss saw the pictures of Zimbabwe he was triumphant. "I knew it! I *knew* I was right all along—only Giorgio could have pulled off something like this! You have to admit *that*." But of course no one would. Giorgio's antics sparked protests and even resignations. He made you feel edgy and anxious. In this the boss demonstrated his own twisted genius. The new energy at the company was palpable. People took the *bordello*—the craziness of everything—for true inspiration.

One evening after his return from Africa, Giorgio and I took a walk in the Piazza Maggiore. It was one of those dark, dramatic nights that make Bologna feel like the most magical place in the world, a stage set to awe. We entered the square from Piazza Roosevelt, passing via d'Azeglio, lined with its elegant boutiques, walking toward the illuminated Archiginnasio, the rose-colored stone school building that was the original home of the University of Bologna. The Archiginnasio contains an intact wooden dissection theater, which witnessed some of world's first medical dissections of human beings—often to cheering audiences—in the early 1600s. "I must have seen Maggiore tens of thousands of times, every night and day since the age of reason," he said as we entered the square. In the distance was the blue-domed chapel of the Sanctuary of St. Mary of Life, rising up like a new moon in the spectral sky. "I never tire of it. For me, there is nothing more beautiful in the world."

Fog drifted in and out of the piazza like velvet curtains, unveiling the clock tower of the Palazzo Communale, revealing the pink-and-white-marble-decorated cathedral of San Petronio, and then, in an atmospheric shell game, making those same buildings disappear and new ones materialize. The air had a delicious cold snap to it and people were bundled in sheepskin coats. I bought a paper bag of roasted chestnuts. *Marroni* carried the smell of fall and their blue smoke filled the city with nostalgia. We crossed the raised stone platform, called the "cushion," that sits in the middle of the piazza, and wandered down via dei Musei, the passageway dotted with mahogany bookstalls displaying chapbooks of medieval poetry and maps of the city.

Underneath an old 1930s sign that read Buca di Petronio

in black-and-gold letters, we encountered a group of African women, swaddled in big, colored skirts and matching head wraps, sitting in the middle of the sidewalk. Their breath formed small puffs of steam as they talked. All the brightness of their garments—saturated tropical pinks and sunset oranges—could not insulate them from the sharp chill of the evening. Women of fashion in sheared nutria coats took extravagant measures to cross the street, avoiding an encounter. Giorgio pretended not to notice the Africans at all, though they were looking for a handout. "Where are they from?" I asked him, as he sidestepped the women, whistling.

"Who knows," he answered. "Aren't *excommunitari* all from the same place anyway?" and he kept walking down the street away from the piazza. He followed the curve of colonnaded via Castiglione—the richest street in the city—to the Sorbetteria Castiglione, the most famous ice cream shop in town. He wanted me to taste his favorite gelato. A crowd was waiting patiently outside, paper tickets in hand. There was none of the usual cellphone chitchat—lest someone miss his number being called—and no cigarettes. Smoking was permitted everywhere, even in church, but firing up a cigarette here could get you banned for life from a flavor like Ludovico, the gelato that mixes, quite extraordinarily, caramelized pine nuts, ricotta cheese, and toffee.

I ordered a simple chocolate-and-vanilla cone. Giorgio chose bitter coffee. He waited for me to taste first. "Here goes," I said, tucking in. The explosion of pure chocolate was so intense I closed my eyes to concentrate. Then I tried the vanilla bean. I knew now why Europeans had fought wars to protect trade routes to Asia, Africa, and the Americas.

Giorgio was triumphant. "Now you tell me, who, anywhere in the world, wouldn't like this ice cream?" The gelato machines were humming—churning and chilling—serving the lines of hungry fans that snaked out under the porticoes. Regular customers ordered their dessert days in advance. It was waiting for them at the cash register, wrapped in cream-colored parcels, next to the black minstrel figurines—with thick red lips and bulging eyes—that were still popular in Italy.

Giorgio never talked much about ice cream in Africa anymore. He had other hungers. He listened carefully to the capitalist tune playing in the executive suite and took to "stakeholder analysis" as a racer takes the corkscrew at Laguna—as fast as he can. Che Guevara may have been an icon to a generation of Italian hippies—his framed portrait appears in bars all over the city— but he was no business role model at the new company. When the boss said that each worker had "a stake in the future," it didn't clash with Giorgio's worldview. When investors were told, "Everyone has an interest. Everyone has a say," Giorgio nodded knowingly. He responded to cries of "Be creative!" and "Be en-trepreneurial!" with great gusto. If a design project came his way and he was too busy with other more interesting things, he sub-contracted it out—often to his own agency.

The man was no simple buffoon. He was a slice of the real Bologna, as rich as mortadella, as red as wine. If an honor guard of policemen riding our bikes attended our events, it was thanks to Giorgio's friendships. (He himself continued to drive a BMW.) If the mayor of left-leaning Bologna came to visit the right-leaning factory for the first time in decades, it was *grazie* to Giorgio's political capital. His Roberto Benigni antics—you loved them or you hated them, there was no in between—were the scrim against which the rebirth of a company was being played out.

Like some clowns and comedians, Giorgio never knew when to get off the stage. His sideshow threatened to detract atten-tion from the main attraction. In a series of *Good Morning*

Vietnam–style missives sent around the company, he called into question the boss's vision of creative chaos. In an e-mailed diatribe sent to all colleagues, he wrote: "I am vulgar and aggressive. I shout and I scream. I treat people rudely, but I am absolutely sincere." It was true enough. "I say exactly what I think and, often, what other people think, but do not have the courage to say." He signed the letter, "Goodbye! Stop busting my balls!"

The details of what happened next were murky. We heard that the boss graciously thanked him for his contribution and the great clown—our own *pagliaccio*—chose to leave the company. "Giorgio has never been an easy person," Max wrote in a memo faxed everywhere. "His aggressive way of doing things, sometimes worthy of censure and sometimes censured, is all the same no doubt due to his great passion for his work, for his results and for the company itself." Colleagues were outraged: passion for *work*? The note went on: "Giorgio leaves us with a great challenge. We now need to do without him what was only possible to accomplish with him—with all the troubles, limitations, and difficulties that he was able to overcome in ways both positive and negative." It was our turn to feel deflated.

Though Giorgio now no longer worked as an employee, he still haunted our hallways. Not as a ghost or a spirit—his bulk and volume would have prevented that—but as an honored guest and sometime supplier. Freed from the pretense of company obligations, he walked the plant like an honoree at an awards show, looking for the flash of paparazzi cameras. He visited the race department to see the latest race bikes. He ate leisurely lunches with the boss in the guest dining room.

Eating was not quite as easy or enjoyable as it once was. Giorgio had recently suffered a disfiguring bout of tic douloureux. The right side of his face was paralyzed with paroxysmal neuralgia. When he spoke, half of his bloated lower lip moved, one big eye bulged, a nostril flared. The forming of words, the making of gestures, and the intake of food were now an effort—a belabored mix of tongue, teeth, spit, food, and air. Giorgio wasn't reduced by the challenge—not at all. If anything, the tic seemed to enhance the portrait of the man, adding an element of improvisational struggle to a face of great power and charisma. His appetite would not be stopped by a tic, his personality not so easily extinguished.

The last time I saw him, he was riding his motorcycle in the center of town on a Saturday afternoon, roaring up and down the cobbled streets in his usual loud way, honking at other cars, flashing his headlights, shooing old men and strolling families to the sidewalk for safety. He was shouting as always—to everyone, to no one in particular. He pulled over at Pino's, a *gelateria* under the portico on via Castiglione, right before the remains of the gate to the city and the Beaux-Arts Margherita gardens beyond. It was a favorite hangout. Giorgio had designed the sign for the ice cream parlor, a Memphis-style graphic in mint green, pink, and salmon letters. Each color of the letters cleverly picked out a reference point in the city—the verdant park, the bronze of old Bologna brick, the rose of the repeated Corinthian columns in the dusk before evening. He parked his bike and I watched him go inside, order a cone, and begin licking, which was now no longer a simple affair. The attack of his tongue, shockingly pink, wet, lurid, maneuvering around the soft chocolate, scooping mouthfuls of the creamy stuff, delivering it to the hungry mouth, all the while gelato dripping down the weakened lips, was an awesome battle to behold. Giorgio relished it all right down to the very tip of the sugar cone.

In the beginning, shy to speak, I would trot out a few Italian words with an improvised accent, dropping the last vowel—like saying *mozzarel* (pronounced "mutz-a-REL") instead of *mozzarella* or *Versac* ("Ver-SATCH") instead of *Versace*—much the way my Italian-American friends did back on Long Island. I thought it might endear me to my new colleagues, but few were impressed. The Bolognese disliked southerners (*meridionali*) and were offended by my preference for another region's pronunciation over theirs. This provincialism is called *campanilismo* in Italian, after the tower, or campanile, that is at the center of every Italian town.

If you were Bolognese, your local campanile—however short, crude, historically insignificant, and built of ignoble brick instead of stone—would be infinitely more beautiful than even the campanile in the Piazza San Marco, let alone the tower down the road in Modena. "All of Italy is *paese*," Alessandro instructed me. Everyone was just a *contadino*, a peasant, when all was said and done, not so far removed from raising pigs or tending sheep, no matter how lofty his pretensions. Since no one spoke much English in Borgo Panigale, he said I would have to learn the language by immediate, full immersion. Painfully, I picked up snippets of what I thought was factory jargon (*gergo*), but turned out to be old *bulgnais* (Bolognese dialect).

Socc'mel, pronounced "SUCH-mel," was the first real word, beyond the basics, that grabbed my attention. Unlike in America, where "suck"—"it sucks" or "you suck"—is among the most common forms of disparagement, here it was a multihued term of praise.[3] Born bolognesi would say things like: "Suck me, what good tortellini *in brodo*," to the waitress in the factory's canteen, if the broth made with ham hocks and hen was rich and the pasta savory. This was the food in the old dining room—the homely *mensa*—before some disgruntled worker blew the whistle, informing the health department that cockroaches had been seen strolling around the kitchen on a passeggiata. The news triggered a food overhaul that ended homemade cakes and casseroles and introduced commercial food service with packaged *primi* (first plates) and tasteless *secondi* (main courses).

"What does *socc'mel* actually mean?" I asked Alè at lunch one day, after he whispered, "*Socc'mel! She* has a great ass," while watching a secretary waltz by in leather trousers and a halter top. The girl had smooth raven hair parted down the middle, wide cheekbones, and honey almond eyes. She was carrying a tray of hot water, a teacup with lemon slices, and a green salad. That was her lunch. But *oh* how she carried the tray! Balanced perfectly against her bosom as if it were laden with a harvest of summer squash and ears of corn, she held her head like an Indian princess.

At the condiment bar, she applied the right proportion of salt to pepper, then balsamic vinegar (to melt the salt crystals), and, finally, a trickle of extra-virgin olive oil to her lettuce. Now she proceeded across the dining hall, pelvis pushed forward, emphasizing each step, serene in her sense of the crowd's admiration. They called her Pocahontas, after the animated Disney character, not the pockmarked historical figure. She was looking for a single seat—this little Indian usually ate alone.

It was an open secret in the company that Alè was having an

affair with her, but he still treated her like any other common figa. In public he praised her physical assets and told his buddies that she was a *puttana*—a whore. Every other Monday, the two would meet down the road at the Quattro Gatti, "The Four Cats"—a pizzeria that was filled with caged tarantulas and copperhead snakes, anything but felines. Over Cokes they would hold hands like two teenagers and chatter among the trapped wildlife. No one from the company approached them. They had created a private lair in which acknowledgment of their relationship was forbidden. Though the meetings took place in public, witnessed by everyone it seemed except for her cuckold of a husband, no one said a word. The lunches went on for years, interrupted only by a honeymoon (she married again) and a short maternity leave following the birth of a baby that most people attributed to Alessandro.

"To answer your question about 'suck me,' " he said after Pocahontas had passed, "Bologna is famous for two things," he pushed a fat tongue up against his cheek and began a slow, pulsing motion, "blowjobs and mortadella. Any other explanation for coming here is a lie."

The free-love atmosphere had a history. Bologna had been the center of liberal thinking in Italy for centuries—just beyond the reach of the Vatican, invaded and enlightened by Napoleon, annexed to the progressive House of Savoy, and finally, in modern times, allied with European Communists.

When the Sicilian Tommaso Laureti together with the Flemish sculptor Giambologna designed the Fountain of Neptune in Bologna's Piazza Maggiore in 1564, they saw to it that the bronze sea god was surrounded by a bevy of erotic putti and naked sirens on the half shell whose breasts spouted streams of drinkable water, piped in from the local river. It became a habit for the Bolognese, who in medieval times had used the marble basin of the fountain to wash vegetables, to suck water directly from the articulated, verdigris nipples when they wanted a drink.[4]

Rumor had it that during the casting of the Neptune, Giambologna, worried about the explicit sexuality of the statue, had asked Pope Pio IV himself for permission to depict such frank nudity in his bronze masterwork. Neptune was to be the symbol of an important Catholic city, and the continued patronage of the Church was indispensable to an artist like Giambologna, who worked on a monumental scale. "For Bologna it's all right," came the reply from Rome, cementing early in its history the city's progressive reputation in matters temporal and libidinal.

The carnal component of the contemporary Bolognese personality was better understood than the predominance of pork in the cuisine. After years of eating *stinco di maiale* (braised pork shin) and *zampone* (boiled stuffed trotter), neither Alessandro nor anyone else could tell me exactly how the pig had come to reign supreme in their diet. Had it been introduced by the Celts or the Franco-Lombards? The Romans or the Etruscans? Some people said medieval Bologna had been a poor place and its citizens were reduced to eating every part of the animal right down to the toenails. Others claimed Bologna's rich past meant that its citizens feasted on bacon, tripe, and ribs while other Italians chewed millet, spelt, and tasteless barley.

My butcher, whose bruised complexion and proud obesity paid tribute to his profession, had the most enigmatic explanation. The cultural centrality of pork was what happened when the neutered pig, fed the leftover whey from making parmigiano reggiano cheese, was so thoroughly chopped, sliced, smoked, cured, and ground up into bits that it vanished completely. My own take was that if every part of the hog was eaten—from head to cloven hoof, from snout to tail—the pig entered consciousness and not just the digestive tract, like Krishna.

Each town has its porcine achievement, from Piacenza's

coppa (salt-cured ham carved from the neck) to Parma's prosciutto (fresh hog thigh massaged with salt and left to hang in a cellar). *Socc'mel* likewise had its own galaxy of dialectal variants. "Suck me, what a nice sweater," a friend would say, fingering the wool of your triple-ply cashmere if it really was *that* soft.

Soccmelo, on the other hand, "suck it for me," meant enough already. *Basta*. After endless trays of green lasagna, two types of prosciutto, and *pesto Modenese* (raw, seasoned pork paste spread on a cracker), bolognesi said "*Soccmelo*" to the waiter at Diana, the Sunday institution on via Indipendenza, before he could make a third pass with the steam cart, laden with larded roast and potted veal, accompanied by mostarda, the condiment of piquant mustard fruits that shone like fat rubies and canary diamonds.

Soccia—a resigned sigh—was softer, almost sweet. "Soccia, I am so *distrutto* (tired), I desperately need a good night's rest." A girl's breast implants were also soccia—so perfect as to make a grown man cry. When a Formula One fan looked at a Ferrari, painted in bright red livery, he sucked in his breath, shook his head, and murmured, "Soccia . . . ," wishing he had the money to buy one. The proper usage of "suck me" and its variants did not come easy to a novice like me. It was a linguistic virtuosity of the locals. My easy out was the simple and vulgar *cazzo*, literally, "prick" or "cock"; figuratively, "fuck." If I applied *cazzo* to any situation I might be mistaken for a real Italian, but never a Bolognese.

20

Offensive language was used regularly at the factory, sprinkled like salt and pepper, the main condiments in Bolognese cooking, which is called a "sweet cuisine" not because it is sugary, but because it tastes so inevitable, so simple and delicious. The assembly of motorcycles was a quantitative affair: the number of bikes to be produced in a day, shipped in a week, sold in a quarter. To swear was to be a creative individual, free from the strictures of grammar, outside social mores. The holy mother of all mothers, Santa Maria Eva, gave sticky blowjobs and took it up the ass in factory Italian. Her son, Christ the Pure, was a pimp, a pusher, and, generally, a son of a bitch down on the line. There was the traitor Judas Iscariot and his merry tribe of petty crooks, cheap rabbis, safecrackers, and flimflam men. There were pig whores, slut whores, and pussy whores—galore.

As our workers would say, *"Che cosa aspetti da un culo?"* What do you expect from a dumb ass—that it write you a romance novel? The derision of buttocks in this case was misleading. Bolognesi didn't often denigrate them—especially if they belonged to a pretty girl. They mostly sang an ass's praises. There was the *culo che parla* (the ass that speaks), the *culo che balla* (the ass that dances), and the *culo che sogna* (the ass that dreams). What an ass never did was sit down and be quiet.

Our workers, self-proclaimed *rompipalle* (ball-breakers) and *stronzi* (shits), never shut up. The factory is freezing cold! The food in the cafeteria is inedible! Management is cheating us out of overtime! Bologna was a workers' paradise, not because the mayor was friendly with Fidel Castro, but because union protection meant that no worker could be fired for any reason, let alone using bad language.

My introduction to Italian labor relations came early on. "The boss needs you!" Elizabeth panted into the phone one winter morning. "The suits from London just arrived and they want to do a factory tour."

"Can you give me ten minutes?"

"He means now." I slipped into my jacket, kept for such emergencies on a hook on the door, and walked into his suite of offices. Elizabeth was dressed like a Spice Girl for the occasion, wrapped in layers of sugar pink silk, offering coffee and brioche to the bankers. She flitted from one to the other, almost giddy, doling out stirrers and napkins, generally yucking it up with a heavier than usual dose of "lovey" and "blimey." With her pasty complexion and candy-colored clothes, I thought she wouldn't look out of place at a Dunkin Donuts counter.

The boss was dressed more seriously. His navy suit came out whenever he had to shill for money. Today he wore buckle shoes. He acted almost surprised when I popped my head in. There was an awkward moment when I wondered whether he would introduce me at all. I stuck out my hand. It hung in midair. Elizabeth came to my rescue. "Would you like a cup of coffee, David? The rest of these blokes are already quite wired!"

"Oh yes!" Max said, his memory now sufficiently jogged. "This is David. I just rescued him from the legal profession!" It wasn't the first or last time I would hear that line. "He's in charge of creating our new company image"—I smiled until I heard his dismissive coda—"whatever *that* is."

I felt immediately small. I started to babble, trying to bury the slight with words: "I'm repositioning the brand—new graphics, new advertising—I can show you the images." But he cut me off.

"Yes, we know all about that." Max turned his back on me to address the bankers. "Now, as I was saying, I'm turning the entire factory into Hollywood entertainment. There are interactive stations that describe motorcycle production. There are slogans—*campione del mondo*—painted on the walls. Everyone from our top managers to our line workers is expected to wear a company T-shirt, smile wide as a Cheshire cat, and act lively for the fans who swarm the plant on a daily basis!" He looked straight in the faces of his audience, sustaining eye contact. "When we go public it won't be as an industrial company." He was shaking his head. "No, gentlemen, I think we all know how miserable those multiples are." And they did. "I'm talking Disney-like valuations! Theme parks, toy licenses, fashion lines!"

"Can we see it?" a suit pleaded, frothing to observe this mythic entertainment factory in the making.

"Of course," the boss smiled. "I was just waiting for someone to ask."

I hung back to have a word with Elizabeth while the group made its way to the stairs. "Don't complain to me, love," she cut me off before I could say anything. "He's the driver and we're in the back seat." She kicked off her high heels under the desk and turned away for a moment to slip out of her silk camisole and into something more comfortable. "Just play your role and look pretty, love." She opened a desk drawer and passed me some Maltesers. "You are in charge of creating our company's image." The chocolate malt melted in my mouth and I thought about what she said. I was just along for the ride.

———

Downstairs, the boss was waving enthusiastically (mostly to people he didn't know) and pointing out numerous improvements to the plant. He took the group to see the new computer milling machines that pumped out prototypes in polystyrene. We visited the paint shop, where computer-controlled sprayers painted motorcycle frames bronze and silver. He called attention to the total ban on smoking—years before law mandated it. As we neared an area of the factory where workers were running "wet" engine tests on expensive "dyno" diagnostic machines, he grew increasingly animated. "This is where something very important is happening," he shouted over the din.

The company had invested a fortune in a computerized testing chamber so that we could simulate engine acceleration and test braking ability instead of manually checking, as we had done for decades, on the pothole-ridden track behind the plant. "The testing chamber is like an advanced hospital surgery unit," he boasted to the bankers. "Everything is super-clean, efficient, even environmentally friendly." It was an impressive claim. "Our workers couldn't be more committed," he crowed. "They are personally involved in each motorcycle we make, because each and every one *rides*." This was even true.

"Do you ever have problems with the unions?" a snooty English managing director ventured. "It is, after all, Italy." He was wearing a chalk-striped suit, a rose-colored shirt, and matching tone-on-tone silk tie. On his manicured pinky finger was an onyx signet ring. We knew that the ponce had never come near a motorcycle in his life. When he said the word "Italy," he almost sneered.

Shocked at the very suggestion of labor strife, the boss looked at me (in mock surprise) and then shook his head forcefully. This was *exactly* the moment he had been waiting for. "Every worker in this company is an *enthusiast!*" he said, eyes widening. "Biking is in their blood!" His audience nodded, entranced. "Go ahead, look for yourselves!" he commanded. He had steered the group toward the testing chamber. "Take a long, hard look around."

Inside the glassed-in box, two fat workers were drinking coffee and the third, the chief tester, was about to light up a giant Cuban cigar. Wetting the tip of the tobacco gingerly with his tongue, the chief nibbled and nibbled and sucked and sucked, and finally chewed off the damp plug and spat it out on the floor. Brandishing a lighter, he began slowly toasting the ash end of the cigar. He had all the time in the world. Igniting the tobacco at last, he put the big Cohiba to his lips and began exhaling great plumes of languorous blue smoke in the test box, lazily scratching his balls every once in a while through coveralls.

My boss pointed to the posted no-smoking signs, hoping to embarrass the worker into action. He pointed again. No go. Frantic, he tapped on the glass. Zero response. Finally, the tester glanced our way through the glass, shrugging his shoulders as if to say, *"Ma che cazzo vuoi?"*—"What the fuck do you want?"— and to my boss's extreme consternation, continued sucking on his torpedo-sized stogie. It was the English bankers' turn to gloat. The tester's assistants, now getting nervous, tried to look busy. They rolled in a new bike and hooked up its exhaust pipes to the diagnostic machine. They started up the motorcycle's engine. They looked at gauges. They consulted dials. The tester wouldn't budge. *He* was smoking. Storm clouds of tobacco gathered overhead.

The CEO, to save face, tried to tell a lame joke. He waited a minute or so more—still desperate to show off his million-dollar testing unit and not *fare brutta figura* (make an ass of himself). He paced. He whistled. Finally, he lost it. Max pressed his lips so close to the glass that his breath formed steam shadows. Anyone who spoke Italian knew exactly what he was going to say next. *"Io, sono capo di questo cazzo azienda.* I'm the fucking boss of this company, now get your ass in gear and start that goddam testing!"

The tester's response was perfect as poetry, summing up centuries of Italian survival against foreign domination, world wars, the comings and goings of various management teams, state ownership, and now American privatization. Pointing his chin up in the air, the tester pulled the corners of his lips down into a full sneer and, with the lit cigar still hanging out of his mouth, he began the slow flick of a pointed index finger up from under his chin out toward the figure of our now livid chief executive officer. The classic gesture could only mean one thing in Italian: *non me frega niente*. "I couldn't give a shit who you are, I'm finishing my Havana."

Menegfreghismo (I don't give a shit-ism) is religion in Italy. No one can be hassled into doing anything—least of all playing the circus bear for a meddlesome CEO. In Italy, a manager can never correct a worker anyway. He can't even talk to him. That's strictly union business. The more pressure we put on workers to turn the building of motorcycles into Hollywood entertainment, the more outrageous their antics became. People stopped shaving. Others stopped washing. Che Guevara posters and Karl Marx T-shirts proliferated like magic mushrooms at a Grateful Dead concert. Beards grew out. Smoking increased fivefold. Red anarchy symbols were painted in the far corners of the factory—just in case anyone was confused about whose side the unions were on. Workers delighted in littering the floor with cigarette butts (Max had a personal vendetta against smokers) and used giant oil drums, not only as ashtrays, but as road blocks in the tourist lanes we had set up for the guided tours, dubbed "The Factory Experience."

Not long after the cigar incident took place, workers circulated a set of faux rules "from the management" throughout the company:

It has been brought to the attention of officials visiting the factory that members of our Italian-speaking staff regularly use offensive language. Such behavior, in addition to violating our policy, is highly unprofessional and offensive to visitors and staff. Please follow carefully these rules for the courteous benefit of all:

Words like *cazzo* (fuck), *porca puttana* (dirty whore), *mi sono rotto il cazzo* (ball-breaker), and other such expressions will not be tolerated or used for emphasis or dramatic effect, no matter how heated a discussion may become.

Creative ideas or projects initiated by management—like the current ban on smoking—are not to be routinely dismissed as *cagate mentali* or *idee del cazzo* (total bullshit or mental masturbation).

You will not say *ha fatto una cazzata* (he fucked up) when someone makes a mistake or *se lo stanno inculando* (they are screwing him over) if you see someone being reprimanded or *che stronzata* (what bullshit) when a major disaster has struck. All forms and derivations of the verb *cagare* (to shit) are utterly inappropriate and unacceptable in our environment.

No project manager, section head, or administrator under any circumstances will be referred to as *figlio di puttana* (son of a slut), *coglione* (a big testicle), or *testa di cazzo* (dickhead).

A chief executive should never be called a *mignotta* (little whore).

People discussed and circulated the memo for weeks, tweaking the text, substituting new insults when they got bored with the originals. It was great fun that took us through a long, cold winter.

Though I became something of an expert on slang and swearing—how could I avoid it?—I eventually got around to learning real Italian. As company fortunes improved, I hired an assistant, Luisella, who had a literary degree from Catholic University in Milan, but had most recently been Max's babysitter. Though she could declaim lines verbatim from the *Decameron*, just a few weeks earlier she had been warming formula bottles and changing dirty diapers. Now she taught me the command form and the past tense remote. After I finally mustered the courage to deploy a few choice verbs in the subjunctive, my colleagues insisted I spoke better Italian than they did.

One Christmas, Luisella gave me the present of a good, comprehensive Italian dictionary. It marked a turning point. In times of distress, bolognesi use a metaphor, *come i portici cosce di Bologna*, "like the arcades of Bologna." *Cosce* are thighs in Italian. The first things a newborn baby sees at birth are the thighs of his own mother. The arcades of this city were like a mother's thighs—they protected you. When a Bolognese walks under *portici*, he feels secure. Bolognesi seek solace in portici—protection from the wind, an escape from the rain. In the cold spring of that year, exhausted from a year of intense turnaround work at the company, I needed a bit of protection myself. On the weekends, I would sit under portici with an Italian dictionary and a thermos of hot black coffee. I learned hundreds of words. The dictionary was my refuge and I slipped into a silent world where there were no tenses, no slang, no sentences, just the glory of words in their hard elegance and crystalline meaning.

21

Max gave interviews during this period saying grand things like "The factory in Borgo Panigale is not strategic from an industrial point of view. It's an element of marketing. It's a theater." The unions went nuts and turned against him. There were three labor unions at the company: the Communists, the Socialists, and the Christian Democrats. Their affiliation had nothing to do with their politics or their priorities. The Communists seemed the most reasonable; they were at least willing to work with management to come up with innovative solutions to the challenges of manufacturing in Italy. The others lived in the Dark Ages. They cared about one thing—the preservation of jobs at all costs— even in a period in which we were adding employees and not firing them. Instead of focusing on strategic issues, namely, flexible work hours, job training, and work reassignment, they wanted simple promises from the boss to hire more workers. There was a semantic problem lurking in their logic: Who was the boss?

Repeatedly, the unions demanded to talk to the padrone— the real owner—of the company. It just couldn't be this nondescript, middle-aged guy in Gap jeans and old deck shoes! They believed a *faccia a faccia*, a direct face-to-face with the owner, would set things straight and win him over to their point of view. Business had been done that way in Italy for decades. But the unions underestimated the wiliness of our great leader—a witch doctor of words and manipulator of symbols—a man who did not want to be pinned down with titles or anything, really. Time and again, Max told the frustrated union representatives, "There is no *padre* here and there is no padrone. This is a modern company, owned by a private equity firm, which is in turn controlled by a group of investors who, having invested their money, expect a return one day."

The unions refused to believe it. They were no fools. When the CEO said, "The only people around here to talk to are management," they insisted on seeing the head honcho. He had to be around somewhere. Their mission was to find him, to ferret him out of hiding, and shine the red light of Marxist truth on his capitalist ways.

"Come on, is it you?" they would harangue Max in moments of distress. "Tell us! Say it! At least, admit it!"

"I'm not the boss," the boss would tell them gently. He was, after all, a fellow traveler. "I'm just another employee—like you—working at the pleasure of my employer." When we began the process of going public, the line was changed to "I am just working for the board of directors who represent the interests of shareholders." The unions couldn't understand that either. It was beyond their cultural ken.

"You're taking us for a ride," they protested, afraid of looking like fools. "We're not stupid, you know."

Understanding their lack of modern corporate experience, Max tried to talk reason to them. "The real owners of this company are teachers' pension funds in Utah and Iowa." The unions stared back at him with eyes as round as fat olives, black and unseeing. "These pension funds do not care a wit about how many workers are employed in Borgo Panigale or even whether we make motorcycles at all. The teachers care about one thing. They want to see profits."

The unions never bought his argument. And I don't think that I would have either. Though they would learn a great deal about modern capitalism in the years ahead, and become quite conversant with the silver tongue of the shaman, they never lost their core belief. "Only a true fool," they reckoned, "would be stupid enough to have a teacher from Iowa as his boss."

Management had its tricks. The unions had others.

Theoretically, we had labor peace at the company. The national labor contract was signed in Rome and the personnel office negotiated odds and ends with the local union representatives at the factory. A section of the company's prospectus even read: "The Company's operations have not suffered material disruption as a result of strikes or work stoppages in the recent past." The document, written while we were preparing to go public, was meant to reassure potential investors. The prospectus did many things. It absolved the underwriters of liability. It gave lawyers lucrative drafting work to do. It didn't mean we didn't have strikes at the plant.

Strikes were the hard currency of union power. Staging chaos how and when the unions wanted would never be negotiated away for cheap talk of stock options or summer flextime. The flash strike—as brief as a thunderstorm and often as destructive—was the performance art of our workers, more creative than any motorcycle they assembled. If we had an important rally or event for customers, the unions were sure to rain on the parade. They would march on the plant, downtrodden, unshaven, dressed in rags and greasepaint, bemoaning to the assembled enthusiasts how management had been abusive. If we launched a new motorcycle model, efficiently produced and more profitable in terms of gross margin (rare though that was!), union journalists would write that we were sneakily shipping jobs abroad to slave labor countries like China and Vietnam. The fact that none of these things was true was irrelevant. The unions could tell a good story too!

When they struck, they would block the entrance gates to the factory with human chains and shout "*Piattola!*" (scab) and "*Zecca!*" (fleabag) to the executives who broke the picket line. These were the same people with whom, just yesterday, they had drunk a cup of cappuccino at the bar, laughing about lovers they had shared and those that had slipped away. Now, they shook their fists with all the anger they could muster and with tears stinging their raging eyes, crying. "*Capitalista!*" as if it were a curse and not a fact of life in post-Communist Europe. If the unions heard that we were thinking of buying a competitor, and rumors were rife, signs went up proclaiming that the jewels of Italian industry were falling into the untrustworthy hands of foreigners. These "jewels," in any case, were paste. We never bought anybody.

One day, not long after the deadly G8 riots in Genoa in which riot police roughed up student demonstrators—and, in a particularly brutal incident, mauled a dozen protestors in a precinct house while chanting Fascist marching songs—the unions decided to strike the executive offices of the plant. The strike was to protest our decision to furlough workers because of a slowdown in summer sales. The unions staged a brilliant spectacle of office agitprop, with ragtag advance groups of workers climbing the stairs of the plant and invading the technical department. Then they moved on to the personnel office, the marketing area, and finally the executive suite. Other gangs of red-shirts followed. They were carrying pictures of Che Guevara, the patron saint of Bologna, and signs that read *Hasta la victoria sempre!*

The parading men were sweaty. They smelled of suntan oil, of foul cleaning solvents and Acqua di Parma. As they marched through the offices, chanting, they smoked long cigars or dragged on cigarettes in spite of the no-smoking signs posted everywhere. The women wore diamanté sandals, miniskirts, and D&G tank tops, and were shouting "Pigs!," "Money launderers!" In lighter moments they sang the "Internazionale" and waltzed through the offices like a merry band of troubadours. The singing didn't last long. Someone started slamming doors. Then everyone was. Doors were slung wide open, whipped shut. The percussive bangs, wood shattering on metal, loud as cluster bombs, reverberated through the plant.

Minutes later, the workers put on earplugs and brandished a new weapon. They switched on electronic police whistles to sear the eardrums of defenseless white-collar employees like me. Work was impossible. I shut my office door and started to sweat. There were hundreds of rabid unionists outside.

22

It was not the first time I felt fear in Italy. Fear is a constant companion of the sport motorcyclist. Every time I went out to ride, I rode with demons. Potholes. Oil spots. Rough gravel. An unexpected car door opened at the last moment. When the heat settled in Bologna and the smell of linden flowers lay heavy in the air like too much cologne, only fear prevented you from riding in flip-flops, running shorts, and a T-shirt. Fear put a full-face helmet on your head and slipped leather gloves with carbon-fiber knuckle protectors over your fingers. Gearing up for a ride—even a short spin in the hills above San Luca—was a claustrophobic tangle of elastic bands, snaps, buckles, and a Kevlar back protector shaped like a tortoise shell that wrapped the rider in a cocoon of approximate safety. Anxiety rode pillion anyway, whispering in your ear to check your mirrors every so often for trouble.

For the professional motorcycle racer, fear was something to be killed cleanly, without much ado or melodrama. That spring I went to my first Superbike race at the Santamonica circuit on the Adriatic coast. There, before a practice lap, I saw a storied French champion pacing the paddock for inspiration, breath sweet with the smell of juniper berries. Old verities about alcohol—that it blurred vision, dulled concentration—were all well and good for the typical enthusiast, but they did not apply in the professional world, where judgment was to be discarded for a higher value—*winning*—and minimum speeds exceeded two hundred miles per hour.[5]

A great racer didn't need to see the track anyway. He intuited it like a medium, conjuring its curves and corkscrews out of thin air. He felt the gradations of asphalt and the slipperiness of a painted line down deep in his soul. If a shot of alcohol helped dull the vibrations of doubt and fire up ambition in the belly of a boy racer, pop open the grappa . . . There was no shame in it. Too much sobriety was a problem on the track, never excessive derring-do. The moment a racer began actually thinking, he was on the brakes—or he was dead. Better to scream Metallica at the top of his lungs, to howl holy *vendetta*—tossing all anxiety to the wind.

I had ridden my bike down to the beach early to look at the house near Misano that Daniele rented each summer with friends. After meeting its owner, a spry World War II veteran who advised me to change my road tires to racing slicks before doing any track work, I rode up into the hills above the house and followed the roar of engines to the circuit. I passed under the storied arches of Santamonica and rolled down toward the paddock.

A racetrack without a race is a lifeless place, rather dull. Mostly, there is the great expanse of asphalt, marked here and there by pits, ridges, and subtle changes in gradient. A semicurve rises out of a straightaway and banks left. The track descends, then switches right. But add speed! The subtlest curve becomes a *big* curve. The smallest hole becomes a *big* hole. Fill the metal and concrete grandstands with fans. Add screaming. The racetrack becomes one of the most thrilling places in the world, a theater of life and death, a place where young men play fast games with fate.[6]

I watched a few warm-up laps from the pit lane. The Misano

track starts out with some well-groomed tarmac and a straightaway. It doesn't last long. A ninety-degree curve pops out of
nowhere, followed by a fast right-hander, then a series of turns
that vary in gear choices from second on through fourth, in plain
view of the grandstand. The twisties and switchbacks of the
course unfold—ascending, descending—on through the chi-
canes to the entrance to the Quercia bend and beyond. Racers
rise and fall, ear to asphalt, running rings around the track.

Truth be told, I couldn't see much of it. The speed of the
bikes was so fast that my eyes didn't register what they saw. I just
felt the snap of my neck as my body tried to keep up with what
senses couldn't follow. Feeling slightly disappointed, I decided to
watch the trials—the qualifying round that establishes grid positions on race Sunday—on television from the pit box. At least
there I had the possibility of some perspective. Gathered in the
box was our racing effort, the mechanics, managers, sponsors,
and support staff—and the racer's family. Now, the motorcycle
industry hates wives and loves girlfriends. Everytime I tell a married man where I work the response is always the same. "Man, I
would love to ride, but my wife just won't let me buy a bike."
Girlfriends are another matter. They encourage all manner of
wildness and irresponsibility.

Watching a motorcycle race with the wife of a champion is a
grueling affair. Though she may feign interest in the technical
aspects of pre-race activity—the tire warmers keeping rubber at
the right degree of stickiness, the starter motor setups—she's really watching for signs of doom: the tiredness, the distraction,
and the lack of focus that could destroy a racer in the clutch.
Wiping a helmet visor, whispering promises, she keeps a sort of
nervous vigil over the box. The night before she may have
treated a partner to an elaborate erotic fantasy—or abstained
from sex altogether—as was her custom. Now she gave tiny
kisses behind his ear, a reminder of pleasures to come—and hid

the helmet spackled with vomit she found discarded in the pit lane.

After the trials—"Prince Louis III" (III for the number of Superbike championships) came in pole—I followed his wife, Alessandra, to the hospitality tent for lunch. Louie was already there by the time we walked in, stretched out like royalty, feet up, feeding off a plate of cold cuts and chatting with the mechanics about tomorrow's race against his archrival, Texan Colin Edwards. Alessandra, a stunning Sicilian blonde with emerald eyes, crouched down on her hands and knees and, whipping a set of clippers from her Gucci pocketbook, began trimming the Prince's dirty, fungal toenails. The parings flew off and made tiny noises—ping, dong—as they struck a nearby metal wastepaper basket.

Louie shifted positions to accommodate her. Now his feet were resting on a nearby cafe table where others were eating. Alessandra took out a pair of metal scissors and expertly pruned his pea green cuticles to the base of the nail. Nothing bothered her. Journalists moved in to ask the Prince questions. She busied herself filing rough edges smooth with an emery board and fielded questions. She kept sanding and talking. Her husband, normally tight and cantankerous pre-race, was utterly relaxed. I don't think that he even noticed her.

23

As fear overtook me, first the trickle of sweat at my hairline, then a catch in a drier throat, I wished I had someone like Alessandra to protect me. But there was no one to preen me, no one to pump *me* up. I was alone in Italy. And strangely scared, barricaded in my office. Ratcheting up the tone again, young anarchists, recently seen drinking beers and smoking joints at after-hours clubs called "Link" and "Kinky," began running up and down the hallways of the executive offices. They were swinging bags, hurling backpacks, and breaking the framed advertising hanging on the walls that I had created. I could hear them howling, looking to provoke management. "Come out, you pigs!" "Show us your dirty, dollar-loving faces!" They opened and slammed my door. "Go home!" they screamed. "Ugly American! Money can't protect you now!"

Shivers coursed up my spine—cold sparks of alarm. I phoned the head of personnel, also a target of the harangue, and announced I was leaving for the day. "I feel really intimidated." After thirty years of experience with the unions—including the late-1970s heyday of the Red Brigades, when Italian executives were held for ransom and sometimes executed—the personnel chief was nonplussed by today's action. "Come and see me when you have a moment," he said. "Let's have a coffee."

I waited till the bands of workers disappeared round a corner and sneaked to his office—cutting through the internal administration offices like a jewel thief instead of taking the normal hallway lined with championship racing certificates. The old chief, gray and grizzled, but with the gleam of ambition still bright in his eye, welcomed me with a formal handshake. "Sit down. Make yourself comfortable," he said. "Would you like a coffee or maybe a little cup of tea? Biscotti?" Like many Italian managers who came of age in the 1960s, he sported a long mane of well-brushed white hair that fell well below his shirt collar.

I ordered a coffee, *macchiato con latte freddo*, sat down, and began telling him what happened.

"You say that the workers threatened you," he interrupted. "Is that right?"

"Yes," I said, kind of embarrassed.

"They came *inside?*" I nodded. "Did they actually step into your office?"

"Well, no, but they were slamming the door and screaming."

"*Allora*, that is a big difference, Signor Gross." He immediately relaxed. He took off his tortoiseshell eyeglasses, rubbed his tired eyes, and began cleaning his lenses with a chamois handkerchief. "Tell me the rest of what happened."

While I told him my story, he crossed his legs, pulled up his wool lisle socks, smoothed his flannel trousers, and rearranged his rep tie. He still dressed formally, despite the abandonment of the corporate dress code, and could not cure himself of using the formal *lei*—the respectful "you" form in Italian—with his colleagues and subordinates, even those of twenty years' standing. All of his fine manners and use of *lei* could not conceal the fact that he was growing bored with my story. "Anything else?" he asked me, as if the case were now closed.

"They yelled that they were coming to get me!"

"They are allowed to say that. But they didn't cross the threshold, right?" I admitted that they hadn't. "Did anyone touch you?"

"No!" I said irritably.

"Then they did exactly what they were allowed to do." He turned his attention to a more pressing matter. An important-looking letter from Rome—parchment envelope, multiple stamps, seals, and postmarks—was sitting on his desk blotter. He slit it open expertly with a silver penknife and began reading.

"But they stuck a hand inside my office and flicked the fucking lights on and off!" He shuddered at my vulgarity. "They slammed my door a dozen times . . . I still can't hear anything!" He took out a white linen handkerchief and patted down his high, aristocratic forehead.

"That's it?" he asked, finally looking at me again. "You are being too sensitive. I think you will survive the affair." He had lived through much worse—troubled times when executives had needed armed bodyguards and the owners had arrived by helicopter and entered the factory through a secret roof entrance. In those days, the unions wielded more than rhetoric and their strikes went beyond histrionics. They had power.

Periodic mass labor demonstrations throughout the 1970s and 1980s paralyzed whole industries, entire sectors of the economy, and ground the country itself to a halt, from Messina to Milan. The era was called *gli anni di piombo*, "the years of lead," a time when Italy's postwar miracle threatened to unravel. For men of his generation, the memory of the terror, the scandals, and the assassination of Aldo Moro still cast shadows in the business conscience. Even today, while the country basked in the unprecedented boom of the late twentieth century, he remembered just how close they had once teetered on the edge.

Now sharpening a pencil and marking up a memo, this head of personnel suggested that I go back to work—things were calming down. "Dai . . . Come on, it's not so bad, is it? I'm sure you have some real business to conduct."

Slinking back to my office I bumped into Max. "That was a disappointing show," he said cheerily. "I was actually expecting more color out of the unions."

"Yeah, the old tricks can get kind of boring," I mumbled.

He went on to praise the personnel chief, who had kept the whole thing moving without a hitch. "He's a real phenomenon," Max said. "That man can talk for hours and never say anything!" As it turned out, he had negotiated the entire strike with the union representatives beforehand. Everything had been choreographed. The only executive who had been left in the dark was—me.

Union tactics never scared Max anyway. They only added to the overall company drama. Dealing with labor issues brought back the nostalgia that every 1968-vintage leftist revisited under the cover of high-count cotton sheets. What side of the barricade you were on today wasn't important. It was the action that mattered. The splashed paint! The sweat! The muscle! The ripped T-shirts fluttering in the breeze like battle flags—dirty, torn, but still flying! The cause! The quest! This time around the cry was the turnaround. Rally the troops! Rev your engines! Build the glorious world of sport motorcycling!

Max hammered home his message in countless interviews. "A motorcycle could be built in any part of the world," he bragged. "There's no magic in it." It was a puzzle of sorts, because he never was much interested, during his long years at the company, in exactly how a motorcycle was actually made in the first place. The bike-building process remained "magic" to him, mysterious and elusive. He avoided the chief product designer like the plague. He rarely walked the line. And he almost never visited the model shop or design studio, all deep within the bowels of the plant. Manufacturing was his black box. He refused to open it.

Max preferred the smoke and mirrors of marketing, much more adapted to his prodigious communicative talents than the gritty details of product development. The guts of the motorcycle—the forged engine block, the tubular, steel trellis frame, and the cast-aluminum swing arm—could never capture his imagination. Inert components—critical though they were—did not possess enough fairy dust to rise above their nature. His engagement with the motorcycle began with the finished product. His attention span lasted as long as it took to create the "flash"—the books, the brochures—that was his professional stock-in-trade. The press was told, sometimes too blatantly and perhaps too often, that the plant in Borgo Panigale (and its workers) existed exclusively as tools to hype product. They had no value in and of themselves. But anyone who could serve up the special effects— the megawatt media fireworks, the laser light shows, the comedic PR stunts—to sell the story was hired immediately and fast promoted up the ranks.

PART TWO

24

Dino, the curator of the museum, had a terrible fear of the cold. He began each morning by wrapping himself in layers of thermal protection—undershirts, down vests, sweaters—preparing for the daily zip over to the company on an old scooter that would send his multiple pale yellow and ivory silk scarves fluttering. In autumn he looked like a late-season bumblebee that had miraculously survived the first onslaught of cold, with his black trousers, striped jumper, puff jacket, and his baldness. A few spare strands of wiry hair sprang from his dome. Even in the office, he kept his guard up, wary of drafty corners, removing a piece of clothing only as the day wore on and the heating system kicked in.

In Bologna that fleeting gust of seemingly innocent air—a draft—could trigger a rash of illnesses ranging from sore throat to even a slipped disk. It all depended on the atmospheric conditions, which Dino could recount like a precise human weathervane: "*Attenzione!* The wind has died in the hills. The sea is calm. The Pianura is a mass of still air, a breeding ground for disease." He approached illness as if it were a sentient being, something to be outfoxed with wiles instead of medicine.

I thoroughly enjoyed his solemn dispatches on the weather and just as blithely ignored them. "Laugh as you may," he would say every time I poked fun at the colorful foulards he tied around

his neck—even in summer—to prevent stray drafts from pene-
trating. "I cannot speak to where you come from, but here on the
plains of northern Italy a draft waits for the fool who dares the
elements with a body part exposed. I, for one, am taking no
chances." He had centuries of old wives' tales, if not science, on
his side.

As company historian he was feverish in his work. He could
produce paint chips from models manufactured decades ago so
that a collector could properly restore a vintage bike. He could
pick up the phone and call long-forgotten mechanics, builders of
early race machines that competed on wooden slats instead of asphalt, for details about an obscure engine part. His interests ran
even deeper—to a more remote past—a time in which the company didn't make motorcycles at all, but was busy commercializ-
ing the radio with its inventor, Guglielmo Marconi.

His desire to talk—in efficient, mechanical English—got
him noticed by the boss, who immediately plucked him out of
obscurity (the accounting department) and appointed him curator of the new museum that we had built in the middle of the
plant. Freed from the crushing quiet of numbers, he effectively
kept up a running dialogue on bikes, Bologna, and things belli-
cose.

"When the Americans came to liberate us a *second* time,"
Dino would say to startled fans during a routine tour, "the first
was when the 456th Bomb Group dropped thousands of pounds
of ordnance on the factory during the war . . ."—he lived for moments like this: a captive audience, the opportunity to play "living link" between the great events of history and the company's
saga—". . . I asked my mother what she thought of Americans.
Her experience was limited. She was about twelve years old
when the Allied army came rolling down the streets of Borgo
Panigale in Sherman tanks, distributing cigarettes and candy in
that raucous cowboy way." Visitors who had come expecting to

hear about racing were now squirming in the red conceptual helmet that served as a theater, fearing a torrent of anti-Americanism. Dino relished their helplessness—and kept right on talking—making sure not to leave gaps of airtime just in case someone had the temerity to interrupt him. " 'Dino,' my mamma told me, 'my experience with Yankees was hard and sweet. Hard, because I got hit on the head by a block of GI chocolate . . . and sweet because it tasted so good! Whatever happens,' she said, 'you can trust an American.' "

Unlike most Bolognese, Dino was not left-wing in the least. He loved America. When the boss described the transformation of the company from a manufacturer of vehicles to a purveyor of entertainment, Dino was right there with him, a kindred spirit. He too longed for what Italians call *un polo*—a powerhouse that would dominate the two-wheeled world and restore Bologna to its rightful place at the apex of industry. "To think that it took Americans to allow us bolognesi to rediscover ourselves," he would say, raising a bushy eyebrow as he showed off the prized collection of motorcycles assembled on the illuminated virtual racetrack. "What's next? French chefs teaching us how to cook tortellini *in brodo?*"

Dino was making entertainment too. He had no pretense that his bit characters and local incidents reached the dramatic pitch of the invasion of Normandy or the firebombing of Dresden. He was a military historian. He knew the difference between the loss of a battalion and the collapse of an entire war front. But still he had his mission to accomplish. "You think you came here just to see motorcycles," he almost threatened his guests, bitterness seeping through his usual curatorial demeanor. "I want you to understand the lives of the people who made them." Dino's mother had recently died of cancer. His father was fading into the fog of Alzheimer's. They had met and married while working on the line in the 1950s. He was trying to keep the culture that had sustained their lives alive for as long as he could.

"Do you want to see something *bello*, I mean really beautiful?" Dino asked, ever the coquette, appearing in my office one day with something in his delicate curator's hands. And then, not waiting for an answer, he showed it to me: a piece of fiberglass fairing, paint peeling away from the base material. He tapped the panel with a long, perfectly manicured nail. "Yes, *of course*, it is authentic!" A few days later he brought me an example of early company advertising, then a couple of vintage motorcycle tanks. He was flirting with me—dangling the artifacts he thought I might find useful in building a new brand that contained seeds of the old.

One time a picture of a Panzer tank got mixed up with a pile of bevel-head engineering drawings. Then a naval uniform appeared along with an old logo T-shirt. And all of a sudden, we were deep in world war: his extensive collection of toy soldiers, model planes, metal helmets, and an unexploded grenade. "It happened right here!" Dino pleaded, "on the very ground on which we stand," as if even I didn't believe him.

"I know," I sighed, hoping to avoid a long discussion about the multiple ways in which the war had touched the company, "I know the Fascists are important, Dino, but we have bikes to sell." I was busy trying to build a sexy, modern brand. He wanted to publish a coffee-table book called *Factory at War!* Who needed to know that we had once built bombs for the Axis? Or had sent the best engineers to Nazi Germany? Or that Bologna's Jews had been deported on the same rail system that shipped our production of war matériel to the front? Not me.

Dino was not so easily discouraged. Like most of my colleagues, top manager or maintenance worker, capitalist or Communist, he was anarchic to the core. We paid him to curate. *He* decided on his subject matter. Today we made motorcycles. But yesterday we had made transistor radios, calculating machines, electric razors, and even munitions! Who knew what tomorrow would bring? His trips to my office became more frequent. Like an archaeologist brushing away debris, Dino unearthed ruins and chipped away at truths. History and politics began to intrude on the fun and fantasy of turning around a motorcycle company. With each discovery, our past grew darker.

Unlike most people in the business, Dino had the soul of an artist. He could make beauty out of horror. It happened one afternoon while we were walking up via Ugo Bassi toward Nicoletta's bar. The setting sun was sending rays streaming down the colonnades of San Felice, turning brick into gold. Dino wasn't interested in appreciating the dimensional quality of the light. Nor did he break stride to gaze into windows displaying lingerie embroidered with sequins and pearls. He smelled flesh and gunpowder. Mortars exploded in midair. "It's always in my mind," he admitted.

"What?" I asked, still ignorant of his near-total preoccupation.

"The invasion. I can't stop thinking about it." He pointed at black-and-white markings painted on the wall, the old indication arrows of the U.S. Army. Here was a bomb shelter. There was a makeshift emergency hospital. He pointed out the word *rifugio* that appeared every so often like rhyme, under balconies, above a window box, marking the shelters for civilians escaping the Allied bombing runs of 1944 and 1945. "All that you have to do," he said in his clipped emotional English, "is to add back the tanks, the traitors, and, of course, the rampant destruction. And then you will understand everything there is to know about contemporary Italy."

Though the statues of Mussolini—lips pursed, chin jutting— were smashed soon after the partisans hanged him and his mistress outside of Milan, signs of his long rule turned up everywhere. The medieval city, the place of the half-marbled, half-brick churches and the raised tombs of saints, receded. The Renaissance city of rich trader houses and frescoed palaces with double Romanesque loggias retreated. In its place a 1930s modern Fascist Bologna materialized.

Mussolini was in the harsh rectangularity of office blocks whose rows and rows of oversized windows created the rhythm of movement. Marble without ornament was modern. Bright light flooding office windows was Fascist. The hand of the Duce could be felt in workers' housing on the outskirts of northern Italian cities. Crumbling into sand, these cement buildings celebrated the honesty of a material that had been new to Italy in the 1920s and 1930s.

Even the thoughts of the Duce lived on. There! Beyond the bridge, right after the curve, entering the tiny *frazione* of a small, country town—written on a wall or painted on a broken bridge or posted on a storehouse—were the dreams of a restless country, the Italy of ambition. *Roma Doma. Noi Sogniamo L'Italia Romana.* "Rome Reigns. We Dream of the Italy of the Caesars!" In the silence of these simple places, the grandeur of one man's voice was still deafening.

A few weeks later, on the way to one of our technical suppliers near Budrio, I saw my first written exhortation of the Duce. *Disciplina, concordia, e lavoro per la ricostruzione della patria.* I called Dino for a precise translation. "Discipline, harmony, and employment for the rebuilding of the country." The message was written on the side of a municipal building in two-meter-high letters, as pristine as the day it had been painted. Had the words been restored or did the letters possess preternatural, long-lasting color? I let their power seep and stew inside me. Divorced from the age and the politics in which they were written, must they necessarily be discredited?

The same sentence, now gray, appeared on a russet-colored building in Brescia, a cement wall in Biella, and a farmhouse outside Turin, rich and ringing across the decades.[7] Dino had been researching similar signage that appeared on barnyards, on decaying farmhouses, along country roads across Italy. "Italy desires peace, but does not fear war" and "Peace rests on the strength of our armies"—drawn in elegant typefaces, Etruscan, rationalist, simple, ancient Roman, that resisted being worn away by rain, sleet, time, and indifference. With his high-pitched nasal voice Dino said, "David, meet the man who invented the original smoke and mirrors." His aristocratic-sounding *r* was aspirated. "More exciting and beautiful, I dare say, than our company's 'More single-race victories than all of the competition put together.' "

What combination of ingredients had been used to make messages that shone through multiple whitewashings, deface-ments, and attempts to subvert meaning? The paint was cer-tainly made with the stuff of poverty: earth mixed with glue, milk swirled with ashes, casein and lime. Modern contrivances could not rub them out. In Novarra a stylish sign—crisp white letters on a blue field—read "Duce." Its pop commercialism was such that it could easily have been an advertisement for Cam-pari. After the fall of the regime in 1943, it had been painted over. The writing reemerged in 1952. From that point, it was treated to three coats of whitewash, various cleanings, and other vigorous attempts at blotting out, but each time the letters reap-peared, clear as day—as grandiose as the Victor Emmanuel Mon-ument itself. This Duce was not going anywhere.[8]

"All letters began as signs," wrote Victor Hugo, "and all signs began as images." The alphabet contains in its design the sum of human history. *D* was a human back, *U* an urn. *X* stood for the crossing of swords.[9] The transformation of Mussolini the soldier into Mussolini *il Duce* began in 1926 with the publication of

Dux, a volume that mythologized the young leader. The process was completed with his conquest of Ethiopia in 1936. Even the poet-patriot Gabriele D'Annunzio was forced to admit that "In all of the history of the conquerors, there has never been a man who was able to create with his own human means, a myth so eternal."

The word "Duce" appeared everywhere: on factory walls, on smokestacks, on gates, on garages—vertically, horizontally, in endless patterns and repetitions—Duce, Duce, Duce—or in stark isolation: Duce! Dino found an old photograph of the factory with the words *Credere Obbedire Combattere* painted on one wall. There was no punctuation. Believe Obey Fight. It was one of the most common of his mottos. According to scholars, Mussolini pronounced the maxim for the first time in March 1939 during an address to the Fascist Guard in Rome. More likely, the charge was invented in 1932, when he changed the old insignia *Liberta e Patria* (Liberty and Country) on military uniforms to something more suitably dictatorial.[10]

Originally, the slogans had specific destinations. The 1939 circular of the Partito Nazionale Fascista decreed that *Credere Obbedire Combattere* be used on the external walls of party buildings. It became so popular that a company like ours probably adopted it anyway. Maybe we put it up in 1938 when the Duce paid his first visit, or later, in 1941, when he came again, after war had been declared. What did Mussolini think when he arrived in Borgo Panigale? He had been traveling up and down the peninsula at a grueling pace. Was he tired, that intrepid seaman, the fearless leader who crossed the Straits of Messina in a launch? Was he hungry, that triumphant aviator, an Italian Lucky Lindbergh, dressed in a flight jacket with a mutton collar? Did he expect to see the appropriate sign that a modern factory was ordered to have painted on its wall? A message that read: Even the most mundane work, minuscule and obscure, can make the country great. *Anche con l'opera quotidiana, minuta ed oscura, si fa grande la Patria.* Or its alternative: Work is the most solemn, most noble, most religious thing in life. *Il lavoro è la cosa piu solenne, piu nobile, piu religiosa della vita.*

Dino couldn't give me a straight answer. Perhaps, almost two decades into his long rule, Mussolini had grown bored with seeing posted what had always been in his mind? Or maybe he had nothing to do with the slogans at all and had left the writing of them to a flunky. The black-and-white photograph of his visit—one of Dino's prized "finds"—provided no clues. The formality of the day and the crispness of the uniforms were all there was. Credere Obbedire Combattere. The words were the only dissonant element. Even in the heyday of Fascism, I wanted to believe that we had offered some resistance.

That was just the beginning. Dino used his position to document exactly what happened to a small company during the dying days of World War II. He did research, visited Web sites, made phone calls, and located the war records of the Fifteenth Division of the U.S. Army Air Corps. He found one Lieutenant Joseph W. Shuster of St. Johns, Pennsylvania. The son of a Lutheran minister, Joe had enlisted in the Reserves and was called to active duty in February 1943. He had been selected—along with nine other men—to be part of a flying unit that would attack enemy positions across Europe.

The crew, all young mechanics and aviators, traveled to Davis-Monthan Field in Tucson for months of ops training in the spring of 1943 and then on to Topeka, Kansas, where it took possession of a bright new B-24 Liberator. In the next few weeks, the men crossed the Caribbean basin to Brazil, flew across the Atlantic to Dakar, traveled through the North African cities of Marrakech and Tunis, then across the Mediterranean to reach their home base in the tiny Italian town of Stornara.

The operation was called "Pancake." At 12:52 p.m. on October 12, 1944, a day full of the fog familiar to all Bolognese from time immemorial, the bombing began. The Italian underground had supplied information to the Allies that a certain factory in Borgo Panigale was making munitions for the Nazis. It could only be one place. In wave after wave, Shuster's bombers dropped 732 five-hundred-pound bombs on the factory and the adjacent Via Emilia. B-17s, the Army Air Corps's Flying Fortresses, simultaneously attacked the Marconi Airport, the bridges across the River Reno, oil reserves, troop concentrations, and the train station, in an attempt to subdue the city.[11]

On the plant itself fifty-three bombs fell. The warehouses were destroyed, the personnel department blown up. The executive offices, from which the three founding brothers commanded the production of munitions, with the grand Fascist rooftop sign that spelled the company's name in towering Futurist letters, were bombed into a fine, gray dust. Another ninety-two bombs exploded nearby, isolating the factory from the critical transport, supply, and communications lines that connected it to Bologna, northern Italy, and the war effort.

Operation Pancake did not achieve the results intended. Dino found aerial photography of "target number 18" from the Maxwell AFB Historical Searches Institute. The bombing report read as follows: "On a single hazy print the factory appears to have been seriously damaged by a good concentration of hits. Two of the small shops have been destroyed and several others partially destroyed. A direct hit on top of the large, flat-topped building caused light damage, but failed to penetrate the roofing. A building near the target area is burning." The devastation was extensive, but the factory, under German occupation since 1943, retooled and continued to make small quantities of munitions almost to the end of the war. Lack of visibility in the fog and the inaccuracy of the bombers meant that the attack was insufficient to allow the Allies to seize control of the city. Bologna remained Nazi.[12]

From a military perspective, the attack had little impact on the larger battle for control of northern Italy. From the company's perspective everything changed. A factory that before the war had been a model of innovation with its gymnasium and kindergarten, an enterprise that had provided employment to ten thousand workers, was now reduced to rubble. A plant that had been, along with Fiat and Pirelli, among the leading lights of Italian modernism—a company that produced goods containing vacuum tubes, batteries, and optical lenses—looked like a pile of charred children's blocks. The damage caused by Shuster's bombers was such that the brothers did not have enough capital after the war to repair the plant and return to their core business, that of producing electric razors, radios, and cameras. The government had no money either, forcing the family to look elsewhere, to other products, to other markets to survive.

In the late 1940s, the beleagured brothers decided to strap a tiny 50cc engine made in Turin to a bicycle frame. They called it the Gattino, the Kitten. Bright red, with chrome details, the Gattino gave Italians a cheap, cheerful reason to return to their warpocked streets. With respect to its competitors of the day, its four-stroke engine was more powerful than its two-stroke rivals and consumed less fuel. It traveled almost one hundred kilometers on a liter of gas. In a country that lay largely in ruins, the Kitten was a technological and commercial hit. It sold in the tens of thousands. We were now a motorcycle maker.

The Kitten was the precursor to an even more important scooter, the Vespa, made by Piaggio, which would become the icon of dolce vita Italy in the 1960s. But that was still light-years away. In the gray Bologna of the late 1940s, the factory pumped out as many Kittens as possible and never looked back. The restoration of the plant was not finished until 1962, by which time the company was state-owned and well on its way to winning race championships in the Motogiro d'Italia road race and the Milano-Taranto.

In March 2002, Dino contacted Joseph Shuster, who wrote back to him via e-mail. "Mr. Dino," he wrote, "I was surprised and pleased to receive your interesting e-mail about the 456th Bombardment Group's damage to the factory . . . I appreciate receiving the pictures you sent me and am sorry it has taken me so long to reply to your message. The Bologna mission was near the end of my tour in Italy, but I have no recollection of the details. Our group's history indicates there was no fighter opposition but the flak was heavy, scattered, and inaccurate. We only lost one plane that day." He went on to write: "While I am only familiar with the company's name, my son is well informed about your excellent motorcycles. I would like to receive more information about them. And last, I would love to visit Italy again and would certainly like to visit your museum but I no longer tolerate long travel distances very well."

Dino was thrilled. He picked up the telephone and began dialing the United States. "Joe, Joe . . . ," he said, his voice almost breaking with emotion, "I am Dino from the museum." Joe was eighty years old. His voice was fading like a weak radio signal, and the conversation, across time and oceans, was inconclusive. A heartbroken Dino had to admit: Shuster didn't remember many details from the fateful fall of 1944.

If anyone showed the least bit of interest in the story of Joe Shuster, and, truth be told, few did, Dino offered to show you other things, like the hidden catacombs under the factory where Jews had supposedly been sequestered when Germans occupied the city in 1943. His current project was to verify whether one of the brothers, rumored to have saved Jews, was mentioned in the

Garden of the Righteous Nations at Yad Vashem. At the drop of a hat, Dino could also show you the secret tunnels through which weapons had been shipped to a depot in town, and from there off to the front. Even more sinister were his field trips to the Wermacht cemetery on the outskirts of the city, filled with dead Germans in narrow graves marked by square, iron crosses. He proposed this excursion to Jeremy, a newcomer at our Internet division. "You know, I'm Jewish," Jeremy protested.

"Jewish, non-Jewish . . . that doesn't matter," he replied matter-of-factly, "This is history." And it was.

It was an early spring morning in Bologna. The sun lit up the sky a luminous pale blue, the color that Italians call *carta di zucchero*, after the original azure-hued sugar packets. I was at my desk working through e-mails, opening stacks of letters. It was always a pleasurable time of day for me, going through the newspapers, checking the headlines on Web sites, making phone calls to my parents who were up late in New York, or just drinking a lazy cup of coffee—extra-*lungo* with hot water—during an hour when most Italians were still sleeping. I looked out the window toward the hills. San Luca was hanging like a paper lantern, glowing red-gold against a forest of pine. Across the street was a stand of loquat trees whose limbs were heavy with new fruit. Borgo Panigale—a forgotten stop on an old Roman road, nowhere important really—was becoming like home.

Bang! Like a gunshot in a comic book, the door to my office exploded. The man, long and lean, in black trousers and Chelsea boots, injected instant anxiety into the room. He paced up and down—gabardine scratching against hairy skin—and started flipping rapid-fire through *Corriere dello Sport*, then *Motor Cycle News*, crunching pages, tearing out articles, throwing the whole mess down on the floor like contaminated pulp. Sighing hard and massaging his neck glands, he muttered about work stress and rare tropical diseases. He coughed, cleared his throat. He mangled a paper clip and used it to clean his nails, flicking the grime on my desk. Still, I didn't look him in the eye.

He took a business card out of the Rolodex, folding it into smaller sections till it disappeared. Then he began swearing. "Fuck this lot. When are they *just going to let me work?*" He blew his nose, cleaning his nostrils with a hankie and a fingertip. Finally, he addressed me directly. "What the hell are *you* so busy doing over there, hiding behind that computer screen? It can't be work." I didn't bite. He tossed the folded card at me. "Everyone is so busy here, nothing ever gets done. Funny *that*." The Australian accent became more pronounced as he picked up steam. "You know *man*, this is a bike company . . ." I called my answering machine in New York. Listening to messages was a useful activity when the man in black, but wearing an even darker mood, came calling. "At *some* point, we are going to have to design some motorcycles around here."

I was tempted to lash out: "You're not the only one working!" But he had already changed tactics.

"You can't avoid me forever," he said, this time sweetly. "Come on, have a cup of coffee on me. It's too early for work." And I relented.

As the turnaround gained momentum and the investment in brand instead of bikes continued apace, the product people got agitated. The chief of design, an utterly determined Aussie who had been in Italy for so long that he had become, as he liked to brag, "more Italian than the Italians," thundered into my office regularly to tee off on strategy. Jacques was a firecracker of a personality—a designer with a hot temper and a sharp tongue who launched puns and put-downs as ruthlessly as clinic models. When he was raging, he didn't just insult me, anyone in the company was fair game. "Selling motorcycles is not like selling soap powder," he would threaten, voice shaking, veins popping, pacing up and down the industrial carpeting, grinding a groove. "You need more than a clever jingle to move units."

The crack was a reference to our chief executive, who had had a short successful career at Procter & Gamble selling Pampers, toothpaste, and, presumably, soap powder before coming to Bologna. "Long after your lot goes back to selling dog biscuits or panty liners or, better yet, 'turning around' the next poor slob of a company, I'll still be here designing motorcycles." Throwing down rounds of black coffee, one plastic cup after another, then cans of Coke, twitching from the buzz, Jacques would stalk the hallways of the plant. *He* was in the mood for conversation. "What I am supposed to do?" he'd ask anyone willing to listen. "Pull the rabbit out of the hat every time?" Smart colleagues nodded their heads, hoping to avoid an escalation.

But the man could not be shut up with understanding. "I can't do the next world-beating bike in five minutes flat—not when the competition takes seven years!" Lathered up one minute, he would sprawl out in my office the next, rolling his head around in an agonized version of yoga. "In Italy you're either a genius or a cunt," he would say, running fingers through a preternaturally boyish brush cut. "Good on *them*! But in the real world, great design takes planning."

When a new, deeply tanned honcho took over (Max had taken a high-end consulting position in Switzerland), the taunt evolved. The new chief executive, a former accountant, had previously run the largest pork processing plant in Italy and told a macabre story about hogs at the slaughter. "The secret of making good prosciutto," said the sweet, diminutive Roman, "is all about keeping the pig in the dark." If the swine, at the moment it met its executioner, got wind of what was happening, it started shrieking, releasing fear endorphins in the blood—ruining the quality of the meat. Everything had to remain perfectly calm for the highest-quality prosciutto—hiding the pig from its destiny. The new boss was just as innocent. His ending was as peaceful as it was inevitable. Max was obliged to return.

Months earlier, a prescient Jacques had predicted, "A sunburnt sausage king won't save us by cutting the salami in thinner slices. We need new bikes—and we need them *fast!*" Jacques did not care about office politics or the even-tone tans admired in Italian business circles. He wanted money to build motorcycles, pronto. When his ire was up (which was often), he would walk the factory floor, knocking on doors, hijacking one executive after another—looking for allies, haranguing doubters—creating havoc in the hallways, the place where real business decisions were made. He ranted about master plans that never got implemented (or made in the first place) and Gantt charts which he called "cunt charts" because only a dumb cunt would pay a consultant to tell him what Jacques already knew and could tell you for *free*—that the company needed to get busy building motorcycles or get out of business altogether.

"In my experience, consultants are expert at one thing only: screwing the company out of its money." His jokes were like roman candles—shocking pinks and acid greens brightening a black sky—or showering chrysanthemums of spark and ash that made you suck your breath in. When he hit his mark. If he took it too far, the pyrotechnics just burned—a cheap M-80 in a mailbox. In the beginning—before I realized it was futile—I tried to quiet him down. "Most of the executive team is made of consultants," I warned. "Everyone here is ex-Bain, ex-McKinsey!"

"Yeah right . . . and I tell you, I've never met a consultant who didn't tell me something I already knew!" He was proud of an ability to produce put-downs for any occasion. "The only difference is that they do it with charts. You know what?" he continued, not missing a beat. "I don't speak '*chart*.'"

"You're in the wrong business," I said nervously. "You should be doing stand-up comedy."

"You can see why no one in management wants to talk to me. I'm a real *cunt.*" In all of our years working together, I never *once* accused him of kissing ass.

He would crush his coffee cup in disgust and cruise the corridors for new victims. The commercial director, a fast-talking former used car salesman, kicked him out of his office straightaway. No one enjoyed being told that he was a "peasant" or a "design heathen" or that the bikes that he was desperately trying to retail to meet ever higher targets were "fat old cows" (cows designed by the previous designer, not Jacques). The product manager cowered behind a locked door. This playboy of noble blood—an "oxygen thief" in Jacques-speak—had nothing in his pedigree to prepare him for a designer who screamed like a banshee and threatened that if said manager didn't help persuade management to build new bikes *right now*, the company risked imminent collapse.

Only the Bolognese head of the technical department, a small grandfather of a man with a smiling mustache, a lifetime of experience, and an iron fist that controlled the product development budget, had the patience to listen to such tirades. He chewed his whiskers thoughtfully and then ignored the designer completely, doing exactly as he pleased: investing his lire in more horsepower. Jacques alternately loved and loathed him like an ex-lover.

Jacked up after more coffee and fully frothed like hot milk in a latte—his passion for product entirely undiminished—he would arrive at my door. In the beginning, I was flattered. I thought he wanted to seek out *my* opinion on company problems. I thought he was interested in what *I* had to say about new model development. Who wouldn't have jumped at the chance to plot future strategy with such a design visionary? Later, I realized Jacques was just dropping the usual bombs, oblivious to casualties, living up to his nickname, "the French Terrorist."

Mine was the last office on the long corridor of executive suites. After exhausting the more seasoned folk, he knocked on my door. "Well, well, now . . . Mister David *Gross* here to save us all with his Harvard law degree and fancy fashion T-shirt graphics!" The sneer in his voice stung. He marched in without further ado and plopped a ballistic aluminum briefcase on my desk. In all the years I've known Jacques, I never saw him open it. Maybe it contained his great big motorcycle idea. Maybe the metal housed a cluster bomb and he was waiting for the right moment to light the fuse. On most days, he himself seemed ready to blow. "Commercial people are like *whores*." Did I know that? I shook my head vaguely. "Every year I see them at the bike fairs. The business cards change. The people remain the same." He was on a tear. "In ten years I've seen ten guys with ten different positions—always doing them badly. At least the mechanics stay mechanics for life. They know what's a screw and not just how to *screw* you."

But I knew better than to think that he was a real friend of mechanics—or model makers or procurement executives or anyone else, for that matter. They were all just pairs of hands or spare sets of brains, "tree monkeys" who last week may have been industrializing refrigerators or engineering telephone poles, but who now had to be put to work, sanding surfaces or ordering parts or calculating mathematics, all in the service of the great project that was design—under his divine direction.

For months—even years—mornings began with an angry visit from "Uncle." I grew attached to his volatility, his overwhelming passion to build things—not just bikes but accessories, apparel, and even motorcycle-inspired furniture with built-in chrome armrests and removable ashtrays. He was an active volcano of creativity, forever erupting in rivers of lava. I craved his roiling personality and, yes, his poetically crass insults. "The company is like a bordello," he liked to tell me whenever I got frustrated. "You can change rooms as many times as you like, but there's still a whore behind every door." Conversation with him was maddeningly addictive—like cheap candy, one fast sugary rush and then a crash.

"What can I do for you today, Uncle?" I called him Uncle because he was endlessly offering me advice.

"Give me half a million dollars. I have a new bike project I want to design."

"I'll give you *ten*," I countered. "Build a whole new range."

"Yeah, *right*," he sighed disgustedly. He removed his matte titanium glasses, rubbing sore eyes. "I'm beat. I've been working all weekend." He glanced at the *Cycle World* on my desk, grimacing when he saw the stunning Yamaha R1 on its cover. "You know what?" I had learned to think twice before answering a loaded question like that. "I'm going to write a memo to the board and tell them what's *really* happening around here." The tiredness was gone. He spoke like a viper spitting its first venom.

"And what *is* really happening around here?" I took the bait, powerless to resist.

"Nothing," the designer said sadly. "That's the problem."

"What's going on around here is that we're selling motorcycles." I held firm to the corporate line.

"This is a bike company, man. We are *supposed* to build bikes."

"And we do."

"Just not new ones . . ."

"They're as new as we need them to be."

"Well, *mate*. I think I am going to write that down. Yes, I am going to put it in a sealed envelope and open it a few years from now. Then we'll see, man. We'll see how these fat pigs designed ten years ago by a plumber"—his great rival and once master—"with engines originally built more than twenty years ago, hold up in model year 2010."

He picked up one of the brochures I had been working on, flipping through the pages. "The Japanese are gaining on us," he said. "Look! Can't you see it? Our bikes are *old*—look at this Beast—wires hanging out everywhere, ten different-colored screws."

"This company is a success story," I insisted. "We're the most profitable brand—"

"Yeah, I can read that in the press releases you write."

"Oh, *come on*, at least have the balls to admit that we've achieved something."

"*You've* achieved? Oh, that is rich, man. All your lot did was start production. Any fool with fifty million could've done that!"

"Next time, why don't you try raising it?" Finding those dollars was no walk in the park.

"This is the other regime's success, man, and you know it," he sneered. "Call me when you're ready to do something new, something *real*." Then he slammed the door behind him, rattling the photographs of vintage motorcycles on the wall—only to re-open it a few seconds later and begin his argument anew, if I was lucky, in a nicer tone of voice, but more often than not, even more riled up than before. The engine covers needed an immediate aesthetic overhaul! The trellis frames required microwelding to eliminate seams! His hands trembled like an old man's with Parkinson's.

"What do I have to do to convince you to help me?" The voice was now small, pleading.

"Nothing," I said, looking away from those haunted cornflower eyes.

"Talk to them, if not for my sake, then for the company. I

don't have the right tone of voice. I get too angry. I'm over-passionate." What he said was true. "But if I have to get on my knees and blow the whole fucking management team to get something done, I'll do it!" It was a strangely generous offer from a man who was a total stranger to the art of collegial flattery.

26

The first time I saw Antonio he was hanging out at an Agip station near the Ferrara exit ramp on the highway that ran from Bologna to Padua, doing nothing much except chain-smoking cigarettes. I thought maybe he was the gas attendant or station mechanic, though he didn't so much as move a muscle when I pulled up on my motorcycle. He just continued taking long, slow drags from a Marlboro—staring off at fields of wheat sprinkled with poppies that flanked the highway on both sides like a parted Red Sea. Poppies always grow with wheat in northern Italy in a secret spring-summer symbiosis of red and green that even local farmers don't understand.

I parked the bike at the pump, unlocked the fuel cap, put the nozzle in the gas tank, and started filling. With a rag from a nearby bucket, I wiped down my helmet and windscreen, which were covered with gnats, sticky pollen, and the occasional bird dropping from a two-hour ride. I became aware of someone watching me, but each time I looked up, he was stretched out against the lamppost, looking off into the flat distance or staring at the big yellow-and-black Agip logo—a fire-breathing, multi-legged dragon—or blowing complicated blue smoke rings that disappeared like genies in the steam of an evening turning orange with sunset.

He was dressed in the simple skinhead uniform that varied little during the time I knew him: a black Fred Perry polo worn close over lean muscle, Doc Martin waders—the cherry-red ones—tight-fitting "bleachers" (Levi 501s splotched with Clorox), and heavy chains—wrapped loose around his waist like a belt, attached to a key fob and leather wallet, linked around his neck like a steel dog collar. As any serious skin would tell you, it was not at all a bad look for a mate—clean and sharp, right for any situation. Matched with a freshly shaved head, in Antonio's case a number one crop, the style became a rallying cry against Italian fashion, against establishment taste and mores. Though later he was always at pains to tell me he was a nonpolitical skin—"I don't believe in anything!"—Antonio flaunted the sexiness of a working-class aesthetic whose opposition to mod fashion and racial integration was its original raison d'être.

As I finished filling the tank with the greenish, flammable fluid, I caught him stealing a hard look at the engine of my bike, eyes half-closed, lids heavy and secretive, the tip of his tongue sandwiched between semiclenched teeth. He pulled harder on his Marlboro, taking monster drags of the smoke that was status among poverty-stricken students. His face colored with excitement and perhaps recognition of his own incipient desire. He was anxious, edgy, and mesmerized. He was looking at a *motorcycle*.

Motorcyclists always talk about their first time. The day they stumbled into Uncle Dan's garage and caught sight of the middle-aged bachelor in stained coveralls, wrench in hand, working on a Harley Softail, polishing chrome, retrofitting gorilla bars, cleaning full dress leathers with Murphy's Oil and Black Beauty. Oh the stink: the burn of smoke, the buzz of silicone! And the noise: the rattle of a clutch, the wheeze of air filling tires, the screaming of screws! The textures to touch: satin steel and polished aluminum. And the colors to choose: powder coat matte black, mirror bright chrome, glossy paint on metal.

These visceral feelings had nothing to do with why rich financiers or plastic surgeons bought our sport bikes—because they were the ultimate object to put on a pedestal or because after having made millions in a world that hardly built anything anymore but offered an array of ever more specific services—iced soy lattes with a pump *and a half* of hazelnut *or* vanilla and preventive "mini" male facelifts—they wanted to reconnect with something physical, something real. No. The teenage boy (and occasional girl) who sneaked a peek at somebody else's rolling thunder or 150-plus-horsepower crotch rocket or an Italian dream bike—all swooping curves, surface dynamics, and billet parts carved from the solid—came closer to the primordial motivation for becoming a biker in the first place: a taste for unadulterated adventure and lust for base metals.

I looked up at Antonio, leaning provocatively against his lamppost, and, for a second, gazed into black eyes that showed no differentiation between iris and pupil and offered no sign of friendliness. I was about to say a neutral enough "*Ciao*" when he looked back at me, then at the bike once again, letting out a low wolf whistle, and said flatly, "Well, well, someone's daddy has money to spend."

"You know, it's not mine," I said, somewhat embarrassed. "It's a loaner bike, from my company."

"*Beh* . . . I would love to ride, too," he said, "believe me." And then he pulled his pockets inside out to show me that they were empty. "I don't even have the cash to go out and get lessons." It was the sweet singsong accent of the Veneto, with a rising tone at the end of the sentence that turned everything into a musical question. "Nine hundred cc?"

I nodded my head.

"Figo." He smirked, shaking his head slightly. And with that he went back to his box of expensive cigarettes and hard stares at shafts of wheat whose destiny was to become pasta and rattle around in a blue Barrilla box in their next lifetime.

We didn't exchange much more than that on our first meeting. I was too shy to say, "I could teach you to ride sometime." I was too timid to ask his name or suggest a date. I was worried about right-wing teen gangs terrorizing immigrants and setting Italian Jewish houses on fire. But I was also riveted—stealing repeated stares, afraid of getting caught, at his finely shaved skull, radiant in the late sun of the plains, a new orb in the galaxy of my desire. I paid the Arab cashier for the gas, bought some Gatorade, and organized my gear for the ride back to Bologna.

The skinhead began to look at me more openly now, appraising my ability to fire up a 900cc motor that produced seventy horsepower at the rear wheel—if not under my domain, then at least back at the test bench in the factory. His blank intensity, staring not seeing, sustaining interest but refusing any warmth, was a show of dominance. He dared me to meet his gaze head-on. As I pulled out of the station, I clicked my helmet visor shut. All I could muster was a muffled: "I guess I'll see you around."

"*Maybe* you will."

Had I heard him say that? I turned to see him one last time—to imprint that image of raw intensity on my senses. What I saw was a boy, as lean as a rail—hard, quiet, still smoking his Red pack—doing nothing more important than examining the lit end of the tobacco, burning orange in the pale evening blue.

Riding on the autostrada back to Bologna, past the stretches of young wheat and fallow brown fields, past the bright Autogrills and the old farmhouses that punctuated the great flatness of the plains, I watched the sun set in the hills to the west, a heavy ball of flame, turning the sky soft and the green mists iridescent, and thought how surprised I was that I had actually found the courage to say anything to him at all. Clouds rushed in. The temperature dropped. The wind picked up suddenly and thunderstorms rolled across the plains, west to east, send-

ing down showers of white, glistening rain and flashes of lightning. Shafts of colored sunlight—greens and yellows, pinks and
oranges—cut through the darkness, throwing patches of land in
stark theatrical relief: a blazing stand of green poplar against gray,
a yellow square mile of oilseed flower amidst marshy dunes, red
roofs in tones of terra-cotta on stone.

Dwarf peach and plum trees, their buds puffed like pink and
purple corn on gray espaliered branches, gave their sweetness
willingly to the wet. Lit by lightning, the orchards became vivid
and electrified like neon signs, testament to that fact that this
was no simple pastoral landscape, but a working place intensely
shaped by man. A land where engines were cultivated alongside
wheat, a place where bikes were as indigenous to the soil as stone
fruit, and a world in which, at some point, many decades ago,
a few farmers-turned-mechanics had taken their knowledge of
engines—the motors that powered plows and moved forklifts
and ran tractors—and transformed it into vehicular art: the engineering of high-performance racing cars and motorcycles.

I crossed from the Veneto into Emilia-Romagna, near Ferrara, pushing harder still, at the limits of my skill, to avoid
getting soaked, and finally saw the sanctuary at San Luca, high
in the hills above Bologna, sparkling red, a ruby beacon of home.
The sun gave its last rays of light to the basilica.

Months later I was surfing the Web (I was tired of the Bolognese
cinni—club kids who talked of nothing except Dolce & Gab-
bana) looking for someone, a mate to go riding with, when I
came across a Web site called "bikerboy.com." The site resembled the apparel catalogs I had designed: well-muscled young
men in various states of undress, wearing carbon-fiber back protectors, black Wescos boots with shiny side buckles and full-face
helmets, posing in groups or alone, silhouetted against sport mo-

torcycles. I scanned the ads and profile postings, skipping the bearded and tattooed Harley bears, and spied the distinct photo of a young, shirtless *veneto*, wearing only a pair of red braces and a hard expression that masked boyish good looks and suggestive lips. I left him a message. *"Vorresti fare un giro?"* Would you like to go for a ride? I sent the e-mail to a user account called "Skind." Underneath his nickname was his personal slogan: "Bastard Inside."

He sent a message back the next day: "I don't know how to ride. Fuck you! But I'll come to Bologna for a beer." He signed the e-mail "Anto." I wasn't sure if he remembered me. He gave no overt sign. The next Wednesday he said he would come to Bologna, "after 2 p.m. because of engineering classes"—he was getting a Ph.D. at the University at Padua—though he reminded me that he would have to leave by five o'clock that same day "to be home in time for dinner with my mother." "And, oh yeah," he added, "wear your full motorcycle leathers when you come to pick me up."

On a warm Wednesday afternoon, I left work early to ride my motorcycle to the Bologna train station, the same place where in 1980 the Red Brigades had planted a bomb that killed scores of people, to pick up my skinhead. The people who remember the bombing—older Bolognese mostly—say that it forever changed life in the city. Like all bombs, it killed innocence as well as people, forever destroying the culture of rowdy political debate in piazzas after midnight and contentious card games that lasted until the break of dawn. It was a watershed event that had made it impossible for working-class families to sit out in the hot dark, as they had for decades, in the Margherita gardens, listening to Puccini on portable radios. The tragedy was the local climax of "the years of lead" and one of the great political losses of Italian life since World War II.

These were different times. By the late 1990s, anything that had a label, a logo, or a name that could be turned into a status symbol was a rage in Italy. Luxury goods were in hot demand and a war was being fought to control the assets. In the midst of the boom, we decided it was the right time to cash in on the cachet of one of our own icon products. That summer, the company unveiled a younger version of the Beast. Management had been looking for a way to introduce a lower-price point in the model range to pump up volumes in anticipation of an initial public offering. What could be done with a bike that was already "naked," with few frills to eliminate? The only thing left to remove (to justify the lower price) was the paint.

The bare bike caused an immediate sensation. It had a sensuous, matte-black fuel tank—painted only with primer, no gloss—that became a cult item in trend-hungry Italy, thanks to entry-level pricing and my "Calvin Klein with Bikes" ad campaign that had been ridiculed inside the company. Every fashion-conscious guy with Diesel jeans, a faux-hawk haircut, and designer sunglasses—and there were thousands of them—rode a Black Beast that year. The rest of the country stared, covetous. The bike was figo.

With the Black Beast between my legs, I raced down via Marconi—past Frette, past the fabric stores, past Gazziero, the modern furniture gallery that displayed Futurist rugs by Giacomo Bàlla and furniture by Giò Ponti, to meet my "Anto." I darted in and out of traffic, flicking the bike side to side, dancing among the cars, trucks, and pretty girls on jewel-toned Scarabeos. Now, a classical sport motorcyclist hates city traffic, longing for the sweeping curves, mountain switchbacks, and silence of the open country. I, a rank amateur, who learned to ride on the streets of New York, specifically on the stretch of West Side Highway between Fourteenth Street and Hamilton Heights, one of the most trafficked freeways in all of America, felt right at home.

Today, with the skies fresh and blue, the sun warm, and the

smell of spring flowers in the air, I was sailing. Tiny bluebells and white daisies carpeted the traffic islands that ran down via Marconi. Linden trees were in bloom, dropping seed and scent. Their smell, canned peaches in syrup, was said to make you dream. Plane trees sent out puffs of pollen in great shimmering clouds. And everywhere, collected in the corners of bars and cafes, lining the porticoes, filling cracks in the sidewalks, dusting countertops, was the floss of poplar trees. Swirling around in gusts of feathery down, the seeds of flowering cottonwoods turned Bologna into wonderland—as if the city itself was underwater—suspended in a sea thick with organisms. I sucked it all in—smelling, sneezing—sensing the anticipation of meeting.

I parked under the big portico at the station, flipped open my visor to look around, and there he was, leaning against a column like an undernourished god. The skinhead was smoking, as usual, and was about to blow a cloud of blue smoke right in my face. "I've been waiting," he said, and took a hard drag off the filter as if life itself was contained in shredded, toasted, chemical-tweaked tobacco.

"Well, here I am now." Maybe I was five minutes late.

He frowned, in that typically Italian way, drawing the corners of his mouth down into a shrug/sneer. "Beh . . . "

His head was freshly shaved, splendid in its shadow stubble, too heavy for the young man who owned it. He did not stick out his hand to shake mine, nor did he try to kiss my cheeks. That would have been normal. He continued smoking and waiting for my first move. I appraised his style, which is what one does in Italy upon meeting someone, checking him up and down, paying particular attention to shoes. He wore black Adidas Sambas, the ones with red, yellow, and green reggae stripes, and no socks. "Don't you know *anything?*" he said when he saw me looking at the trainers for too long. "Skinheads don't always wear boots."

"Yeah, well, I've never met one before."

He grimaced. "Fuck, first time for everything!" He said nothing more. He just kept staring, eyes calm, showing no color, betraying no emotion, pools of hard observant glass. I looked at his stillness, his total composure in those bleached jeans. They were the same ones from the gas station, now rolled to the calves, matched with a Lonsdale T-shirt, sleeves shorn.

"I am sweating like hell in these leathers," I said, breaking the edgy silence. "Hop on." He jumped on the back of the bike, refusing a helmet, took a last hit off his smoke, and then with nicotine-stained fingers threw the lit butt into the crowd of immigrants.

"Let's get the fuck out of Africa!"

Starting up the engine, I clicked into gear. Passing the seedy train station hotels, I turned onto via Indipendenza, fast-dodging taxis, buses, Philippine maids on grocery expeditions. I hoped that speed would distract Antonio from my nervousness. My hands were shaking. At the intersection near the Grand Baglioni, an old pile of a hotel, full of rococo furniture and soiled velvet swags, we saw a middle-aged woman with a fluffy white dog about to cross the street. Antonio rapped my helmet and started yelling: "Swerve! Hit that old bitch! Give her the fucking scare of her life!" The cursing was in lightly accented English, the tone and inflection of a young lord.

Down the road, we approached a stylish girl coming out of the restaurant Diana. Her boyfriend was classic fighetto: tan linen suit, deep blue shirt with lots of starch. They were the perfect targets for Antonio's ire. "Slow down!" he commanded. "Get those bastards nice and dirty! I touched the rear brake slightly and he turned his big head round to face them. Opening his mouth, he let fly a massive luggie of spit and mucus. I couldn't see if anyone had been slimed, but the skin was ecstatic. He grabbed my waist as we sped off and shouted, "Che figata!"

"What happened to your nerve?" he shouted into my helmet at the traffic light.

I flipped open the visor to say: "I couldn't spit if I wanted to, I'd be drooling all over myself."

"So?" he said. "Drool! I'd like to see that!" The light changed and I pulled out—shriek of tire on stone. Revving the engine hard, I drowned out his laughter in the rattle of a dry clutch. I rode toward the bronze statue of Neptune and then down Ugo Bassi to the two towers, guarded by San Petronio, patron saint of the red city. We turned onto via Castiglione, passing Santa Lucia, the sixteenth-century church with the unfinished brick facade, in the direction of the Margherita gardens. The tires were heating up. You could smell them. People in slower vehicles made way for us. Elderly Bolognese, hanging onto shopping carts for dear life or gripping canes, steered clear. Boys gave us the hand gesture that meant *cool*.

At eighty kilometers per hour, fast for streets paved with granite, we were now approaching Porta Castiglione, a remnant of the old medieval walls that once encircled the city. I passed the monumental gate, turning right on the *viale*, opened the throttle, and touched five thousand revs. We were now, as the Bolognese say, *fuori porta*, beyond the gate, out of the box, free to roam. I put the bike through its paces, loping around the viale, passing restored Liberty-style villas in faded stucco with carved wooden doors. This was where Bologna's upper class lived at the turn of the last century before fleeing the city for the modern conveniences of Casalecchio.

If Antonio didn't like Bologna's *borghesi*, I thought, maybe he would go for its low life. In the right lane next to us, the cars were downshifting to a slow roll, appraising, in descending order of preference, the Russian, Romanian, Albanian, and East African whores who worked the viale. The drivers—executives on lunch break and laborers with wages to spend—were checking out today's catch. Though it was hot, the women were elabo-

rately kitted out: feather boas and platform boots, fur-tinged neg-
ligees, and hair extensions. Nothing was too much for their
johns. If a whore got in a car, a contract had been struck. Twenty
minutes and ten euro richer (more without protection), she was
back on the street, working the beat.

As we passed the African section near Porta Saragozza, with
its towering women in melting candy-colored makeup, Antonio
cantilevered himself out over the saddle to flip hookers twice his
size the bird. "Fuck you, you big black mother-fucking *puttane!*"
he shouted with delight. "Men should never have to pay for
figa—ever!"

"You're a thug," I told him. "A real prick."

"*Vaffanculo!*" he laughed. His whole body was radiating pleasure. I could feel it. "Those whores should pay *me* to fuck them,"
he bragged.

"Who taught you such filthy English?" I asked.

"I am a clever little *bastardo*, aren't I?"

We arrived at the apartment palazzo hot from the ride. I chained
the front wheel to a pylon and we began to climb the long flights
of stairs to what was my first real apartment in Bologna, near
the Piazza Malpighi. Antonio was immediately short of breath.
"Cazzo che fatica!" he grunted. "Your apartment must be really
cheap. *No one* wants to walk up this many stairs." When we
reached the first landing, he stripped off his T-shirt. A fine mist
came off him, disappearing like the last gasp of moisture in a
river during a drought. He rested a moment, caught his breath,
and we climbed the last set of winding steps to the iron gate of
the vestibule.

I opened the heavy door—Antonio said, "Permesso," asking
permission before entering—and we were met with a blast of
summer, the not unpleasant smell of hot dust, scorched leaves,
grass, and wooden filings. I took off my gear, leaving just a tank

and shorts, and began opening the shutters to the apartment. Antonio immediately went to the refrigerator. "I'm not very Italian, as you will soon find out," he said walking down the corridor, sweat glistening in the hollows between his shoulders. "I don't drink wine." He drained a fast Heineken and came into the living room with beers cooling his pits.

He took out a cellophane wrapper of *maria* from his pocket and with one hand rolled a perfect joint. Good rolling is a point of honor among young Italians. Antonio's spleef was a symmetrical cone, Amsterdam style, with a big bulbous end stuffed with Drum tobacco and marijuana. It was called a "mushroom." Only the "artichoke" is bigger, but that requires scissors, string, a straw, and a larger quantity of pot than most students can afford. Now he lit the cigarette and began smoking luxuriously. Italians do not light and pass, they light and smoke, leisurely. He took hit after hit, watching himself smoke in the round Deco cherrywood mirror hanging next to the fireplace, trying out a variety of poses. "I'm a real bastard you know," he said to his reflection, exhaling. He pursed his lips, then made a fist. "One fucking mean little punk!"

I slipped a Leonard Cohen disc in the CD player and sat down on the couch, saying nothing, though I clocked his every move through squinted, half-closed lids, listening to the sensual growl of the music pumping through the cheap sound system:

> I saw you this morning.
> You were moving so fast.
> Can't seem to loosen my grip
> On the past.

"No one else is around, right?" Antonio asked suspiciously, closing the doors to my terrace and the Italian mamas who were frying sausages in big black pans.

"Of course not, who would be around?"

"Just checking." He flexed his tight little frame, all unmarked skin except for a dusting of hair on his stomach and three beauty marks on his left shoulder shaped like a trident. His nipples were those of an adolescent boy, almost translucent in color, like clear gloss on a nail.

> And I miss you so much.
> There's no one in sight.
> And we're still making love
> In My Secret Life.

"Skind is one tough little fucker," Antonio said, now turning to face me directly. "A real hot number." I wondered what "Skind" stood for and where the dialogue in this script had originally came from, a porno magazine, a comic book? The good mood of the ride had turned abruptly. "Right?" Antonio wanted to know. He grew very quiet, serious—almost severe in his expression. "Right, dog?" He walked over to the couch and with his fingers began drumming my lips. He tapped my teeth like a percussive instrument. Then, leaning over, he pressed his lips down on mine in what I thought was to be a kiss. I closed my eyes, full of expectation, waiting for the first touch of this rough prince.

It wasn't a kiss, though, that he was looking for. He slapped my cheeks hard and with fingers that tasted like old leather pried my lips apart. "Don't you want a hit, mate?" He smiled strangely at me. "Open up." I looked up at him leaning over me, staring straight into his dark eyes. Afire now, sparkling with the colors that black absorbs, memory of orange opera at the arena in Verona, of soccer uniforms under a hot yellow sun, of blue light in the Piazza San Marco. He pressed down on me with chapped lips and, with my mouth now wide open, exhaled sweet tobacco breath into my lungs.

Emotional wheelies popped in my head, whirling across distances. The soft breeze brought the smell of jasmine planted in my terrace garden, top note of all great perfumes, into my nose. He was in my mouth, on my tongue. The maria seeped into the depths of my body and filled deep empty parts of me. We exchanged breath smoke back and forth like this a number of times, two bodies connected by sensation, lost.

> *Hold on, hold, my brother.*
> *My sister, hold on tight.*
> *I finally got my orders.*
> *I'll be marching through the morning,*
> *Marching through the night,*
> *Moving cross the borders*
> *Of My Secret Life.*

After a few minutes, he took a sip of beer, bent over, and dribbled it into my mouth, mixing it with his spit. It was like cool water from a well. I drank, then he licked my lips clean and said, "*Geil.*" Sexy. We spoke little. Just sharing the smoke and beer.

> *Moving cross the borders*
> *Of My Secret Life.*

Antonio's cell phone began beeping. "Don't answer it," I said. "Come on, let's hang out some more."

"I have to."

"Who is it?" I asked as he read the incoming text message.

"Never mind. Anyway I have to go . . . I told you before." In a flash, his T-shirt was back on. He had to go back to Padua. He tucked his shirt into his underwear, as Italian men do, pulling the shirttails through the leg holes of the briefs to create a smooth "line." He splashed cold water from a mineral water bottle on his face and, in two minutes flat, was ready to go. It was as if nothing had happened at all. I was too stoned to ride the bike so we walked back to the train station together awkwardly. There was no sign of intimacy between us at all, no speaking. I waved goodbye to him without ceremony one block before the station. From that time on we were together.

27

It was the height of the boom and we were feeling pretty giddy from our triumphs, including passing Triumph of England in sales. With little in the way of new product, that is, original motorcycles designed from scratch, we had doubled production. Much of the increase, as Jacques was eager to point out, was due to the company's liquidity crisis, when suppliers had not been paid and production had ground to a virtual halt. The pipeline was dry as a riverbed in Lucania. The instant we turned on the faucet, our market sopped up the added volume like a sponge. But there was more to it than that. We had begun revamping our distribution network. In major markets, we began building stores to properly position our "World of Sportbikes" vision. These dealers offered a full range of bikes, spare parts, accessories, and apparel in a branded environment that featured modern Italian furniture and a wall depicting the history of racing. At first the stores were laughed at as high-end makeup counters. But they quickly proved their viability by boosting sales.

Beyond these structural changes was a harder-to-explain fact: we were becoming a "hot" brand. We were also "cool," "edgy," and all of the other adjectives that magazine editors throw at consumer goods companies that somehow resonate in the fickle belly of the customer—that wealthy surgeon or soccer star who is looking carefully, rather desperately actually, for something exquisitely expensive to buy. Jacques was unconvinced. With stock market indices at record highs, the dot-com boom in full bloom, and managing directors of investment banks playing minor deity in corporate America, he said we were listening too closely to outsiders. In the Wall Street lingo of the day, we were "smoking our own Kool-Aid."

At first I thought that Uncle was just feeling left out of the game. "I don't have to act like this, trust me, I don't want to," he would say by way of explanation for every rude outburst. "I could let half of this stuff slide by me if I didn't care so much."

"Be collaborative, give new management a chance," I kept telling him. "Once in a while, let them think *they* have a good idea too."

"You really know nothing about Italy, mate," he answered coldly.

"But you have to build support for your ideas. That is Management 101. Design is not everything."

I had hit the hot-button issue. To him, it *was* everything. Design was what let him dream: of a folding, hybrid fuel-cell scooter that performed like a motorcycle but had luggage compartments large enough to sleep in. Design was imagination and innovation: a motorcycle with variable suspension and adjustable ergonomics that at the flick of a switch transformed into a Harley-style cruiser and then back to a European sport bike for twisty roads. *If the product was beautiful it sold itself.* He believed only in that.

In late-night sessions that went on for hours, we argued about design. I tried to explain to him what I really thought: that design was important, critical to our success, but that modern companies required teams with complementary but different competencies to get the right product to market, on budget. Jacques knew all of this already and didn't need it retold to him with an American accent. His objective—clear as any data point on a consultant's chart—was money and the green light to build.

To get it he was willing to spend months teaching me about product development. He took me through a crash course on concurrent engineering. He gave me books on modularity that explained how shared components reduced cost of goods across product platforms. If the imparting of knowledge failed to convince me of his righteousness, there was always insult. Cracks about the uselessness of marketing were common. I was responsible for it. He liked to pull out examples of how consumer focus groups had predicted mediocrity for products like the Renault Twingo, a surprise cult car in Europe that he just happened to drive. "Marketing can never promise you the future," he railed. "It only explains the past. If you don't understand that, you understand fuck all."

Each morning he raced his Twingo down the mountain to teach religion to the heathens. He loved that little car—and not just because it had tripped up marketers. The Twingo was the antithesis of what any layman would ever call "design." It looked like a flying soap dish. Jacques's was the color of Irish Spring, with interiors done up in dog hair, the silky detritus of his loyal hunting Segugio named Pluto. The great decorator Andrée Putnam had a Twingo too, a silver one. She declared it to be one of the most beautiful objects in the world.

The Twingo suited Jacques perfectly. It was cheap. It was ugly. It was French. It spit in the face of the taste of a nation of label-loving automotive enthusiasts for whom driving German was practically ordained by God. "It's the most successful car in the automotive history of France. Did you know that?" he asked me.

I had heard him say it at least a hundred times. "I didn't know France had an automotive history."

"Cheeky American. It's a fucking good automobile. Not a lot wanking else you can say about the thing." But if you gave him even the slightest opening, he would describe a pet project in which he intended to put a high-performance, turbo-charged engine in his soap dish, "Mega!," and whip the pants off all those hairdressers who drove Boxsters but couldn't get around the roundabout. I drove a base-model BMW 318i coupe that he never let me live down.

Sometimes I couldn't resist provoking him. "You know, I just don't get the Twingo."

"What do *you* know?"

"Nothing."

"*Exactly*." And he would laugh, satisfied at last. *I knew nothing*. "But maybe you're right," he said, not really wanting the conversation to end. "I should have played my cards differently in Italy. Here, you have to drive a Porsche Carrera to get any credibility, and wear designer suits. That's what a designer is to these peasants. A twat in a Prada suit." His long ash-blond eyebrows were trained on me, twitching like antennae, hoping that this lawyer who spoke "consultant," but was beginning to understand something of the importance of design, could help him get the bucks to build his dream bike.

28

In the months after meeting Antonio, messages would come in to my cell phone in the middle of the night—beeping and buzzing like dogs yelping in the dark: "Are you sleeping?" It was usually around 2 a.m. and I *was* sleeping. "Can you talk now? I'm alone!" Italians text-message each other in exclamation points. "Everyone else here has gone to sleep!!" For the life of me, I couldn't understand what was so exclamatory about sleeping.

"Okay, call me," I wrote, drowsily.

"I have no fucking money on my phone, dog," Antonio barked back. I called him but there was no answer, just the computerized ring tones of Telecom Italia.

"Why aren't you answering?" I wrote.

"They might hear me."

"*Who?*" I wanted to know.

"My parents in the next room."

"So what?" There was no answer from him so I messaged: "What's the big deal? They know, right?"

They didn't.

With a few keystrokes and a beep tone, I was thrown back decades, caught up in the politics, inhibitions, repressions, and repercussions of the Veneto. After the war, ambitious *veneti*, the children of rough peasants and peddlers, had transformed cities like Treviso, Padua, Vicenza, and Verona from some of Italy's poorest places into its most entrepreneurial. Companies like Benetton, Diesel, and Luxxotica had created riches, but a strong parochial culture remained. It was not uncommon in the Veneto to see businessmen fingering Padre Pio medals during meetings or requiring the local priest to bless a deal before closing. In Bologna the signing of a deal was an occasion to order up a round of private call girls (not the trash from the viale) and party for *real*: fat lines of cocaine and French champagne.

Now I understood why Antonio's availability was limited. He would show up at my doorstep early, telling me he was in Bologna "on business," though I knew he didn't work and had no money except pocket change. "Let's get an early pizza with everything on it," he would propose, thinking that sausage, pepperoni, mushrooms, and onion, "irresistible to an American," would make up for a month of not seeing me.

"But it's just three o'clock."

"You're the New Yorker. You're the one always telling me that you don't like to follow rules. Let's eat early."

So we would eat. Antonio ate little, usually just a white pizza, no cheese, with rosemary and salt. Later, I realized he was saving his appetite for his mother's cooking, a few hours later. Sometimes, he would forget himself—telling me what a great pasta fagioli she was going to make and how many bowls of it he planned on consuming. With me he mostly liked to drink. He would order rounds of "bicycles"—half blond beer, half Sprite—and sometimes, if he wanted to get drunk, Guinness. While he drank he would place one hand under the table, squeezing my thigh every once in a while to remind me that, while quiet and introspective, he was still present—communicating in his private, coded way without words.

If his parents went away to their villa in the Dolomites or to visit his grandparents on Lake Garda, he would send me a hasty message to come to Padua "immediately." We would walk around the great squares of that city, making long loops around the Prato della Valle with its marble statues and treed canals, or wander under the long, low, golden porticoes of the old city, inspired by Bologna's. In the beginning I think he was afraid to show me his house, and after that he preferred to walk because he enjoyed the freedom conferred by his parents' absence. Home was a reminder of his shackles. At least the city was still his.

While we walked, he would chain-smoke cigarettes or chew Happydent gum to freshen his breath, and ask me to talk to him in English about America. This way, he said, he became, like me, a tourist, seeing everything through exotic eyes. He listened to my American voice and dreamed of places that he never knew existed: of St. Mark's Bookstore, of the Russian baths on Tenth Street, of the Cozy Diner where I used to eat split pea soup every day. I tried to explain to him the taste of Katz's pastrami and how I longed for it. "Think of roast beef, but sour." Then, "Imagine sausages but sweeter." Finally, I said, "Think of something German-tasting, like sauerkraut." "Sweet and sour" and "pickled" were things mostly foreign to the Italian palate.

"Don't worry," he assured me when I was about to give up on his understanding, "I *get* it, dog." Lest I think that I had the upper hand.

As we walked around the city talking about New York, the erotic tension between us grew to a pitch. Sex was like a summer Coke—too little ice and just the thinnest wedge of lemon. Refreshing for sure, but it didn't slake thirst. A sliver of time, though, was what we had, and we made the most of it. We fucked with passion, in haste, at innumerable seedy hotels along the autostrada; in towns like Mestre and Rovigo, in the tiny Formica cabins of surprisingly clean saunas, in parked cars, out of doors, at a friend's house, on the banks of the river near the university, in the dark rooms of discotheques squeezed against other sweaty Italian couples of all stripes, straight and gay, married and not, people who had nowhere else to go but intense desire to satisfy.

"Enough of this, A! Look, let's just meet over the weekend and hang out," I had hoped to convince him. "I'll come up *on the bike*."

"No. My parents are around."

"I have new Dainese leathers I want to show you." He didn't take that bait. "Can't you just say I'm a friend?"

"They'd be too suspicious. How could I have a friend like *you?*"

I should have ended the relationship right there. I had worked for years to accept my own sexuality, forcing it on my family and friends, proselytizing, protesting, and pushing boundaries. Antonio still lived with his parents, overlooking the second-biggest piazza in Europe after Moscow's Red Square. His mother was a successful architect. His father was a physician affiliated with the United Nations. He worked three weeks out of the month in Budapest and there, I imagined, maintained a girlfriend, a couple of whores, or, perhaps, a whole second Eastern European family. He returned to Padua rarely, usually to have his shirts ironed by his wife or to eat polenta with cuttlefish with his boys on occasion, and then, just as quickly, disappeared.

Antonio's younger brother, Michelino, was the real power in the family. A teenage soccer star with a harem of high school girls from Vicenza to Verona, Little Michael's achievements were talked about as if he were a sports Einstein. "It's those *genius* soccer legs of his," Antonio would brag. "They never tire." Apparently the kid would seduce the mothers of his own girlfriends, bedding one after another with great talent and endurance. Family life revolved around *his* schedule: soccer training, sport massages, and a complicated social calendar of coffee dates and discotheques. There were blackout periods when the house was just his. He was the *gran bel ragazzo*, a real Italian stallion (yes, they really say that), and the whole clan was proud of his virility as if it confirmed theirs.

And if I had any doubts, Antonio would raise a bushy eyebrow—at least *his* were not plucked—to intend that his brother's equipment, his *"mega-cazzone,"* was really something worth marveling at. "You should *see* it," he would say, shaking his head with pride and disbelief. "It's like a small porpoise!" What was I supposed to say to these provocations, that I wanted to inspect it for myself? That I wanted to sample it too?

Dinner conversation in Padua, as Antonio described it, consisted of recounting its exploits, its adventures, and, sometimes, its laments and misfortunes. Once in a while, just to be polite, I would ask, "How swims the dolphin?" But this apparently was not the accepted way to ask about someone's sex life in the Veneto. Antonio was forced to remind me that there was much more to his brother than his outsized organ: "Not only is he a great *figone*—a big stud, Davide," he lectured, "but he has a beautiful *soul*." By this I understood that he made girls fall in love with him in addition to fucking them royally. Antonio, named for a patron saint, stand-in for an absent husband, was expected to be respectable.

"Dave, don't get angry!!" *Double exclamation point.* "Please!"

"I am not angry, A. Wrong word choice."

"Remember, I am just a young kid ☺. I need time to clean out the closet." I always bragged to my friends that Antonio was a great linguist, that he spoke perfect English. The reality I suppose was a little different.

"Look, I'm just frustrated. I really want to see you. It has been weeks," I wrote.

"Please, be patient with me. First, I have to finish school . . ."

"And when will that be?"

"In about two years."

"I thought you said you were in your late twenties."

"Soon I will be!!!"

Antonio got younger the longer I knew him. After several years, he grudgingly admitted that he was only twenty-two when we first met. I was ten years older, though I confessed to half as much. Even that was totally incomprehensible to his young mind. "You can't be a day over twenty-six," he told me once when we were kicking around a soccer ball. "You look like a little puppy taking his first steps." He was so young he couldn't imagine someone over thirty. That would have been his father, whom he saw as often as me. Which was not often.

The real part of our relationship existed courtesy of Telecom Italia. Text messages were the kisses and caresses of an affair that existed mostly in digital 0s and 1s, backlit by a liquid crystal display screen. But how important were those fragments—snippets of sexual innuendo and moments of affection—that beeped or buzzed on a well-worn Motorola Timeport! Waiting for the vibration of an incoming message, the promise of a tidbit of contact, was exquisite agony. I would finger the keyboard of the phone at meetings unconsciously, under the conference room table, hoping.

In lonely moments, I would scroll down the list of his saved messages, holding the silver handset like Jerusalem rosaries, stroking the olive wood bead-buttons, hands warm and sweaty. I would read the blue LCD texts aloud as if he had really said them to me in the first place . . . letting the letters of his thought seep into me, like tea sending its liquor into hot water. Sometimes, I'd show funny or tender messages to Alessandro just to prove that the kid existed at all. "Italia, the land of poetry, the place of a thousand lamentations and more, of infinite regrets, of failed passions and frustrations . . . *Madonna*, this cocktail is strong! It has gone straight to my head! Anyway, good night, sweet dog!" There were always plenty of exclamation points in Italian text messaging, as if each utterance needed a pat of butter to make it richer, tastier.

"Look, Antonio, this is all too much for me. I just want to have a normal boyfriend."

He wrote back immediately: "Give me time! Please, come to Padova one of these next afternoons. Let's fuck!" Oh great, twenty minutes shoehorned in between his brother's soccer practice and his mother's return from the office. He canceled that date too because he got a terrible case of bronchitis that turned into flu. "In a few days I will be better and ready to meet you!"

"Okay, feel better," I wrote back, figuring I would never see him again.

"Ti voglio bene. Ricordalo!" he wrote one week later at midnight.

"Yeah, right. I love you too," I e-mailed back in English without thinking, though the throwaway line set off a crisis in our textual universe.

"You *love* me? *Mi ami?* Or are you just hot for me? Maybe you just like me a lot. Like a friend? Like a sex buddy? Please explain yourself to me. Tell me dog! I am very curious. But I can't write too many messages because I am running out of money on my phone."

I wrote back that I felt a mixture of things for him, love, lust, brotherhood, and friendship, but that I wasn't looking to define our relationship just yet, especially since we rarely saw each other.

I thought I might have offended him, but the message seemed to click. "I understand! I really do—bodies, minds, and feelings! We must stay together. We will talk about this tomorrow." But of course we never did. Weeks later an orphan message came in: "Your words r so nice . . . I like it." Then: "From the deepest part of my heart, thank you for your support." Antonio sounded like a politician addressing donors at a rubber-chicken dinner.

One night out of the blue, he wrote me this: "Can I ask you something David?"

"Of course, A."

"It's something serious."

"Okay."

"Am I still your bro?"

29

Jacques, the Aborigine in the occasional tribal-print shirt and khaki shorts, became a frequent visitor to my office. It was a relationship based on one thing. Like Enzo Ferrari, who always claimed that the best Ferrari was the next one that he was going to build, Jacques was a product man through and through. He was a designer of bikes, yes. But he loved anything powered by a motor: go-carts, speedboats, scooters, snowmobiles. He was even interested in vibrators—one of the "overlooked areas in industrial design," in his opinion. His pet project, if things went "tits up" in the bike business, was to design a line of superfunctional sex toys all "carved from the solid, hand-polished, with chrome and strip titanium accents, quality details and Bakelite bits." (There is something about a designer of a certain age that just cannot resist Bakelite!)

When I commented that polished metal sounded cold, Jacques shrugged his shoulders and snorted: "If it's beautiful, it sells itself." Sex toys packaged in butter-soft leather and brushed aluminum, he predicted, would be a hit with business travelers. "I know I'd be proud to show it off on my hotel nightstand." Many of his detractors—much of Italy, for example, which could not stomach the fact that we had turned to an Australian for design—would have been delighted by the news that he had given up on motorcycles and taken up dildos.

Were Jacques's designs beautiful? It was a question that launched a thousand chat rooms. There are motorcycles that when you look at them make you feel. There are other motorcycles that make you think. Jacques was an intellectual provocateur of a designer. He made you argue. We had hired him away from perhaps the greatest motorcycle artist in the world, a man who was not even a professionally trained designer. This master used to style motorcycles for us, but defected to the competition when we acquired the company. Most of Italy thought he was a living genius. Jacques was more down to earth about it. He called him "a plumber."

I had seen the man's fabulous, no-expense-spared studios on secret missions to San Marino to lure him back to Bologna. He was a natty perfectionist of a plumber, that much was clear: a quiet fellow with a wrench and a mission, a dedicated duffer who built, rebuilt, tinkered, and then fiddled some more until every detail on his motorcycle, right down to the fuel cap, was absolutely perfect. If a simple thing like a handgrip could be colored, embossed with a logo, or further enhanced or improved by his design, and if that project required a special stamping machine to press hot rubber, he bought the equipment without blinking.

If it took multiple paint jobs to get graphics to pop—the right red, the right width stripes, the right metallic engine finishes—let's say on his latest superbike, a stunning competitor to our top of the range, so be it: to hell with budgets and timetables. He was the master of what bike design aficionados call "the phallic female"—motorcycles that were, on the one hand, unmistakably aggressive, but also silky smooth, sensual, even highly arousing.

Whenever talk turned to design at the company, and it inevitably did, since all Italians are born style mavens with a sixth sense for what is stunning, from supermodels to superbikes, there was an elephant in the room. That animal was the slim icon of modern sport motorcycling, the plumber's 9X7. This was the red race champion that sat on a plinth at the factory's entrance. This was the sport bike exhibited on pedestals in rich men's living rooms. And this was the piece of rolling industrial art and thunder that added ten fat points of sweet gross margin to our bike averages. Not just a motorcycle icon, the 9X7 was our meal ticket.

Launched in the early 1990s, the 9X7 had revolutionized the motorcycling world right from its debut. The motorcycle was downright sexual—a sloe-eyed, slippery fox with a wedge-shaped front end that looked like Sofia Loren and a tail section that was pure booty. Bikers never tired of looking at her. Even nonriders were seduced. Factory workers would sneak out to the parking lot during breaks to marvel at her simple yet sophisticated collection of curves. What did they see, staring at the same bike, week after week, month after month? (It changed little in the ten years we sold it.) They were looking at a piece of machinery that dissolved divides, between engineering and art, between transportation and kinetic sculpture, a bike that championed the idea that the motorcycle was not necessarily the poor stepsister to the automobile, that it had the power, on its own terms, to conjure up dreams.

This was the monkey on Jacques's back, his bogeyman and the yardstick against which all his future designs would be measured. "I am going to make that plumber's motorcycle look fucking old one day," he promised me so often and with such conviction that I wasn't sure if he himself was convinced. The odds sure looked long. Bikes like the 9X7 happened once in a lifetime. Arguably as much of a fluke as it was a masterpiece, it had taken almost seven years to build, had practically bankrupted our predecessor company, and had racked up a string of record championships in a series—Superbike—whose rules were originally stacked in our favor.

On top of that, the 9X7 was displayed in museums around the world, including in Tom Krens's landmark show, *The Art of the Motorcycle*, at the Guggenheim Museum, where it was named one of the motorcycles that defined the 1990s and one of the most distinctive styling jobs ever seen on two wheels. The 9X7 didn't look designed. It looked inevitable. There wasn't actually that much else to say about it—especially if you were a literate motorcycle viewer. Every component was exactly in its place, as if evolution had decreed that that particular part, that specific detail, could go only where it was and nowhere else. The bike was in harmony with itself.

To compete with this historic moment when engineering met motorcycle art, Jacques turned to the future. His was a Buck Rogers vision, a comic book version of the world of advanced fighter jets and ballistic missiles, chrome Waring blenders, and dueling Dualit toasters. Fairings were covered with swoops and cutouts, with visual zips and complex surface radii. Components—always a strong suit—were cast in aluminum, carved from the solid, polished to a mirror-bright finish. Jacques had obviously never heard of the Jewish rule about being overdressed: when in doubt, take one thing off. To him more was more. So fuel caps recalled finely tooled silver belt buckles. Exhaust systems looked like high-tech telescopes. Fans and critics alike agreed on one thing about Jacques's design: love it, hate it, there is no room for indifference.

Jacques marched ever forward, implacable, adding complexity or seeking simplicity—looking for new technologies, cutting time to market. He spewed torrents of drawings, plans, and projects—scrambling like a deejay. He tricked and tweaked, sampling bike ideas like so many musical styles—desperate to make something new, something of his own.

One spring morning he came in ranting, all of his thick blond hair standing straight up in attack mode. "I swear I am going to kill someone!"

"What happened?"

"If those peasants change the details on one more bike of mine, I'll club them into a bloody pulp." He had sweat straight through his shirt. "If the technical director—or his dog—decides to change something that I worked on for years because he was too lazy to haul his ass up and down the motorway and see me in the design studio, I'll rip out his heart and lungs and feed them to Pluto."

"Calm down." I was worried he'd have a heart attack.

"Heads are going to roll. I am going to come into this office one day and ax someone to death. That's the way we ex-convicts do it in Australia."

I tried to distract him. "Would you like a cup of coffee?"

"There will be pools of blood to clean up!"

This morning he was angry because his new motorcycle, an advanced supersport, had been criticized in the press as a medieval torture rack. The riding position was wrong—too much stress on the wrists. He claimed the technical department had secretly changed the ergonomics without telling him. He may have been right there, but the real issue was a larger one. A war was being fought in engineering departments all over Italy over who controlled product development. In the past, it had been enough to build a superb engine and cobble a chassis around that. Engineers ruled the factory and designers styled plastic panels. Now, with reliable high-performance engines widely available (Rotax, a division of Canadian giant Bombardier, sold them off the shelf) and many components (brakes and shocks) standard, the emphasis had shifted to industrial product design. A modern sport motorcycle had to fully integrate engine and chassis, components and *style*. Total design, right down to the screws, was what made for success. Our company, whose reputation was based first and foremost on motors and second on design, had not yet accepted the reign of the men in black Prada suits.

"Double espresso—from the bar, not the machine," I said. "I'm buying."

"Oh, okay, so now you are offering. Isn't that rich? I was getting tired of always courting you, you know." We walked down to the bar in the bowels of the factory. "Enough of the niceties," Jacques said more calmly. "Let's talk business. You guys hired me to design motorcycles. So let's fucking start designing them. Come up to the house this weekend. I want to show you something—a new project that no one knows about."

Jacques lives in a converted barn and stables behind San Luca. Long ago, native plant life in this part of the Italian peninsula was cleared to turn the plains—the Pianura Padana—into the nation's breadbasket and pasta machine. Here in the hills, the birch copses are still dark and green enough that one can understand why woods were once frightening to Italians, thick as they were with medieval wolf, wild boar, fox, and foreboding. Today, a pheasant is about as hairy as it gets.

I careened past Porta Saragozza in my hairdresser's coupe, rounding the corner where pilgrims begin their procession up the winding arcades to the basilica. The road was tight and steep, as difficult to negotiate as my relationship with Uncle. At the hairpin turn, the BMW stalled suddenly and began rolling backward. Unable to engage the gearbox, not knowing what to do, I called him. "Use the hand brake, then shift into first!" Jacques shouted into the cell phone, laughing maniacally. "Fast, mate! Or I will have to extract you from that sardine can at the bottom of the hill." I pulled the hand brake hard as he instructed, jolted into gear, and raced the rest of the way to his villa in a cold sweat.

At the gravel parking lot I was met by Pluto, Jacques's usually sullen doppelgänger, who was urinating all over the neighbors' flowers. "Good on *them*, Pluto," laughed Jacques, egging him on from the doorway. He was wearing a Hawaiian shirt and shorts. "That's why we live up here—so we can walk right over to the edge and piss down on all of them." We took Pluto for a walk, then climbed the stairs to Jacques's stone-and-stucco farmhouse-cum-condo.

The place was covered with boxes, crates, and collections of objects. On the walls were framed lithographs by the graphic artist Billal—beaten, scarred men lashed to their jail cells. In one lurid image a moody prostitute walked the night beat. Jacques talked about Billal as others do of Picasso. "Of course, you know him, he's a *giant*." There were drawings of women in spiked patent leather heels, nailed to crosses, locked in cages. "I love his stuff," Jacques said blithely, as if the work were watercolor flowers. If you mentioned "great art" to him, say, a Beckmann or de Kooning (my favorites), he was utterly dismissive: "Nobody looks at that old *cac* anymore, man. For Christ sakes, give me something new!"

We sat down in a pair of vintage leather club chairs Jacques had bought in Paris so that he could sit comfortably in his living room and admire his things. He was an acquirer, a tireless purchaser of anything old. His preferred period was the 1920s through the early 1960s. The rest was all cac. He didn't care much about the intrinsic worth of things. A fine gold watch was displayed with the same importance as a well-designed matchbook. Only aesthetics mattered. One living room wall was dedicated to glass-and-chrome display cases containing ephemera—inkbottles with magnificent labels, exotic dyes and pigments. Other cabinets held pens, amber medicine bottles, chemist's funnels, and Pyrex beakers. He collected antique wristwatches and wore his favorites in rotation—bubble-cased silver Rolexes, vintage Longines, and, my favorite, an English military-issue Smith with a gray-green canvas strap.

He bought whole lots of things, sets of things, in duplicate, often in multiples. His eye was not for the item itself—set in splendid isolation like a jewel solitaire—but for the repetition of that item, the juxtaposition of that item with other like (or different) items, and the impact that such exhibition could have on the senses. There was nothing fussy about Jacques's passion. When he ran out of space, he dropped prized collectibles right down on the floor. Junk spilled out of drawers and closets. A restored flame red Moto Morini was the centerpiece of the living room. It still dripped oil. Jacques's pleasure was not in perfect restoration or prissy connoisseurship, but in the original moment of acquisition. He was generous with the most precious of objects, letting friends borrow almost anything. Often, he just gave away things outright. It was easier than keeping track of who had what.

He took me to the kitchen and brewed a pot of coffee. I reached down to pet Pluto, who was sitting near my hand. He snarled, then snapped. "Bad dog," I corrected.

"We know who our *real* friends are," Jacques said protectively. "Right Pluto, good old doggy?" The bastard had slithered under the diner-style Formica table to receive belly rubs and "scruffles" from his dad. I love dogs, even nasty ones, appreciate antique pens and vintage movie posters, but had come expecting to see a new motorcycle. "Okay Jacques," I said, losing patience, "show it to me."

"Hey, man, there is no rush," he said, stretching his arms behind his head—his mellowness was the true novelty. "Let me finish showing you around."

The kitchen was filled with appliances, both usable and ornamental, and now he showed me everything, piece by piece. There was the midcentury icebox and the powder blue test tube warmer that looked like an umbrella stand. There were collections of old steam irons, Fiestaware dishes, two-tone Art Deco fans with rubber blades and Bakelite bases. Exhausting his treasures, Jacques walked me toward his sanctum sanctorum, where his bike designs were presumably born.

On the way, we passed one last collection: vintage Bakelite radios lining the staircase down to the studio. I thought this must have been his most serious passion, more personal than motorcycles, since he was loath to talk about it. When he caught me looking too closely at the collection of Packard-Bells with the front grills of automobiles and a rare ebony Tesla with fins and fat dials, he said almost shyly, "I'm not like you, David. I'm not hoarding my money in a bank so that I can drop dead one day at fifty. I do what I want. I buy what I want. I never feel guilty."

The smell of urine rose up in a wave of acrimony. Angry that his "dad" left him most of the time in a basket in the back of the Twingo, Pluto had pissed all over everything. "Sorry about the smell," Jacques said, when he finally got around to looking at the pinched expression on my face. "He's an old dog. I guess I'm just used to it." Besides the stink, the studio was filthy, filled with stacks of motorcycle magazines from the 1980s and beaten-up Disney figurines.

"Jacques, you have all your stuff here . . ."

"Yeah, I know. I really need to get this place organized into a proper studio. I wanted to show you something, though." He was distracted and began sifting through files. "One of these days when I have the time . . ." I opened up some of his portfolios to look at drawings. I found the plans for the interiors of an Audi, which was among his first professional projects when he went to Germany. "Don't waste your time with that old car crap," he said. I saw early drawings for a dual bike, a highly rated hybrid that had won numerous magazine awards but never found a market because its maker went bankrupt soon after its launch.

"Christ, you have hundreds of drawings here," I said, astonished at the breadth of the work. I picked up sketchbooks of futuristic sport bikes, of commuter bikes that folded into suitcases and doubled as coffee tables, and exquisite renderings of advanced urban attack scooters that anticipated every market trend.

"Yeah, man, I've designed enough bikes to keep the company in business for the next century and they don't even fucking know it." Bike concepts were imagined every which way, the single-seat version, the *biposto*, the entry-level, and the "R" model with all the fancy racing bits. Most designs were done in simple charcoal pencil or ballpoint pen with washes of magic marker. Sometimes a headlight or a mirror was touched up with a fillip of metallic paint. This was before the era of 3-D computer graphics. You couldn't just push a button in Alias to create a model range. Everything had been drawn by hand, colored by a febrile imagination.

He pulled out a portfolio case thick with drawings. "Take a look at these and tell me what you think." Inside were sketches of lean, muscular cafe racers in black, chrome, and acid yellow— motorcycles inspired by the bikes he had admired as a boy. It was these models that had encouraged him to travel from Australia to Europe, to look for design work at Audi, and then later to attend the Royal College in London and finally, one day, after all that effort, to pack his bags for Italy, carrying these very same sketches in hand, to knock on the doors of fabled motorcycle manufacturers. "What do you think if we made a neoclassical version of our 1970s sport bikes?" His voice was very quiet, almost vulnerable. I kept looking, lost in the sketches.

The bikes were no simple replicas of vintage bikes. They were history reimagined, the past coaxed into the twenty-first century. "Has anyone seen these drawings?" I asked. No one had.

I was looking at sketches that took you to that moment, of torture or inspiration, that place of bubbling, broiling creativity, when pencil crossed paper for the first time and an idea was born. You could feel the energy of every graphite gesture, the passion and intensity of the man himself. "Water-cooled or air-cooled engine?" I wondered aloud.

"Air, I think," he answered, looking over my shoulder. "Go for simplicity."

"Most guys can't use the existing power on our bikes."

"Give me a fucking break!" He was immediately piqued. "All this horsepower is like having three dicks, each nine inches. Sure you're fucking proud of yourself, but there are still only two holes." Classic Uncle.

And then he showed it to me: his retro-futuristic master-work, a take on the most important motorcycle in the museum, the 900 Supersport that an English racer had ridden to victory at the Isle of Man in a great comeback victory that marked the be-ginning of the modern era of our race dominance. "Let's build something the Japanese can't!" he declared. The project was a celebration of Italian heritage, the one thing that no Japanese maker could take away from us, allowing us to sell an essentially low-technical-content bike for a premium price.

Looking up from the sketchbooks for just a moment, I said: "This is brilliant. The vintage trend is going to be huge."

"Yes, David, I know that." He could never just accept a com-pliment. "If these guys would only let me work . . ."

"The range could be sold for years . . ."

"Of course," he said dismissively.

"You could work your way through the museum and build a whole family of related bikes . . ."

"Really?" That familiar grin had crept onto his face. He could not find it in himself to humor *anyone*—not even me, not even now.

I imagined the marketing possibilities: the vintage leather motorcycle jackets in sky blue and orange, the collectible foun-tain pens, the reintroduction of the glorious double-line motocross logo designed for us in the 1970s. I thought of the poignancy of the story: the young, poor Jacques, who could only *dream* of owning such a bike; the designer who had to wait twenty years, travel to Europe, get educated, join the company, and finally design the motorcycle that he had always wanted to ride as a teenager. It was a story that would resonate with the press and with our fans—enthusiasts who had themselves dreamed similar dreams.

"Perceived quality and visual performance will be the key," he said, "if we ever produce the thing."

"Which we will . . ."

"Yes, but just don't tell anyone."

"Let them think it's just a design exercise, right?"

"This way it won't threaten the cunts."

After the initial burst of excitement, we each fell into a deep silence. It was one of those rare moments of stillness. It wasn't that we were exhausted. The project was too exhilarating for that. Rather, the quiet was a kind of closeness. I think it was the best time we ever had together. Sitting there on the piss-stained floor, each left to his thoughts, surrounded by chipped Donald Duck and bitten Mickey masks in the stinking study, I experienced a moment of beauty. I watched a shaft of light move across the rough concrete floor, catching motes in its beam. Jacques had been dreaming so many years about this motorcycle; it must have been a great release to finally talk about it. This was his triumph, his personal fruition. Later would come all of the work, the disappointments, and the eventual success. But the poignancy, I was sure, was caught up among the collected dog hair and urine-scented designs—the pure dreams of a boy—shared on a Sunday afternoon.

Breaking the spell, I asked Jacques if it would be a problem finding talent to build the bike in time for the September motorcycle show in Munich. "Don't worry," he said. "It is a piece of piss. I can do the whole project with outside people. Maybe in England where I know a lot of bike people and design studios." For a guy that hated marketing, he had done a perfect job of selling me.

Selling the big boss was easy. It took twenty minutes. Max gave us a couple hundred thousand euro to build the prototype and three months to do it. He didn't care so much about the technical details of neoclassic sport bikes or the fact that we were bringing back one of the most beloved motorcycles of the modern era. Those were just details. What excited the chief executive was that we were building a motorcycle in an innovative way, without the involvement of the technical department. Jacques was to recruit a virtual R&D team: a brilliant Dutch engineer who specialized in suspensions and an English design consultancy with Formula One experience. I would put together a crack public relations outfit to tell the story of the birth of a dream bike. We would prove to the biking world (and, not insignificantly, to Wall Street) that new management could build beautiful things too.

Max loved the words "dream bike." It wasn't your typical show bike: a futuristic clinic model that automobile companies unveil to hide the fact that they have nothing exciting to sell. Our project was more subtle smoke and mirrors: we were giving our lead designer a chance to express his personal vision—a no-compromises, no-excuses motorcycle. If no one liked the prototype that would become the 900 Rivoluzione, a twin-engine sport bike inspired by the original, but with a modern 900cc motor, ceramic monodisc brake, and a video camera instead of rear mirrors, we could say that the whole thing was Jacques's idea. If the dream bike was a success, it would open the door to many things, not least of which would be reams of press about management savvy.

For the next three months we worked like demons. Jacques shuttled back and forth between Bologna and England, where, in a shed designed by the imperial architect Lutyens, the Rivoluzione took shape. First came 3-D CAD designs, then components cast in fiberglass or resin. In addition to realizing a bike, Jacques was testing advanced design methodologies. Everything would be designed directly on the computer, working in a linked virtual way among his studio in Bologna, the Dutch engineer, and the English designers. "Our new design center innovatively integrates the traditional skills of hand modeling and sketching with the disciplines of the computer screen and the CNC milling machine. An advanced digital design process enables the team to incorporate all of the engineering hard points—the fixed parameters of engine, frame, and chassis—at the outset of development." I wrote that in the press booklet.

Reality was slightly different. Three weeks before the bike presentation in Munich, I received a nasty phone call from Jacques. "I need more money."

Heart racing, I asked, *"Why?"*

Jacques exploded: "The designers here are total idiots! The surface radii are all wrong! I need to hand-model the bike and I'm running out of time!" Ignoring all of the promises he had made about working in a networked team, maintaining budgets, and allowing each person to do his part, Jacques had effectively hijacked the project. "I have no time to explain all this to you—

trust me, you wouldn't understand anyway—just give me the fucking money." It was three weeks before delivery date.

Crisis details emerged in other ways. I got a phone call from the director of the English design studio, saying that Jacques had made off with the prototype in the middle of the night. "Where is he?" I demanded to know. But no one could say. Another call was a simple request for an address.

"Should we just send the bill directly to you?" asked the man with a bold Birmingham accent. What choice did I have? The Formula One design consultancy Jacques had sold to me as the most advanced automotive studio in Europe had become, suddenly, incompetent.

Jacques spent the next week, up to twenty-four hours a day, hand-sanding the surfaces of the Rivoluzione in Birmingham. After that, he spent more time supervising the painting of the prototype and the application of the historic graphics from the 1970s. He slept in the model shop, taking breaks only for Coke and candy bars. The paint was still wet on the prototype when Jacques packed the bike onto a pallet and drove a van from England to Germany in the middle of the night, arriving on the morning of the show with his precious dream bike in tow. He walked straight up to the stand, unloaded the bike, and began mounting the mirrors and license plate.

"You fucking lazy ass," he screamed the moment he saw me. "Where the fuck have you been for the last three weeks?" I was shell-shocked. My cheeks turned hot like exhaust pipes.

"Who do you think did all this work, the stand, the video, the press release?" I started protesting.

"You should have fucking shown me the pictures before you put them up."

"What are you talking about?"

"The design of the stand! I should have been asked for my opinion and approval." His anger was not the garden variety. He did not turn red in the face or begin sweating. His hair did not stand on end. His rage was coldly measured, pitched, and brutal in its focus. The only physical signs were the blue veins in his temples, pulsing, feeding blood to the furious brain. "That image over there is wrong." He pointed to a descriptive wall panel that told the story of the development process of the prototype. "That wasn't the inspiration for the bike at all. Take it down immediately."

"Okay, calm down." Tears were in my eyes.

"Yeah, you be calm. You've been on fucking vacation! I've been on my hands and knees working like a slave." Jacques wouldn't look at me. "You didn't even come to visit me. *Not once.*"

I had one of the workers remove the offending pictures. Ten minutes later, I grabbed a microphone, shaken, and presented the bike to the hundreds of journalists. Here is what the public saw: a slim torpedo of a motorcycle whose sculptured bodywork immediately recalled the original. The tubular trestle frame was similar to the Verlicchi racing versions that had appeared on our bikes since the 1970s. The single-sided swing arm was made of braced steel, triangulated, and pivoted on the back of the gearbox. Five-spoke magnesium wheels by Marchesini were fitted with racing slicks. Shocks had been made by the Swedish suspension specialist Öhlins, but mounted in an endurance racing position. The front brake was a single ceramic rotor, based on Sputnik Russian technology that combined the advantages of carbon fiber with cast iron. When braked the material glowed red. The front suspension solution employed upside-down forks, hand-polished, to make the metal look soft, custom-made. A cast aluminum dry sump incorporated the oil cooler. The headlight recalled the classic chrome bezel lamps of the period, updated with a monofocal lens. To sum it all up: the bike was pure eye candy, a buff cafe racer, with just enough gas in its tank to get you up in the hills, eat a plate of mortadella and *tigelle*, and return.

No one was expecting the Rivoluzione. The house was floored by it. There were gasps and cheers. It was Jacques's moment of career glory. Fans roared with excitement and demanded that we actually build the thing. I didn't speak to him for days. A few weeks later, he came to my office. In his hand was the Smith military watch with the gray-green canvas strap that I had always admired. "Here, why don't you borrow it," he mumbled. When I protested he said sheepishly, "Really, I don't need it. Just take it."

Company executives were divided as to whether there was a market for the bike. Many, furious they had been left out of the development process, badmouthed the project from the get-go. Yes, they admitted, it had been a brilliant media stunt. Some even said (privately) that the bike was beautiful. But no one thought that anyone, besides a few die-hard collectors, would buy a single-seat cafe racer that could be ridden only an hour or so on a tank of gas.

My team went into high promotional mode. The bike went into *Fortune*. It was placed on CNN. Krystle, recently promoted to head of advertising, came up with an idea. She had been talking to Sotheby's in Chicago. Fast on the heels of the huge success of the Guggenheim's *Art of the Motorcycle* exhibition, Sotheby's had decided to mount their first motorcycle, scooter, and bicycle auction in Chicago. Krystle had persuaded them to put the prototype Rivoluzione on the catalog's cover. Though they agreed not to list a bid price, it was understood that we would entertain offers in the six-hundred-thousand-dollar range.

Krystle was the most professional of professionals, a brilliant PR woman and a born diplomat. For weeks she planned what she would say to Jacques. She settled on this: "The auctioning of the

Rivoluzione prototype establishes the project, not just as a bike, but also as a work of art." Jacques went completely nuts. How could we auction off his baby? It wasn't the company's to sell. He shook and he threatened. He shouted at the top of his lungs. "I am taking this to the CEO!" he railed, his threats echoing down the hallways.

I was called into the CEO's office for the confrontation. "That bike belongs in our museum," Jacques began shouting, "not in some rich tosser's living room." The boss was very calm, very measured. In his office were wall-sized pictures of the motorcycle that was taking the biking world by storm. Reprints of the *Fortune* article containing the Rivoluzione (and him on the cover) sat in stacks on his desk.

"Well, Sotheby's seems to think it's worth hundreds of thousands of dollars," Max said carefully. "Let's think about that for just a moment. We could build three other prototypes with that money."

"You can build them. I'm not."

"You're enjoying a huge success with this bike, Jacques. Don't you see how this builds value not just for the company, but also for you?"

But Jacques was shaking his head. "I'm not interested in seeing my face in magazines. I just want to do good work."

"Good. Then we can build a second prototype in how long—a month's time? I'll make you a deal," Max went on. "If we sell the bike for six hundred thousand, I'll give you the money to build others."

Jacques refused.

"Let me ask you something personal," the boss asked, now looking directly into Jacques's raging blue eyes. "If the prototype is so important to you . . . if it is so truly and totally valuable, please tell me where all the other prototypes are?" Jacques's face went pale. Where was the first prototype of the Beast? "It must be worth millions." The designer was utterly silent. "Where is the prototype of the 9X7?" the boss continued. "And for that matter, where are the clay models of all your own bikes?"

Jacques turned all the colors under the sun, like the opera singer in *The Rabbit of Seville*. When he finally found his voice again, he yelled that previous management folly was not his own and stormed out of the meeting.

A week later the Rivoluzione prototype went up for sale. Krystle got a call from Sotheby's saying that there had been a bid just under the minimum asking price, in the neighborhood of five hundred thousand dollars. I thought the boss would sell. But I was wrong. The man's true class shined through. "Of course, we will not sell it," Max told me privately. "But if the bidding had reached the offer price it would have been something to think about, wouldn't it have?"

I immediately informed Jacques that the bike didn't sell and that he could sleep easy. But by this point he had moved on to the production issues related to the real Rivoluzione, a bike that on January 1, 2000, was put up for sale on the Internet, beating the millennium bug, to sell out all five hundred units in just forty minutes.

At the very back of the factory, just outside the model shop, there is a gated area filled with broken-down motorcycles and prototypes. Some are missing seats or fairings like so many limbs. Others have no wheels. This part of the factory, despite rounds of Disneyfication, has not been renovated. Just beyond, outside a mechanical gate that opens with the push of a yellow button, is the test track that our head of research and development built, years ago when no one was looking, to the tune of tens of thousands of euro.

I rarely go outside, though. Instead, I like to poke around the pen of chipped clay models, test fiberglass mules, and rush-painted prototypes. A significant part of sport motorcycle history can be seen amidst the rusting fuel tanks and superannuated suspensions, parts discarded like last year's Christmas presents that no one wants to play with anymore. There are three-valve test engines in heaps. There are Sport Touring prototypes painted in burgundy and gold, periwinkle blue and silver, colors that never saw the light of production. In the back of the pile, wrapped in a greasy tarpaulin, covered in pigeon shit, sits the original Rivoluzione prototype. It is gathering dust, entirely forgotten.

Whether or not Antonio was my brother, I needed to see him. I was skin-addicted. That summer he had begun work on his engineering dissertation. The topic was advanced cellular telephony. I didn't know much about the specifics, but it couldn't have been a big stretch for him. He was already an expert on extracting maximum value from his Telecom contract, knowing the cheapest times to send and receive text messages, to make phone calls. When he finally ran out of credit and there were no more promotions, trials, or other freebies to be had, he would sweetly extort a recharge from me and—I was sure of this—from others. "I want to call you bro, *badly*, but I have no money left on my phone. Is there something you can do?" What one could do was to go to the local tobacco shop, purchase a prepaid calling card from TIM, and recharge his account for twenty-five or fifty euro, depending on how generous (or lonely) I felt.

His study grant came from the communications division of Siemens. As part of his research he would need to spend a week in Germany. "Let's meet at the central train station in Munich, right near the café where they sell the giant pretzels," he wrote one July day. "I want to make everything up to you!" And with little more than that, I bought tickets to fly to Bavaria. If Antonio didn't show, at least our ending would be definitive.

In Italy real skinheads are rare, and punk teenagers co-opt elements of skin style to match their pink-dyed mullets. Munich was full of the real thing. Skins were prowling the station in packs, coyotes in combat boots, cadging smokes and drinking tall boys out of paper bags. If some poor tourist was caught sipping without conviction and there remained a mouthful of beer left in the bottle, there was no compunction in asking: "*Oi!* Mind if I finish that off for you, mate?"

I was so busy watching that I didn't notice Antonio get off the train. He clapped my shoulder from behind, spun me around, and gave a tight bear hug, drumming my back with his fists. His face was hidden, so all I could feel was the pressure of his body. "Dog, I can tell that you missed me," he said in a low voice.

"Really, how?"

"You smell like you haven't cheated."

"What does that smell like?"

"*Clean*—like a shave."

I had my head buzzed right before the trip and now Antonio took it in his hands and began rubbing the short hairs back and forth till my whole skull burned warm like a campfire. Then he licked my stubble. Swipes from a big tongue, right there in public. I flushed like a girl, excited. The other skins, I could not tell if they were gay or straight, looked at us for a second and then moved on. We were nothing special to them, just two mates fooling around on a lark.

"Are you hungry?" he asked. "There's a great sausage place near here." It was nothing more than a garishly lit hot-dog stand in the middle of a square, but to Antonio this was the most beautiful spot in the world. "Just look at them," he said, amazed, watching the parade of teenage hustlers, punks, skins, and rockers. "Fucking magnificent!"

We ate gelatinous white sausages served in pots of hot water and fresh pretzels studded with sesame seeds and salt. The waiter, cradling a heavy tray of *Weisbier*, a cloudy blond brew made from wheat instead of barley, said to me in English, "Your friend here speaks good German. You should be proud of him." But Antonio was ignoring me, transfixed by a punk right out of *Sid and Nancy* getting loaded off schnapps. "Italians are not usually good with other languages," the waiter went on.

Antonio interrupted the cruising to drop his fork and knife: "I am not a *usual* Italian." Then he smiled—a clean smile— showing nicely shaped teeth. It was the first natural smile I think I had seen on him. He reached over to squeeze my nose and then began playing with my mouth and lips. "Don't be jealous, bro. I'm not really interested in him anyway."

"Yeah, right . . ."

"You could look like that. Let me pierce you . . ."

I pointed to the white bicep of the kid, branded with blue letters and a heart. Antonio finished his beer in two fast gulps. "I'm no Romeo and you're not my fucking boyfriend." We went back to the hotel where our bodies continued their erotic corrida, tangled up in sheets and pillowcases.

At the crack of dawn, Antonio woke up to begin his regimen— long rounds of alternating sit-ups and push-ups. Gyms, he said, were for fags. After a forty-minute routine of grunting and groaning, he went to the bathroom to shower and shave. Shaving is a ritual of no small importance for a skinhead. All the hair on his body required careful grooming by an electric razor with an expensive gold-plated screen. He would set the razor on the lowest setting and begin buzzing his scalp, his underarms, his pubic hair, and then the rest of his body. Everything was clipped down to the same height: seriously short. He said that this way his features came into the proper relief. Then he showered, in water as hot as he could stand, toweled off, and applied unscented cream—no perfumes or colognes were allowed—all over his body, including his now shadowy skull.

He came into the bedroom in just a towel, body glowing, and pounced on me, licking me everywhere. Under my arms, toes, neck, nipples—breaking his skin code of silence and severity. "I'm so happy to see you, dog!" he growled. "There! I *said* it!"

We got dressed. Antonio put on all of his elaborate skin gear. I chose a tank top, cargo pants, and biker boots. We walked in the direction of the English Garden, occasionally touching, though Antonio was uncomfortable with any public displays of affection. His fear was that he would bump into a friend from his exchange program. I thought it unlikely. Most people crossed the street the minute they saw us coming or heard the insistent clomp-clomp of our boots.

"Keep up with me, don't dawdle," Antonio ordered, if I strayed to look at a window display. "Don't play the Italian with me. We're not on via Montenapoleone! No strolling." If we saw another skin, he refused his greeting. "That is not a real bonehead." If he saw other gay Italians, he clenched his teeth to hiss, "Stupid queens! Pretend you don't see them." But if a good-looking guy appeared, that is, a muscle dude with silver-pierced ears, nipple rings, and big tattoos, Antonio stopped dead in his tracks to let out a low wolf whistle . . . sucking in his breath in Aryan awe to say in German, "*Geil.*" Hot.

I felt that twinge of jealousy.

At the entrance to the park, we encountered a group of park rangers. They were shirtless and sweating, perspiration running down their backs to darken short shorts that only Germans wore. Antonio grew stone still, like a pointer, tracking their thick-muscled legs and fur-covered chests. The men wielded power saws and were reducing large branches to firewood and sawdust. The buzz gave Antonio the cover to say, "Slurp, workers!" out loud, unembarrassed. A couple of the men began popping open cans of beer from a cooler—their shift was apparently over—others started stripping. The process of getting naked was a romp of slapped ass and bawdy jokes that Antonio pretended to understand. It was a scene rarely seen in other parts of the world, never in Italy, one that existed, if at all, mostly in the pages of Tom of Finland.

While we watched the men splashing in the river, all of Munich was entering to spend a Saturday in the park with nature. Unlike the perfectly plucked and styled Italians, these Germans were raw, undone in ways both beautiful and grotesque. Many were almost naked like the workmen, young gods and goddesses with good complexions. Others showed signs of age, businessmen and their wives, as exotic in their Bavarian way as Nuba photographed by Leni Riefenstahl.

Nearby a team of teenage boys was kicking a ball around in nude unselfconsciousness. Wading in the river was a group of much older men, bodies ravaged by years of triple therapies. Though their cheeks were hollowed out and their chests sunken, the men were radiant in the warm sunlight, pouring buckets of water over each other quite tenderly, lest the temperature of the river be too cold for someone's compromised immune system. When a young Adonis kicked the ball into the river, a man with a handlebar mustache, a bone drilled through his nose, and hanging balls as large as grapefruits, headed it right back to him. Everyone laughed, because the old man was quite accurate.

The atmosphere, mostly unsexual, had a studied casualness that was particularly German, in that it required all of German civilization and culture to mask the brutality that existed just underneath the surface. Antonio's eyes sucked in everything, hungrily, the same way he smoked a cigarette. In the park he dropped most of his skin affectations—the cold staring, the exaggerated erect posture, the paced walking—and allowed himself to wander, to drift, to look at things leisurely and just soak it all in. I didn't speak to him much, just watched his watching: look-ing at boys' penises in their infinite variety, considering the way a floppy pair of balls moved in their sack, examining the firings of muscle fiber in the calves of a young athlete kicking a ball.

On any given day, the beer garden in the middle of the English Garden, with its Chinese pagoda, greasy pork chops, drunken tourists, and true Bavarians dressed in lederhosen, struggles to overcome cultural cliché. The capital of Bavaria is, after all, the epicenter of Teutonic myth, of Wagnerian opera, of mad King Ludwig II's Disney castle. Kitsch is part of the landscape. Today, when we arrived, skinheads in kilts were turning fairy tale into combat zone. Ostensibly they were waltzing to the strains of an oompah band playing Strauss. "Beer hall putsch meets soccer hooliganism," I said to Antonio when we saw them. But he wasn't listening. He dove straight into the center of the mosh pit, shouting with delight: "Filthy human animals!" Hours later, wiped out, he peeled off his shirt and stretched out on a picnic table next to me. "I need some color, mate." Though he had been born hundreds of miles north of Rome, Latin blood still coursed in his veins.

We dozed under the broad leaves of chestnut trees, listening to punks belting opera, which had been embraced by the move-ment for its pure bombast. Late in the day someone scribbled a name on the back of a matchbook and passed it to Antonio. The bar was not far away and the clientele not so much different— just older. Everything was dark and the patrons were way past ordinary drunk. "So as not to feel the blows from the first punch-up," Antonio said when he saw the first guys passing out. It was the first time I heard him express any negativity toward the movement.

In the bar, there was very little speaking, just heavy posturing. Some skins sat on the wooden bar, feet propped up on beer kegs. Others commanded stools, kicking out ska rhythms on the brass fixtures with their boots. "There are no girls at all," I whispered to Antonio. "What's the deal?"

"Don't assume anything," he warned me. "This is Germany." He grabbed a stool and set himself up near the cigarette machine. I ordered a round of beers and, afraid of locking eyes with a Nazi, drank. I sipped as slowly as possible, gargling, swishing the liquid around in my mouth until it had no taste. I rearranged my belt buckle. I adjusted my briefs. I busied myself with a variety of activities: chewing gum, sucking breath mints, and every once in a while taking a drag off Antonio's cigarette. I flexed my stomach muscles to pass the time and was hoping either that he would get drunk and fall over or that someone—*anyone*—would come over and talk to us.

A blond skin with a bright green Mohawk was watching. "He has been looking at you all night," Antonio said in my ear, bending over from his stool. "Ignore him." The skin inched closer. Suddenly he was standing next to me, starting a ritual that was all too familiar from a lifetime ago: the bumping of elbows, the brushing of thighs, looking at/looking away. Letting a hand wander, tentatively in the dark, testing to see if touch would be rejected or embraced. It was a gay bar, after all. The guy was dressed like all the rest of them—I guess that was the point—but he had a handsome face, clear slate-colored eyes, and the lean build of a soccer player. He saw me looking and hooked his fingers in the belt loop of my jeans to pull me closer. He smiled and spoke in soft German. I looked up at Antonio, hoping that he wouldn't be too jealous to translate. As I did, the skin slipped his hand down my jeans to feel my ass.

Antonio slid down from his stool even quicker. "First of all, he doesn't speak German," he said in English, for my benefit. "But I do. So go fuck yourself before I do it for you!" He took his

Bundeswehr-issue boot and planted it deep in the stomach of the skin, kicking him clear across the bar. Antonio climbed back on his stool and lit a cigarette in triumph. He didn't look at the defeated German, but made sure to blow lazy circles of blue smoke in his direction. "Just in case you forgot it," he said, wrapping his arms around me, "you are *mine*."

"Hey, this place wasn't my idea."

He drained his beer, belched, and said, "Let's get the fuck out of here. Enough of these Nazi bastards—I'm fucking sick of them." Later, eating spaghetti in a restaurant run by transplanted Neapolitans, Antonio accused me of having encouraged the flirting in the first place. "If you do it again, I'm going to kick *your* fucking ass." In this respect, he was one typical Italian: jealous to the core.

The afterglow of Antonio's public acknowledgment that we were together didn't last long. In the weeks after Munich, things went back to normal, that is to say, a relationship that was lived more across radio waves than in real life. Many Italian relationships exist happily in this universe for years, separated by a few hours, a train ride, a convenient marriage, or by career obligations. The limited nature of the contact, circumscribed by circumstance, creates a physical zone of privacy that is cherished, even nurtured in Italy. The ability to step out of one's own giro, to have a truly private affair—outside of family or friends, unintegrated with the rest of one's life, is considered a high art form. Affairs, even the quick ones that last a month, a weekend, or even just one night, are not considered frivolous. They are the central moments of beauty, the possibility of creating art in one's lifetime.

But I was not Italian and soon got frustrated. "Can't we make a simple plan?" I would write, hoping to tie Antonio down. "Next week, next month? You tell me when, I don't care . . ."

"I have to wait until my parents are away."

"And when will that be?"

"It's always a sudden thing."

Sure, Antonio came to Bologna a couple of times. If I got mad enough and threatened, he would show up like a truant child, forced to go to school, still defiant. "Let's go fucking wild," he'd write on the phone before pulling into the Bologna train station. "Drugs, beer, sex, orgies . . . I want to get really lost," as if expressions of anarchic desire covered his absence and so many other things. Then he would disappear again. He would keep me waiting for days about a plan, only to change it at the last minute or cancel outright. Once I wrote back, "You're finished," after he had failed to show up for a scheduled Sunday lunch that just happened to be my birthday. I sent him a final SMS that said, "Goodbye," then deleted every message I had stored in memory.

A few hours later, a lame text came beeping in. "I'm in bed ill 39 degrees plus antibiotic. Sorry, but I slept all day long. Look, I've got no excuse . . . David u re an important person in my life . . . Please do not leave me alone." When I didn't respond, he wrote, "David . . . Please!" Then: "I really understand you, you're angry. I know you. You are my brother, but I am not as adoult as you are . . . not as mature. I am afraid of what I feel for you. It hurts. Please let me come to Bologna one of these days soon. I will make it up to you." He wanted to see the basilica at San Luca "to ask for forgiveness in front of God."

My friends advised me to drop him immediately. "Come on, can't you see it?" Alè warned. "This is your classic *mammone*, mama's boy. He could be having the best sex of his life, but he would run home in a minute to eat a plate of pasta if mommy made the special sauce."

Daniele agreed with his assessment. "Dai, why don't you find yourself a nice Bolognese? Sure he'll have shirts ironed by his mother and won't miss the chance to eat tagliatelle al ragù on Sunday, but at least he can be independent. In Emilia, no one cares whether you fuck girls, boys, or animals at the steps of San Luca, as long as you dress like a figo and show up for Christmas dinner."

How could I explain to them that his destructive energy was

intoxicating? That he made me feel alive? Antonio took wanton pleasure in breaking things. He broke plans. He missed appointments. He burned family photographs, as if the incineration of images could extinguish memories. He rent his garments—cutting off sleeves, slashing collars—mourning his innocence as others remember the dead. I read the signals he was sending out: *I'm not ordinary. I'm suffering.* Each painful part of him helped *me* feel. Every tantrum triggered a galaxy of jealousies, insecurities, and frustrations that no other lover had managed to elicit in me—enhancing my fantasy that what I felt for him could be turned into something sustainable, something real.

He was a dirty fighter.

He purposely created situations in which he knew I would lose my temper. And when I did, he took credit for it, as if it were an accomplishment. "See! I knew you were feeling rage! I could see it in that false American smile! I could read it in the nasty milk blue of your eye!" When I disagreed with his diagnosis, he would wrestle me to the floor, "Don't deny it, bro!," pinning my arms behind my back. "Don't tell me you didn't want to kill me, to beat me to a fucking bloody pulp! How *much* do you hate me? Tell me! *Tell me!*" It was imperative to know the very depth of my feeling, to have it calibrated in precise emotional rungs: Rage! Hatred! Killing fury! Only after I had confessed everything—true or not, he didn't care—could he soften his tone and become a real lover. "*Piccolo, cucciolo* . . . Don't you feel better, now that you've gotten that evil out of your system?" He kissed me in those moments and called me his "puppy."

A promised apology, sanctified by San Luca, I could not turn down. The next weekend he appeared in Bologna as if nothing had happened, his usual skin self. He still wanted to see the Madonna of San Luca, but dressed in army shorts and combat boots. We began the pilgrimage at Porta San Mamolo, walking in the direction of the via dell'Osservanza. At Porta Saragozza we started to climb, making the long ascension up the four kilometers of porticoed hill, to eat a pizza at the trattoria and look at the majesty of the elliptical sanctuary that, according to tradition, had been given a Madonna by Luke the Evangelist himself.[13]

After lunch we went inside the darkened church to see the Madonna and take in the view of Bologna from on high. Antonio, a true believer, washed his hands with water three times before entering, crossed himself, and lit candles for each of his family members, two for his little brother who had an upcoming soccer match. In the church he refused to walk close to me. "Just focus on your confession," I told him, which he elaborately made, on his knees to the priest. Afterward I felt a little uncomfortable in the presence of such religiosity: "I guess I didn't realize that you were so observant," I said guiltily. "How often do you go to church?"

"Never, as a matter of fact." I immediately felt better. Motioning to a priest carrying a box of votives toward the altar, Antonio nudged me. "The guy is eyeing us."

"You're imagining it."

"If that fucking brother keeps looking at my dick," he said, raising his voice, "I swear I'll take it out right here so he can suck it."

"Jesus, have some respect."

"Americans are making such a big deal about churches—now." He was sneering at the man. "Italians haven't been inside churches for decades for just this reason. We *know* they're filled with sodomites—just like *him*." It was the same priest, I was convinced, to whom he had just made his confession.

We walked out of the cathedral and stopped to smoke a cigarette on the portico. Beyond the sanctuary were fields that grew vegetables and meadows that sustained small dairies. Toward the horizon line was the forest, a place where many centuries ago, in a wood much darker and wilder, wolves had wandered. Antonio was not much interested in nature. Down the road he saw, and his eyes were always sharply focused for this, a young worker laying down fresh gravel. I knew what the worker looked like just by watching Antonio's lips. The boy would have a shaved head and no shirt on. I thought of his chest, hot and salty from a day's work, but now that the afternoon was wearing on, cooling. His nipples would be large, protruding—perhaps even erect in the freshness. If they had been adorned with silver piercings, I would lose Antonio with a fast "Slurp!" and "See you later!" But today, after his confession, he was well behaved. "Let's go for a hike," he said, a glint in those fathomless eyes.

We walked down San Luca, under porticoes, passing the parked cars of Italian couples, perched out on a ledge overlooking the autostrada twisting toward Florence. In the back seats of cars, amorous Bolognese were rocking back and forth, suppressing moans in the shadow of the Lord. We tramped through mountain laurel, found a quiet spot near a tuft of late-season snowdrops, and within moments, Antonio had my shirt off and his hands all over me. He licked my chest, my underarms. His tongue trailed down my torso, chasing fur, wetting down everything with his hot spit, until he found the black skull and bones that pierced my navel. He took the titanium ball in his mouth, rolling it around, letting it rattle against his teeth, and pulled me closer to him. I took his shoulders and turned him around, not letting him slither away this time, pressing myself into the small of his back. Antonio smothered gasps, at pains to conceal his pleasure.

We didn't see each other for six months. All communications went dead. He refused to answer phone calls or respond to text messages. I had been totally played, again. Just as I was about to strike his cell number from my phone, the real death knell of a relationship in Italy since no one exchanges last names, addresses, or home phone numbers, a beep came in. It was like the chirping of a tiny sparrow, a *passerrotto*, nickname for a lover. The message read: "Kiss." I couldn't process the significance of something so childish, so utterly meaningless. But instead of plotting a spiteful retort, I just wrote back: "Where the fuck have you been?"

"Great troubles here."

"What?"

"My mother found out about me. She went thru my drawers and found my porn, a black dildo, and a bottle of poppers."

"You use poppers?" I wrote back, pissed off and jealous. "Certainly not with me."

"That's irrelevant right now, Dave. I'm scared. What is going to happen?"

"Stay calm."

"On Friday my father is coming back from Hungary to confront me. My mother says that I am *contro natura*, against nature and perverted."

"Well, I agree with her there!" I wrote.

"This is not the time for silly jokes. Call me later."

When I called Antonio, there was no answer. He didn't take my calls for weeks. I was left to my own imagination, interrupted now and then by bits of text data that I could not altogether trust. "She has stopped cooking for me, she won't make my favorite pasta!" I struggled to understand the cultural significance of these particular losses. "She is not showing me any affection at all, no cuddles, no tucking in at night."

Allow me to delve into cultural stereotype. Italians never speak of their mothers with irony. There are no "mother jokes" in this country. The idea of mother is pure poignancy. When the *festa della mamma* comes around, Italians rush to the bakeries to buy the very freshest chocolate tart. The quality of the baking must be exceptional. The cakes are decorated with just one word, *Mamma*, in white or yellow frosting. Anything else would be superfluous, even diminishing. In my family, my mother is a figure of comedy—the blonde birdbrain who backs the car through the garage door, smashing it to splinters, not once but twice. Okay, that is understandable. Anyone could do it. But then two months later, she drives through the same door again, this time going *forward*. That's vaudeville.

Antonio couldn't see any humor in his forced "coming out." "The gay world is dirty, scatological," he wrote to me, distraught. "She said that! She is obsessed with beasts and perversions." His communications to me, in a mix of fragmented English and Italian, ricocheted from total catastrophe to all clear and then back again. Since we could never have an extended phone conversation about what was really happening, my own fantasies and preoccupations took over.

Why does a mother go searching through her son's drawers in the first place? Antonio told me that it wasn't the gay pornography or the dildo that tipped her off about his homosexuality. Rather, it was the half-used bottle of "Rush" that I didn't even know existed. I had thought, in my humble ignorance, that poppers had died out in the 1970s. Who knew that they had been embraced as party drugs by skins, punks, and ravers?

Antonio's mother, ostensibly young and sophisticated, had gone online to find out more about Rush. I Googled the word myself—coming up with this title: "What are poppers?" I clicked on it and up sprang a yellow-and-red vial with the telltale lightning logo. The description explained that poppers, amyl or butyl nitrites, are often marketed as room deodorants, video head cleaners, leather polishes, but their real use is otherwise: "Poppers cause muscles in the anus and vagina to relax, and they are often used during sex."

How did his mother connect drugs and homosexuality? Did she actually handle the black dildo, that fleshy facsimile of the real thing? What did the silicone phallus feel like in her hands? Was it exciting? Did she think of Africans, of Arabs, of the thousands of immigrants who were flooding the Veneto, changing its demography and its cultural complexion, not to mention its color? Or was the color of the shaft overshadowed by its intended purpose, the penetration of orifices? In her image of beasts and criminals, was her son included as a demonic abstraction? Or was he a specific sinner among the corrupted masses of practicing pederasts, sodomites, and adulterers?

Antonio had forwarded me a message in which she described "the gay life as evil, like being an assassin." Did she think of her son, the same beautiful boy who did her shopping each day so that fresh fruit and vegetables would be on the table when she got home from the office, as a murderer? The same child who drove his father to the airport every time he had to leave for Budapest . . . the same brother who watched his brother's soccer practices, never missing a match, even though he hated the sport—seeing it as the representation of every conformist tendency in a nation of sheep? In many ways I was in the same position as Antonio's mother, mostly in the dark, and, for my own part, angry. Antonio never told me exactly what he was doing with those talismanic objects. In our long relationship together, they never spoke. They stayed in the background, and in my imagination, hidden away in the drawer, like old lovers in picture frames.

The biker world is tough mostly in the imagination. Testosterone and horsepower get most of the attention, but motorcycling is a fragile sport—cleverly masked by gruffness. The mechanics of the motorcycle, especially a handmade Italian one, are always ready to traduce: a popped piston, a failed alternator, something as simple as an antitheft device—the so-called immobilizer on our bikes—that did just that, locking up the engine whenever the cheap electronic part burned out. Human error looms even larger: a surprise low-hanging tree branch, a truck suddenly in the wrong lane, an abruptly opened car door in stalled city traffic—these are just a few of the threats.

Even the best protection, the most carefully laid plan, is inadequate to protect the vulnerability of skin. The sport motorcyclist pushes on anyway—riding faster—girding himself to go beyond his own limits. Knee down on a mountain road—even when there is gravel. Taking the turn wide, crossing into the opposing lane—just for a second—to taste what perfect asphalt feels like, even when skill can't guarantee a proper line out of the corner. Downshifting to weave between trucks on the highway— escaping a double blind spot—feathering the clutch like a pro, letting the bike float between the legs more like steed than bucking bronco. The lure of the road dangles many charms: the wintergreen charge of nature! The druglike addiction to hard acceleration! Experience can teach you many things, but it doesn't make riding any safer. Skill drives you *harder*.

A sport biker invites fate to dance—just one quick waltz—praying that if he can keep rhythm, she will keep her distance. It's a risky proposition. For it's just as the rider goes faster, rushing headlong into the unknown—fueled by horsepower, pumped by adrenalin, encountering new turns, never-before-seen vistas—that he feels most free. Free-styling. Hot-dogging. Sweat breaking on the brow. The senses become acute, discerning. To hear the grit on the road! To smell the jasmine and magnolia! Differentiating blooms. Understanding how smells mix and mingle yet remain separate. Drunk from exhaust fumes and flowers, a biker screams into his helmet—horror and joy—flirting with the ever after, but stopping just short, just shy of losing all reason.

Luck was not always with our riders. The head of the model shop, an experienced motorcyclist with a career's worth of design work for Moto Morini, had his arm "clipped" while riding home one day. (The world of accident is full of euphemism.) The *incidente*—"accident" in Italian—happened just a mile or so away from the factory during a lazy afternoon on the most ordinary stretch of road. The man was a crack designer, expert mechanic, and had helped perfect the chassis dynamics for a new motorcycle developed by my team.

I played the aftermath over in my head for months, daydreaming about the limb, now cradled in a muslin sling, swollen, without any signs of life but for the blood pulsing beneath. If only he had received specialized medical attention—a trip to a major New York hospital—rather than what was on offer in Bologna, his dead nerves might have been stitched back together, soldered like the wires of an old Marconi radio, and sparked back to life. But he never complained about his medical treatment. Like most bikers, he was a stoic, resigned to fate.

My friend Willie, aka "the pocket Tom Cruise," had a "spinout"—no one called them crashes if the victim lived to tell about it—on a roundabout late one night. I can't say with certainty if he was drunk, though he certainly had been partying. No amount of Acqua di Giò could cover the alcohol stink on him some mornings. He doesn't remember the circumstances of his accident, though the aftereffects were clear enough. It was as if someone had taken a needle and scratched a skein of symbols—tiny stars, fine skeletons—on his face, an unambiguous warning to others: here is road hazard. Avoid! A sharp instrument had punctured his chest. It might have been a pole. Tree branches had lacerated his shoulder.

He was rushed away, on a stretcher, by the ambulance that found him on the traffic island, unconscious, blanketed by shards of glass and candy wrappers. A tow truck hauled away the crushed metal and plastic remains of his defunct wheels. (That was always an efficient operation in Bologna.) The accident was nothing much: nothing broken, nothing burned. The pocket Tom Cruise lived to ride again. His only shame was that it happened on a scooter, a lowly 150cc—not even a motorcycle.

The star engineer of the high-performance motors unit went off-road in a tragic accident during an endurance race across the Sahara. The telephone call to the management team at New Year's had a sickening, inevitable quality to it. No one knew how or why he lost control of his motorcycle in the dusty wilds of the North African desert. No one could second-guess his bike (it wasn't ours, thank God!), his choice of gear (he always wore full body protection), or his riding talents (the man was an experienced off-road racer). We only witnessed the horrifying results. His lower body withered away. Muscle retreated from bone. Skin went slack and lost its human color. His head grew more prominent, more intelligent-seeming. When he returned to work confined to a wheelchair, he was more determined than ever to build engines that gave our racers a performance edge. Here was true biker culture: no tears, no laments—just the quest for more horsepower.

People died regularly at the company. We lost at least a handful of testers every year or so in freak accidents and unexplained circumstances. The ordinary crashes caused by weather, by road conditions, by car drivers—postdiscotheque—lost in rum-and-Coke daze, were easy to explain, if not accept. But sometimes a biker would just drift—inexplicably break concentration—wandering across a double yellow line to crash head-on into two tons of truck. Was it really just that—a loss of focus? Tired road eyes? It was a subject of much speculation among enthusiasts.

In one of the great tragedies of modern racing, Ayrton Senna, the much-adored Formula One driver and motorcycle fanatic, hit the wall at the Tamburello curve of the Imola circuit during the San Marino Grand Prix. The slim, handsome Brazilian, an idol to his fans, was removed from his race car while an audience of millions watched on television—holding its breath. The driver with the big yellow helmet and the heart of gold was not moving. Shocked announcers broke the long broadcast silence with their sobs. The champion was prounced dead at the scene, Sunday, May 1, 1994.

More than a decade later, the mystery of his death remains unsolved. Missing seconds from the videotape recorded by Senna's onboard camera—just before impact—give rise to countless conspiracy theories. Absent data from the black box behind the driver's seat throws fuel on the fire. Did the steering column of his Williams Team car break in two? Rumor has it that Senna lowered the column to his specifications. Did the drive shaft rupture upon impact or just before? Was it a cracked weld or was the quality of the metal itself in question? What were race conditions like that day at Imola, then one of the world's fastest courses? Web sites broadcast the crash frame by frame, looking for clues. Despite multiple investigations, lawsuits, and incessant theorizing at the bar, no single convincing official or popular explanation has emerged.

Speeding down a tunnel of light, wall fast approaching, what was Senna's thought at the moment of collision? Could it have been this: that he should not go out in a simple car accident like Mike "the Bike" Hailwood? Oh, the mawkish embarrassment of such an ordinary end! That he should not limp into old age battered by injuries like Giancarlo "the Lion" Falappa, the perennial underdog of Italian motorcycle racing? Half mad and often mumbling, the old beast, as famous for his crashes as his pole positions, was hustled off from department to department whenever he came calling. The deep humiliation of a professional no longer able to compete!

Maybe the great champion, Senna, approaching the checkered Kronenbourg sign, had decided that he had just had *enough*: enough of the leggy blondes, enough of the corporate sponsors, enough of the tax-free Monte Carlo residences and the luxe accoutrements of Formula One racing. With one glorious explosion, a fireball of fuel and fiberglass, he invented the perfect ending. He went across to the other side, still in the prime of his career—halfway suspended between dream and reality. Racing toward death, rushing toward life—because what is fate if not acceptance of one's humanity—Senna found his climax, his personal conclusion. And whether his decision was one of bravery or just boredom, it sealed his reputation. He would remain a legend—a rock star of the racing world—forever riding high above the cheering crowds, beyond the reach of the bleachers.

35

Every time we organized a motorcycle rally, the specter of death—or at least grave injury—hung above our heads. It wasn't a gloomy cloud of cliché. The mood was electric, more like the charged rush right before a thunderstorm. It was the buzz that we felt firing up our engines in the morning, fingers stiff in cold leather gloves, breath frosty. Would this be the last time? Sweat trickled across our foreheads. It was the dizzy satisfaction of pumping a tank full of gasoline—and the promise of burning it up right after—that had our pulses racing. Remembering the last time on the road, that day in the mountains when we just missed hitting a Porsche that pulled out in front of us without so much as signaling (car drivers are *always* blind), or later, while riding home through a mile-long diesel spill on the motorway, which we navigated successfully, or the giant pothole, unseeable in the purple dark, which we did not.

   Che culo! What dumb luck! We escaped without incident— just a scratch, a few scrapes. The gods of biking were still there smiling down on us. In ancient Greece, centaurs were real creatures, half man, half horse, running free in the woods, in the valleys, at the foot of great mountain ranges, guided by their master Chiron.[14] Living out their time on earth, they gave us a mythic story. To ride a motorcycle is to remember, to taste their freedom.

Setting off on a bike—any make, any model, on journeys long or short, challenging or just wandering—is transformation, throwing off the shackles that constrain us, escaping the prisons of the ordinary. Every time a helmet's visor is lowered, the shroud is removed from weary eyes. And the everyday awesomeness of the world, shimmering right there in front of us, is revealed. The motorcycle makes a man young. The motorcycle takes youth and molds a man. It contains in its mythos, which is the source of its psychic power, the classical paradoxes: life and death, beauty and destruction, freedom and incapacity. In the saddle, perspectives change, rules bend, and we can *see again*. Unafraid, we *long* to gear up—we hunger for it—to give the bike gas, to measure our humanity against all that is great, mystical, and enchanted.

Bikers have specific rituals to follow before testing their mettle. Ordinary things, like kicking tires and flipping on headlights, like wiping down windscreens and repositioning mirrors. There are also more esoteric procedures, like checking chain tension, monitoring brake fluid, and sometimes applying a little cleaner to clear debris embedded in a caliper pad before riding out. Each rite has its place in the firmament of road religion. Superstition plays its part too. Faith in technology has not eclipsed fear.

At our races and rallies even hardcore bikers took precautions, tying red string to handlebars and pasting tiny crosses to windscreens. If a MotoGP champion like Valentino Rossi had a procedure for stretching his legs, flexing his toes, touching his balls, and then squatting down on the tarmac to talk to his bike personally before each race, I could carry a picture of Antonio in my back pocket and wear a silver chain with a Roman coin and a Star of David.

I always felt churning, suiting up for a ride in the mountains, especially on unknown roads. Squeezing into my Gore-Tex and nylon pants (stiff, but thankfully not new), pulling on Axo boots (more performance than my ability required), I would check my gear and tighten my straps like everybody else, praying that my skills would be sufficient so as not to make a *total* fool of myself— *not today*—not in front of this many journalists. I would beg the biking gods (I'm not superstitious—this was self-preservation!) and make several trips to the bathroom. Queasiness didn't allow me to eat before a ride. I waited until lunchtime to *mangiare*— after I had found my rhythm and could trust my riding companions. By then the mood would be lighter, especially if the riding went well, and I could gorge all of the tiny olives, fatty ham, and pecorino cheese set out at roadside stands tended by country folk dressed in traditional costume.

In the afternoon there was camaraderie—a shared bottle of water, a spare pair of gloves. Once, a colleague, an old dirt bike racer, quietly adjusted the ride height down a peg for a long trip with veteran riders. It was a discreet way of giving me, a not so tall, not so experienced biker, more control over the motorcycle by lowering its center of gravity. Brotherhood was in the simple gesture, the silent nod—an almost imperceptible dip of the chin—that bikers gave each other before clicking their visors shut, as if to say: "All clear. Good luck for now, and if we should lose each other along the way, don't lose your head. Keep strong." It was like going off to a little war—winnable—nothing to worry about really. But no one could be sure. If the conditions were right, even the most mature biker could revert to a boy. And then it was off to the races. When someone, usually a neophyte on a whim or a dare, decided that this was going to be his race to lose. Because once that fool's plan was hatched, nothing we could do could stop it.

36

Every year we staged a re-creation of one of the oldest motorcycle races in Italy, the Motogiro d'Italia. From 1914 through the
late 1950s, "the lap of Italy," on the roughest of roads, was the ultimate test for bike and biker and attracted thousands of fans. In
those days, much of motorized personal transport was two wheels
(not four), and a cottage industry of bike manufacturers (up to
two hundred manufacturers at the peak) vied for the attention
of enthusiasts by racing their latest, greatest machines. Each
marque had its own design particularity or technical innovation,
from the flying saucer–shaped fuel tank and banana frame of the
MV Agusta Disco Volante to the single-cylinder, shaft-driven
overhead camshaft with Cosmodromic valves of our own bike.
Lessons learned on the road quickly found their way into production, establishing the essential sales and marketing formula that
continues in Italy to this day: win on Sunday, sell on Monday.

The idea for a re-creation of the Motogiro came from Mario,
one of the student curators pressed into service by the boss to
help us "recuperate" our history. He was writing a book about
restoring vintage bikes on a shoestring budget "all by himself."
At least that was the story we told. I remember weeks spent with
Krystle, translating his convoluted but deeply felt treatises on
vintage models into passable English. Besides his passionate love

for old motorcycles, Mario had one great talent: laughing. In the face of any challenge, any organizational problem, any affront to his large, sensitive ego, his lips would curl upward in a giant grin to reveal broad white teeth, thick as china. Then, out would come peals of rat-a-tat-tat *romagnolo* laughter, accompanied, when necessary, by smothering bear hugs and sticky kisses. When the company wanted to acquire a particular bike for the museum, Dino sent out Mario, who deployed his "charm." After a few hours of his dramatic pleadings and emotional embraces, vintage bike collectors would do anything to get rid of him.

Now he wanted to re-create the Motogiro. He sold the project to management by stressing that a new Motogiro would serve as an extension of the museum ("Something alive, not dead!"); as a window for the retro-futuristic Rivoluzione, nearing its production date; and as a general celebration (the company was marking its seventy-fifth anniversary). For Mario, the vintage road race was even more. It was a personal platform for fiery cultural exhortations and government-sponsored coffee klatches on "Emilia-Romagna, the Land of Motors!" When I expressed doubts about state funding, Mario stopped laughing for just a moment: "Davide, you wouldn't understand. In Europe the government actually *likes* spending money like this."

He got the necessary permits from the Federazione Motociclistica Italiana (FIM), worked out logistics with a riding club, Libero Liberati (named after the legendary 1950s racer who died in a crash), raised funds from the region, and mapped out a route—Narni, Amelia, Muccia, Loreto, Recanati, and Siena—that included many of the stops on the original Motogiro, which last roared through Italy in 1957.

Oh, the dramatic excitement of those times! When it was still possible to race on public roads and a rapt nation turned out to watch pilots (who in real life were just kid farmers) giving shape to their dreams. Before Italy was a modern nation, on a par

with Britain and France. Before there were speed limits and traffic controlled by video camera. Before Benetton privatized the
country's highways, installing a Telepass system at tollbooths and
building Autogrill restaurants every fifty kilometers that sold
chocolate glazed doughnuts. And, perhaps most significantly,
before cars took over as the definitive status symbols on the
road, eclipsing the evocative power of the motorcycle to define
modernity.

It was a time of heroes. A time when centaurs took to the
streets and, in a spectacle of great daring and verve, ran free.
When the Motogiro came to town, everything else stopped. The
roar of engines echoed across fields and valleys—replacing memories of bombs and bullets. For just a few hours, fierce political
battles subsided. Priests and anarchists agreed to a truce and
masses of spectators lined streets and piazzas, pressed tight against
barriers, to taste, for just a moment, the mythical elixir.

It took great courage to race back then. In northern Italy the
streets were clean and police-monitored. But in the south there
were animals and excrement on the road. Each segment of the
race was long, up to eight hours. And the weather in April could
be a bastard's mix of sleet, hail, snow, rain, and baking sun. The
risks were great. Motors failed on mountain inclines. Braking
power was intermittent. Dozens died on the Motogiro before it
was banned (along with all other road races) after a tire blew out
on Alfonso Cabeza de Vaca's Ferrari (he was the seventeenth
marquess of Portago), twenty miles from Brescia, during 1957's
Mille Miglia car race, causing a spectacular crash and the death
of the marquess, his navigator, and ten spectators.

In his travels up and down the peninsula, Mario discovered
that many of the men who had raced those early sport motorcycles, legends who brought speed and light to roads pockmarked
by history, had not yet passed into it. They were very much
alive—and far from being forgotten old men, were still riding.

Giuliano Maoggi, the Tuscan-born "Italian Knight" who took part in the Motogiro from 1953 to 1957, still rode like the limber-limbed *ragazzino* who had won the championship. There he was—a young man sitting on a slender 125cc at the end of one of the lengths of his 1956 victory. Pushing the Gran Sport with squat, muscular legs, wearing a circular-striped helmet emblazoned with the letter M, he captured all of the arrogance of those times. A grimace twisted across his face. Pressed between his lips was a cigarette. I chose that photograph of Maoggi as the poster image for the reborn Motogiro. Using letters supplied by Dino's exhaustive research on Fascist fonts from the 1920s and 1930s, I developed a logo and ad copy to promote the Motogiro: *La leggenda ritorna*, the Legend Returns.

The glory days of the original Motogiro masked a problem that would become persistent: waning Italian competitiveness. In the late 1950s, Soichiro Honda built the C100 Super Cub for a war-devastated nation that couldn't afford cars and whose public transportation system was all but in ruins.[15] With its overhead-valve, horizontal, single-cylinder 49cc engine and simple plastic-enclosed bodywork, the Super Cub became an instant best seller in Japan and then abroad, paving the way for a stream of similar products. Honda sent its first factory team to race at the Isle of Man Tourist Trophy in 1959 and lost. Two years later the Japanese won in both the 125cc and 250cc classes. By the end of the decade, Honda was dominating all racing, exporting bikes to Europe and America; by the mid-1960s it had become the biggest motorcycle company in the world.

Japanese bikes were clean and efficient, and if they weren't technologically innovative or superstylish—then as now Europeans dismissed them as copies—their high manufacturing quality was reason enough to ride them.[16] It all happened so fast, at the speed of a sport bike. Though there was no immediate death knell, the shakeout of the Italian industry commenced. Bike maker MV Agusta still won a record number of world titles in the late 1950s. Its Works 350 was and is a paradigm of the partic-

ularly Italian marriage of design and performance, with its tubular frame, box-section swing arm, ventilated twin drum brakes
with double air scoops, magnesium engine cases, and a double-
overhead-camshaft four-cylinder engine.[17] Piaggio managed to
define la dolce vita with its midcentury Vespa—a wasp-waisted
scooter with monocoque chassis and single-cylinder, fan-cooled,
two-stroke engine that took the world by storm.

But the times were changing. A postwar economic boom
brought cheap cars like the Fiat Cinquecento to the masses
and the need for bikes as a primary means of transportation
was obviated. The contraction of the domestic market in the
1960s forced many historic Italian marques to shutter. To survive, Moto Guzzi, Laverda, and others went up-market with
larger-displacement bikes that were still profitable, and began to
export their products.

When Mario revived the Motogiro in 2001 as a timed trial
"race," most of the makers of bikes that had run in the original—
the Bianchi 175s, the Motobi Catrias and Imperiales, the Aer-
macchi Ala Rossas and Perugina Sports—were long gone. The
remaining niche manufacturers were kept on life support only by
a trickle of financing from rich enthusiasts who could not bear to
see a historic brand like Moto Morini die a natural death or an
exotic builder like Bimota (whose innovative hub-center steering on the Tesi 1D replaces conventional forks) cease to push
the boundaries of handling. It was a time of consolidation. Just a
few factories could even hope to compete against the size and
scale of the Japanese behemoths.

Though Italian bike makers were dead or dying, the racers lived
on. I remember the departure of the Motogiro from our parking
lot, in the shadow of the huge billboard of the reigning World
Superbike Champion. No longer black-and-white, no longer

frowning, but deeply tanned and dazzlingly alive was Maoggi himself. Today he was once again riding a historic 175. Now in his late seventies, the white-maned racer would teach us young-sters a thing or two about racing. "Going fast is not just a twist of the throttle," he said, scrutinizing the lineup of historic metal. "In our time, the whole body had to be used to will the bike for-ward, conserving power for downhill sprees of nearly unlimited velocity so that the bike would have enough momentum to make it up the next hill." This was his Indian summer. He was enjoying giving advice to young weekend warriors mixing fuel—one part gasoline, one part oil—and to journalists kick-starting reluctant engines, hoping that their motors would spark to life before it was time to roll up to the starting gate.

Here in the parking lot there was no debate about the beauty of an old scarab-shaped gas tank. A banana-shaped swing arm was singularly beautiful, a silver dustbin fairing unquestionably sexy. Everyone understood the accomplishment of these vintage motorcycles, built with great attention to detail. All this in a time before there were designers! Today, product standardization, design modularity, and rationalization ruled. Keeping costs down was the name of the game. But the determining factor in our commercial success was still our ability (or inability) to design and build beautiful motorcycles. Gorgeous product would have enthusiasts salivating, willing to pay any price premium—to cover the cost of manufacturing in Italy. But as much as we talked obsessively, collectively, about design—wrote about it in countless magazine articles, promoted it at industry conferences and symposia, plastered it on our Web site and in our catalogs—simple, modern beauty still somehow eluded us.

This year the Motogiro was going off without a hitch—following a route from the factory in Borgo Panigale through the cities of Ferrara, Rovigo, Piazzola sul Brenta near Padua, ringing the ski resorts of the Dolomites, and then returning to Bologna via Verona. I spent a few days of glorious mountain riding on a Beast, trying to keep pace with a superfast American girl named Julia. We raced across Alpine meadows and abandoned apple orchards. We roared through the mountain towns of Bocenago, Arco, and Folgaria. I didn't see much. My eyes were glued to Julia's ass, a beacon in black leather, shifting from side to side in the saddle. We carved corners through pink limestone passes and barreled across lunar bowls of sand and scree.

Julia didn't need any encouragement to become a biker. She was one of those rare females—sexy and still able to take a four-valve out on the racetrack and tangle with the best of the boys. Once every twenty minutes or so, she would stretch out her legs, boots almost grazing the ground, then drop a fingered glove to give me the signal: pick up the pace. Hillsides covered in grape vine whizzed by. Stands of white birch and fir flashed before us in shades of silver and green. The dreamy shapes of the mountain— or what we could see of them from a bike—rivaled the domes and towers, spires and minarets of a Mogul's palace.

I stayed close to Julia's tail, eating her dust, occasionally spotting in the corner of my eye the purple tongue of a late-season crocus poking out of an icy hollow. As thundershowers turned into hailstorms of marble-sized ice, we began passing many of the old men of the Motogiro, now stalled at the side of the road. Hailstones hit the tarmac like bullets. Sheets of water came down. I thought about the changing nature of biking, watching snapshots of these patient riders huddled under tarpaulins, tinkering with their sputtering motors, trying to nurse old hounds back to life, using practiced hands, ancient tools, and even soft words of encouragement. If mechanical failure couldn't be remedied, they sat at the side of the road, heads bowed, waiting for the sweep van and a last-ditch chance of a specialist mechanic.

The last thirty miles through a series of narrow-bore tunnels was a trip in psychedelia. The roads were grooved to prevent freezing. Rubber rolling on ridges created disco hum. Clerestory holes in the rock cast pulsing light as dizzying as the dance floor. We arrived at Madonna cold, numb, drenched in sweat, but exhilarated. Conditions had been heavy. The long ride from Bologna up to the mountains in pissing rain, in traffic, had caused many vintage engine failures. These bikes were air-cooled and needed constant speed to be properly radiated. They couldn't handle modern stop-and-go traffic. We apportioned spares to those who had spent the day in the sweep van. And after rounds of warming grappa, I went to bed. I had decided to skip the mostly dull ride back to Bologna, leaving the event a day early to meet Antonio in Catania, where he was studying on another grant. This running of the centaurs was going well. The next morning I took a train from Trent to Bologna and then, leaving the vintage world behind, hopped on a modern charter to Catania.

I was sitting in the Sicilian sun eating pistachio-flavored ices when my cell phone rang. Despite the heat, I felt a chill. Italians never call early on a Saturday morning. "Pronto," I said into the phone, forcing cheerfulness. It was Krystle, calling from the Motogiro near Mantua. The event had just a couple of hours to go until it reached its conclusion in the center of Bologna, where a gala dinner was planned in the Palazzo Re Enzo, named after King Enzo of Sicily, who was imprisoned there from 1249 to 1271. It is said that his imprisonment was a luxurious one, spent in the company of nobility and rich quantities of food and drink.

"Oh, David. *Thank God.*" I knew already from the tone of her voice. The long lull after the word "God." It spelled disaster. "I'm so glad I found you . . ." Krystle, with honey in her heart, couldn't chase away shadow or change the fact that joy was chased with sorrow at motorcycling events.

"What happened?" I asked, my voice quiet, calm.

"It's terrible."

"Tell me," I said, thinking of Maoggi's luminous smile.

An English rider from the Gruppo del Mondo club had had an accident. He was carving up curves at full speed on state road 62 when a small white car, probably a Fiat Punto, made a left turn onto a country lane. The police report didn't say whether the driver had had his turn signal on or not. The biker, Mr. H., was riding a rented sport-touring bike that made better than 120 horsepower. According to witnesses, he was "flying by" at "at least 130 kilometers per hour," "oblivious," "in his own world." The group had just a few more hours to go before arriving in Bologna. Perhaps pensive, certainly tired, most likely musing about the splendor of these days, riding perfect roads, air soft and flowery—he had been wandering, traveling in a personal world of time and space. After days of sleet and hail and mountains thousands of kilometers in height, his luck (and ours) had turned.

What did he see on the road? They said he had been riding too fast to see anything. I wondered how could he have missed the procession of orchards with new fruit and the square fields of green wheat that covered the plains? Maybe, lost in a daydream, he had been paying too much attention to birds—screens of swallows returning north—or to bees swarming over poppies. Was he watching the sky too closely, considering its chalkiness instead of concentrating, as he should have, on asphalt? He had not been drinking. He wore protective leathers and a full-face helmet. He was a family man, as they say, with "everything to live for."

In a simple but devastating highway accident, he hit the Punto almost head-on. The elderly driver of the car walked away from the accident without a scratch on him. The motorcyclist and his bike went on a journey—high in the air, wheels spinning—then over the barrier and into the ravine below. The momentum didn't end there. Water took over. The current carried the motorcycle downstream, past rotting tree trunks, through rapids and eddies. Eventually the bike lodged underneath a natural rock bridge, tangled up in reeds and watery debris.

Krystle arrived at the scene of the accident within minutes in the sweep van. "She almost saw the dust settle," one witness told me later. "She could have watched the skid marks dry on the road." It took precious little time to reconstruct the accident. The rubber traced a path to the embankment, then straight off the cliff. A bystander pointed to the bike far below—lodged precariously in the rocks—water running over metal and plastic fairing. "Where is the rider?" I asked on the cell phone, over the sound of river rushing in my ear. For better than twenty minutes Krystle searched the narrow shoulder of road, the hollows of tree trunks, and in patches of wild wheat on the muddy banks of the stream—with me on the phone. She couldn't find him.

"Oh my God!" she whispered into the receiver, voice thick with terror. About a kilometer downstream, blown up like a balloon but otherwise unmarked, she found him. I put down my coffee cup and grabbed Antonio's thigh under the table. I needed to hold onto something solid.

"Okay," I said, "take your time and tell me."

Krystle was short of breath, almost choking. "It's awful . . ."

"Breathe," I said, "it's okay." My own body was shaking.

"I don't think he's alive, David."

There was heaving.

"Can you see his face?"

"Yes. It is enormous and blue."

"Are his eyes closed?"

"Open."

"Is he moving?"

"I don't think so. The water is moving him."

I thought about the body, preserved in the icy runoff, Apennine water washing everything clean and cold, preparing the body for burial. "Don't make any announcements till we have a death certificate," I advised. "Stay calm."

"Okay."

"Do not touch him either. Call the police immediately."

"I'm so sorry. I'm going to faint . . ." I heard muffled noise. Gasps? Sobs? ". . . will go to the hospital and then call you." And then she dropped the line.

While I waited for her call, I drank rounds of coffee at that plastic cafe table in Catania. I chain-smoked Antonio's cigarettes and thought of liabilities. Who was responsible for the man's death? Did he have insurance? Did *we*? I called colleagues and friends who were riders. "Is there a biker way to handle tragedy?"

They were very clear: "Do nothing." "Let the police apportion blame and determine guilt." The insurance company would calculate whom and how much to pay. There would be no drama, no lawsuits, and no legal pyrotechnics.

Antonio said: "A motorcycle death in Italy is just a number on an actuarial table." He was holding my hand.

When Krystle called back, she apologized for fainting. "No need," I said. "You're the one doing the heavy lifting here." She was sitting with the body in the morgue, waiting for identification, going through standard death procedures. We informed our team on the ground of what had happened and then called the boss in Bologna. He had ridden the event for a few days and agreed to speak about Mr. H. at the closing ceremonies of the Motogiro that night in Bologna.

"What about the widow?" Krystle asked.

"If you like, I'll call her," I said. "It's the least I can do."

"No, I need to do it. I *owe* it to her."

When Mr. H. was pronounced dead by the authorities, Krystle mustered the courage to make the call. Mrs. H. was not at home. Krystle was crazily relieved. She left a message talking about a grave accident, not specifying exactly what had happened, and urged the widow to call her back as soon as possible.

By the time Mrs. H. finally rang, her friends had already broken the news to her. The eventual phone discussion was all bureaucratic detail: insurance arrangements, consulates, police reports, death certificates, and the logistics of shipping a body internationally.

At the closing ceremony of the Motogiro, the boss made a speech in Mr. H.'s memory. His words were simple, unemotional, but Max was visibly moved. A fellow rider followed with: "I knew him only for the few days that we rode together on the Giro, but I know he truly loved riding. He went out of this life the way we all would like to—riding our bikes *fast*." That was it, nothing more. The bikers ate their pasta, drank their wine, ate a fat slice of celebration cake, and went home.

The aftermath of Mr. H.'s death created a buzz of excitement, shock, and sadness, but no time for mourning. The company moved on to a new endurance race in the Dolomites. There was a whole season of Superbike races left in Europe, Laguna Seca in California, the completion of our debut season in MotoGP, and the Speedweek in Austria to think about. For a moment we talked about Mr. H. over a dinner at Anna Maria's trattoria, famous for its tortellini *in brodo*, braised rabbit, and *stinco di maiale*.

The latest gossip was that Mrs. H. had been just about to divorce her husband anyway. "So his death served a purpose," someone dared. There would be no fighting about his assets or custody battles over children. "Mr. H. rode off gallantly, like a true biker gentleman." Then the talk turned to the eyewitnesses. Hugh, an English guy who worked for me in promotions, said, "It was bloody hell, like war. Finally, I felt like I had some purpose in life! I felt *alive*." His trademark enthusiasm was coming on: "After the accident, I was talking to his friends, riding with them, keeping them all together. I helped them make phone calls back home since they didn't speak Italian . . . so *exciting!*"

"But imagine what it was like for poor Krystle," I said. "The muck of the ditch, searching for the body . . ."

"Quite a comedown for a princess. Instead of fashion shows and red carpets, she was dragging a dead biker body out of a muddy ravine." Hugh didn't say that. But a veteran biker did. The approach to the business of death was always like that, callousness masking fear. To a man, the hard-boiled bikers among us said in well-rehearsed set pieces: "Well, that's the way he would have wanted to go, riding his motorcycle right up to the very end."

I couldn't say that going out on a bike was the way that *I* wanted to end it all. Maybe I was too cautious, too conservative, too attached to the life that was lived off the road—the dull, motionless life that bikers laughed about. Was I not the real biker that these men were? I could never just *let go.* I thought about it all the time. But the years at the company changed me. With each passing accident, with each loss, I became more accustomed to the matter-of-fact injuries of our testers, our friends, and our riding companions. With each crash, with each broken bone, I understood that we were building a bridge. Each untimely death, another paralyzed rider, the losses brought us closer. I thought about how sadness and injury, suffering and tears, linked together to form an indivisible chain, an invisible necklace that bound us all together, tracing back in time and looking forward, connecting us to the legendary deaths of past champions and those tragic losses that were still to come in the future, allowing ordinary people to inhabit the space of their heroes.

"Pain is the enemy that becomes accepted and then a true friend," writes Dr. Costa in the book that recounts his lifetime experiences healing injured racers, "because in suffering are seeds of hope, which become beautiful flowers, creating a tapestry of colored petals strewn over the most difficult of roads, where courageous men run."[18] His own father had built the Imola race-track and designed the infamous Tamburello curve, where so many racers had crashed and burned.

When our bikers died—and they tended to die in unlucky batches of twos and threes—I thought about the spells they had fallen under, what flowered paths they had been traveling. Were they entranced by long stretches of mesmerizing asphalt? Enchanted by sparkling angels and insects—the giant gnats and yellow-jacket wasps and sticky sacs of pollen that popped when they hit a helmet visor? Or had they simply failed in their personal quest for greatness? *Trying* to make that perfect turn. *Almost* touching their knee down. Roads in Italy—even highways—are not the boring repetitions of truck stop, gas station, fast-food outlet rhymed with streetlight, traffic sign, and toll-booth that they are in America. Roads here are twisted, unmonitored, unkempt, and sometimes elegant, as full of risk and excitement as the wild. The rider doesn't die of boredom. Perhaps he dies as Senna did, or Mr. H. did, of ecstasy: unable to stop, unable to resist the glow of headlights in the opposing lane. Impelled forward, ignoring rule and reason, trying to get a bit closer to hear nymphs and road maidens calling a biker to dance. To meet them on the shoals, to kiss them on the mouth, to cross that median and come to the other side—peril be damned! When I rode, I watched the hood ornaments of cars and trucks suspiciously. As seductive as dice and just as treacherous, those streamlined speed angels, chrome-bright Indian chiefs, winged princesses, and flying goddesses sang a biker's song. But I always kept my distance, because not all music is sweet, and not every siren's call must be answered.

After the great success of Jacques's dream bike, and with a few fits and starts, we finally went public. I hired an investor-relations expert, an ex–Hollywood actor down on his luck, who taught us to "throw" our voices to the room's sweet spot, to leave five seconds of air space after each new concept, and—here was his secret weapon—to eliminate titles from our PowerPoint slides. "This way the audience is forced to actually listen to your presentation and not just read it." We updated our charts and graphs, went shopping for new suits at Zegna, and the big boss finally had his moment. He chose a Gulfstream 4 with the oversized picture windows.

Though he never admitted it, I always suspected that he was behind the decision to go for a dual listing—on the New York Stock Exchange and Milan's Borsa Italiana. Two listings meant ten blissful days in the air! Previous claims that he could float the entire company by calling three friends in Milan were forgotten. Max and his management team were now hopscotching across the continent on a private jet, squeezing in meetings in far-flung places such as Lisbon and Edinburgh. The schedule was grueling—up to ten meetings a day with junior analysts whose attention span was mostly limited to the number of management options to be exercised on trading day. "It's a really big payout for you guys, right? House in the Bahamas time?"

"Bankers are too stupid to understand our story anyway," the boss concluded back on board. "I've always said that, right?"

"Dumber even than lawyers," I seconded.

But as much as he complained—about the jokes not laughed at, the questions not asked—he loved every last minute of it. When we got to London, he was presented with a real decision: keep the Gulfstream or go Concorde. It was touch and go for a minute. The bonanza of supersonic frequent flier miles and lavish Concorde goodie bags won out.

SEC rules prohibit forward-looking information during a road show. Management was not supposed to talk about future bike registrations or new products or impending joint ventures or anything that might give the institutional investor who came to hear our IPO presentation an unfair advantage over the ordinary investor. No matter. The boss ordered "flash" reports to be faxed from Bologna daily so that he could look for fresh ways to spin the numbers. With each new city, with every press interview, our future grew rosier. One minute he was talking to CNN about more horsepower for our race bikes. Next he was giving an interview to Bloomberg promising gross margin improvements. He never crossed the line, but he couldn't resist flirting. "No one has ever looked at the factory," Max crowed. "It's a gold mine—for savings!" By the time we reached Boston, our cell phones were ringing nonstop.

"I'm watching his lips move again on CNBC," one of our bankers on the deal shouted into the phone. "He's talking about next quarter's sales! Make him stop!"

I tried, but it was futile. "What can I do? You know he can't say no to a microphone."

"The SEC will pull the plug on this circus if he continues." Sensing commotion, the boss came over to see what was going on. "Do they like what they see?" he asked, eager to know how he was playing on air.

"The lawyers say you can't talk about forward-looking results," I told him. "The SEC may not let us price."

"Give me the phone, I'll handle this." When I passed him my cell, Max lowered his voice an octave. "Now, just what is the problem, gentlemen?" The words were sweet but barely audible. "Hey guys, it's getting windy up here," he blew into the phone. "The connection is weak. I'm about to lose signal." He tapped the mouthpiece with his finger for good measure. "Boston is going stormy." We were, of course, indoors. "Call me back later." And then he hung up. Whether he actually listened to the concerns on the other end of the line was moot. The cameras were setting up for his "get close and personal" and he was never one to be late for an interview.

"Everything okay in New York?" I asked mildly.

"Keep those fucking lawyers out of my hair, David," he ordered, passing me the dead cell phone. "I have a job to do." He slipped into his blue jacket, sat down in the director's chair set up in front of the Rivoluzione, and looked straight into the bank of blinking television cameras. "Now boys," he said, opening his green eyes wide, "how does a small company from Bologna, land of luncheon meat, beat the pants off the Goliaths?" He was cool and collected, his delivery perfect as any anchorman's. "I'll tell you. When the Japs have a problem with a race engine, they rush a fax to Tokyo, desperate for a technical solution. When Italy breaks down—and we break down not infrequently—our mechanics, poor guys with nothing but wits and wrenches, march right out onto the track and get their hands dirty!"

He was off to the races. No lawyer was going to rain on his parade—not today.

The company priced at a multiple of twelve times earnings before interest, taxes, depreciation, and amortization (EBITDA), more than twice the value of an industrial company. It was his victory. When the investment bankers told Max that the deal was "many times oversubscribed," that is, there were more offers to buy than stock to sell, he begged the leveraged buyout company to release its remaining shares. He was not a greedy man, just practical. "Twelve times EBITDA is a tidy profit for anybody." A modest man when it came to money, Max had no need for megayachts or exotic cars or plantation houses in the Caribbean. But after four years of hard work at the company, he felt he deserved to ring this bell. He had earned his payday. And management's stock options were tied to the fund's exit.

After the last presentation to potential investors in New York, we gathered in the conference room of our lead investment bank to discuss the final allocation of company shares. I looked at Max in his shirtsleeves, tie askew. He had sweat stains under his arms and his cuticles were chewed red raw. Stockbrokers in the field, bankers in the room, accountants in Bologna, and our lawyers in Washington were already on the conference call, debriefing the billionaire who controlled the private equity fund that owned us. Max tried one last time. "For years management has been working for peanuts . . ." he started out.

"The history of the world tells us," a Texas voice drawled from the speakerphone, "that it would look mighty funny if we sold everything . . ."

"No one is fleeing the company," Max said curtly.

". . . like we were abandoning a sinking ship."

"I think of it more as a question of delayed compensation."

"Pay is not the point." The man on the other end of the line controlled dozens of portfolio companies. He had his reputation to consider. And investors had long memories. "I just don't want anyone to think that we don't believe in the story."

Max mounted his final futile effort. "There are risks ahead. Maybe now is the time to sell." But the Texas billionaire bested him.

"We *are* the other great brand in motorcycling," he repeated from our roadshow presentation. The boss could hardly disagree with his own words. "The company is firing on all cylinders. The market is red hot. Six months from now the shares will be worth even more. Why leave money on the table?"

On the morning of the day we went public, we donned biker boots and leather jackets and rode our Beasts and superbikes downtown to the six massive Corinthian columns of Eleven Wall Street. We looked up and saw the pediment sculpture, called *Integrity Protecting the Works of Man*, that crowns the New York Stock Exchange. Inside, we toured the hivelike building, visiting the specific location on the trading floor where our stock would be listed, and met the specialist trader who would "make a market in our shares." We shook hands and took pictures with Exchange officials. Then we gathered on the wooden balcony that looks out over the great trading floor, the place where money meets the market, and passed out company baseball caps in anticipation of celebration. At 9:30 a.m. on the button, the bell rang and we revved our engines, filling the canyons of Wall Street with our trademark Cosmodromic roar.

And then the bombs began dropping on Kosovo. We waited for demand for the shares to materialize. We watched the electronic ticker and our specialist down on the floor. Our stock remained lifeless, stillborn at its listing price. Six months later the longest bull market in history ended its run and the bubble economy collapsed. Though we weren't a dot-com and actually made something, the world's attention shifted away from top-line growth stories (like ours) to more concrete things—like profits.

Seasons came and went. No one much cared when we hit record sales targets or won championships. Then, inexplicably, sales began to slow. First we blamed the weather. Summers were late, then long, then too hot to sell anything. We blamed the Japanese, who were exporting deflation around the world, slashing prices in a market that had become cutthroat. We blamed the euro, which had grown mightily against the dollar. And eventually, we blamed our head designer.

Embarrassed by our flop on Wall Street, the boss went looking for other scapegoats. "Damn the Yugoslovians," he railed. "Not only did they start a world war, but now they ruined my IPO!" When the stock kept sliding, he turned his wrath on our bankers. "I told them to sell," he whined to managers who were increasingly complaining about the evaporating value of their own options. "I said to them, 'Why wait? Sell now.' " And then to me: "Do you know the difference between being a really rich man and just being comfortable?" I knew where this was going. "Well, it's the difference between a twelve times EBITDA multiple and where we're trading at right now!"

Our stock price was still drifting.

I thought back to my arrival at the company. During those

first honeymoon weeks, I was invited to the houses of my colleagues as a guest of honor. Their parents, excited at the prospect of a young American executive at their table, would produce feasts of impressive proportions—giving credit to Bologna's nickname *la grassa*, "the fat." But before the first forkful of tagliatelle al ragù was eaten or glass of Sangiovese poured, they blurted out the question they were most hungry to have answered: What engineering school had I gone to? MIT or Caltech? RPI or Stanford? They had read the college guidebooks. They knew the rankings.

In Italy engineers merit an honorific before their surnames, *Ingegnere* (*Ing.*), just like *Dottore* (*Dott.*), *Professore* (*Prof.*), and *Avvocato* (*Avv.*). In Bologna, capital of Emilia-Romagna, home to Ferrari, Maserati, and Lamborghini, the engineer is more than just a professional. He is deity. When my hosts discovered that I was a corporate attorney by training and worked in the motorcycle industry mostly for adventure, their esteem fell away as *grana* cheese crumbles when you stick a small, tear-shaped knife, called *la coltellina*, into its core. *Their* son had a boss who was not even an engineer! "*Ma pensate*," they would say, astonished, "Imagine that!" Guglielmo Marconi, Bologna's most famous son, was an engineer. "Did *I* realize *that?*"

The murmuring and plotting against us, always present, became more open, more virulent. When new models didn't lead to growth, the boss became frustrated, piqued, and eventually kind of bored. There wasn't really much left to do but sell the stake in the company that wasn't already public. He talked to the Malaysians; when they didn't bite, he opened negotiations with the Chinese.

That summer the Italian newspapers were full of stories about a coming invasion—a tsunami of cheap Chinese shoes, cheap Chinese textiles swamping the market. All of Italy was up in arms, its industry under attack. It was a hot, tense July of recriminations between labor and the right-wing government in power in Rome. But not as hot and humid as the factory of our potential acquirer, whose plant was located in a southern Chinese city of thirty million people with a name that no one had ever heard of. "That's more than half the population of Italy," the boss reminded skeptics before departing. He wanted to stay positive.

When Max came back from China, he tried to get himself fired up about everything Asian. "They can make a front fork for half the price of ours," he said to procurement executives one day in the cafeteria over a lunch of spaghetti *alla norma*, which he ate quite dexterously with chopsticks. "Can you imagine that? And the market there is going to be huge one day—hundreds of thousands of big-bore bikes. I'm certain of it."

"Once they build roads," I drolled.

"More than that," he went on. "They know nothing about marketing. David, I think we can help them." I could see the old hunger in his eyes, the refusal to concede defeat on any front. "Imagine the story we could tell! Marco Polo rides to China— *again!*" I could see him trying to pump himself up, attempting to massage a massively bruised ego—desperate to get lost in the next chapter, the next great adventure.

PART THREE

The most important road in northern Italy is the Via Emilia, a Roman road that traces the history of these lands back to antiquity and crosses Bologna at its dead center, where two towers stand. Built two millennia ago by Marcus Emilius Lepidus, the artery runs northwest to southeast, linking seven provincial townships—Piacenza, Parma, Reggio-Emilia, Modena, Bologna, Forlì, and Rimini—and smaller towns like Imola and Faenza. Over the course of centuries, it has seen Roman armies on the march—away to battle in faraway outposts of empire. It has witnessed Crusaders—off to holy war in Constantinople and the promised land beyond. The road has been host to hordes, Huns and Nazis, invading, marauding, retreating in an ever changing tide of conqueror and conquered. Today, the lanes—asphalt over ancient stone on original dirt path—are diminished, hardly used by major traffic at all.

The Bolognese take a parallel highway, the A14, to the beach. They no longer see the pigs shipping out from farmhouses —fattened, doomed—riding the roads to a long curing process. Young people don't see the vans painted with gold letters that read *prodotti ipici*. When older Italians see such signs, their mouths water. "When was the last time *you* ate *cavallo?*" they reminisce. "You know horse is a specialty in these parts—not right here in Bologna, of course, but once, when I was in the hills outside of Modena, where they eat such things, I had the most delicious stew . . ."

On the autostrada one would not get caught in a windstorm of wheat chaff after the harvest, swirling like dervishes. Or stare at a mass of starlings moving like a silver thundercloud across the plain, creating shadow. At two hundred kilometers per hour there is no time to take a detour—to bump into a team of middle-aged cyclists in pink fluorescent Lycra, legs shaved and oiled, bodies tanned dark, dark—fast-pedaling alongside sunflowers that stretch into fields of forever. All of that is the other Italy, the older Italy, the Italy we think we know (and *perhaps do*); the Italy that Italians themselves have lived in for centuries, but not the place where a younger generation wants to pass its time. My giro skips the lost Guelf roads that encircle Imola in a maze of imperial design and the Byzantine mosaics of Ravenna that venerate saints and feed the senses. My friends take the highway to the coast in search of sand, sea, and hedonism—ignoring all else.

Oh, the pleasures of a seaside town in summer! The boardwalk stands that sell skewers of fresh-grilled calamari and shrimps served with piadine! The steaming heaps of linguini with tiny cherry tomatoes and baby clams! The myriad sights to take in at a mint-green cabana run by a wrinkled grandmother and her Adonis of a *bagnino*—all lean muscle and the smallest of Speedos. The ripeness of teenage girls with new breasts as brown as cups of coffee! The swagger of young boys racing trick scooters in little more than flip-flops! The graphic perfection of striped lounge chairs and coordinated umbrellas—waiting for sun worshippers who long to lie all day in the heat—motionless, like lions.

All smoky winter long, Italians talk about beaches: "Give me heat!" and "I need the sea!" The exodus to the riviera romagnola begins in trickles at Easter and finishes in waves. The season peaks in July, with tens of thousands of bolognesi at the shore, packed like sardines in oil. Though the sand is the same up and down the coast, from Marina di Ravenna to Cattolica near the border with Le Marche, there is a strict hierarchy. Marina attracts teenagers with its bars set amidst the dunes. Cattolica is family-oriented and mostly German. Lido di Classe and Lido di Dante have pine barrens and nude beaches. Rimini, the largest town, with its Grand Hotel made famous by Fellini, is considered high kitsch/trash. Just farther south, below the *colonie*—the Fascist summer camps built by Mussolini in the 1930s for disadvantaged children—is Riccione, the pearl of the Adriatic.

It takes about fifty minutes to get there from Bologna—racing in the left lane, flashing headlights to pass slower-moving traffic. At this pace, few landmarks of any kind are visible. Landscape is blood and white oleander atop a median that starts in Forlì or the occasional billboard for Mirabilandia, a theme park in Ravenna whose copycat cartoon characters smile so wide they threaten to crack their paint. Overhead, newly installed LCD signs blink intermittently—attempting to scare a country whose highway mortality rate rivals the Third World—into following rules. "Your car is a weapon. Don't use it to kill!" Italians think these travel tips are bad luck and floor the gas pedal on sight.

Autogrills slip by in neon orange. A bright Agip gasoline station stands out in chrome yellow. Stacks of ceramic factories near Faenza (they make tiles and toilet bowls) spew cottony smoke. At the exit for Rimini, I roll down the windows and let the salt air purify my soul. At the bottom of the pack of beach resorts, rarely mentioned in any guidebook, is Misano Adriatico. Here, just down the beach from Riccione, is the tiny house I rent each year with my friends Daniele, Nicoletta, and Willie, the pocket Tom Cruise.

Misano is down at the heels, working-class. It has no

Liberty-style villas from the turn of the last century. Or grand marine pine gardens. The place does not set style trends or entertain celebrities. What it has in abundance are locals: electricians, auto mechanics, carpenters, fishermen, retired factory workers—true *romagnoli*—and a smattering of Eastern Europeans who reside in the 1950s hotels that haven't yet been torn down.

The amenities are particular. Across the street from our house is a bakery called Pasticceria del Mare where women fry doughnuts filled with custard that Daniele swears taste like beach roses at five o'clock in the morning. Next door is a butcher who cuts bite-sized lamb chops, stuffing them with hot peppers and breadcrumbs. In walking distance is a pizzeria that pounds wild herbs to fill *crescioni* and a fishmonger who sells periwinkles. No one is sure if they are meant for eating or as bait. Misano has its own train station, a cafe, a discount shoe store, and a motorcycle dealership. Most of its inhabitants are elderly—or club kids. I come here for one reason: it's the only place on the beach my friends can afford.

The owner of our house, a former pilot, is named Villa. Everyone is named that in Romagna, so people know him by his nickname, Jock, short for Giacomo. On the first day of every season he welcomes us home with a guided tour of his "kills" at El Alamein. "Yes, *bambini*, don't worry, I'm still alive . . . I didn't survive the war to die an early death!" he says upon seeing us. "I eat well. I digest. I move my bowels twice a day." His voice is squeaky but strong. His healthy colon is a compliment to his wife's cooking and his own constitution—something to brag about when you're eighty-five.

Hanging on the walls of his living room are models of the British planes he shot down fifty years ago with his Fiat G50 Freccia, the story of each dogfight authenticated by a historian. Grim stuff, but Villa is merry. A tiny man with a white-waxed, Hitler-style mustache, he loves motorcycles and admires Americans, who, for some reason, he thinks are particularly hygienic.

Villa's house is two blocks away from Santamonica, the raceway where Carl Fogarty, then reigning Superbike champion, pulled a hat trick in 1999, and fifteen minutes from Predappio, the birthplace of Mussolini. Once a year, without fail, Villa visits each, to see the superbikes run and to pay his respects to his commander in chief, the great Duce of his youth. On summer mornings we wake up to engine music—riders shifting up and down their gearboxes, playing scales. At night we drift off to sleep with the smell of *benzina* in our nostrils. It is strangely peaceful—despite the din of dune buggies, dragsters, and superbikes—to sit on Villa's flat, fifties rooftop in the early evening, drinking homemade bellinis and eating figs stolen from his garden, while watching the sun set in the clouds of iridescent exhaust that rise above the autodrome.

On the other side of the house—facing east toward the periodic strife of the ex-Yugoslavia—is the sea. The Adriatic is a flat expanse of gray or green that, depending on conditions, is covered with the sheen of suntan lotion or brown algae, effluence of the organisms that swim in its waters from June to September. Between shore and paddock are the squat square houses in which we live. They are simple stucco affairs, pale pink or lemon yellow with wraparound terraces, sometimes decorated with cheap ceramic tiles. If any beauty is to be found among the painted cabanas that line the beachfront or the cake-colored houses or the boardwalks with their mosaic renditions of sea maidens and monsters, it is the freakish charm, the very audaciousness of a spit of sand that dares to call itself "Paradise" or "Olympus," when the attractions on offer are just tattered umbrellas and cement bocce ball courts.

There were few bellini moments that summer. Everything was fast and furious. Nicoletta had decided that it was time to find a proper boyfriend, a Bolognese of good breeding. "Not some greasy bricklayer or office monkey," she emphasized at our house meeting where it was determined which cleaning fluids to buy, how much time each person got in the shower, and who was responsible for washing out the garbage pail so it didn't stink. "And I don't need some *checcha disperata*—some silly queen— who only wants to borrow my clothes. It's been hard enough with Daniele all these years." She slipped jewel-encrusted sunglasses on her short, narrow nose and went to the closet to get the mop. "I want a *real* man."

"*Bella,*" Daniele yelled out from the bathroom. "Your clothes are not exactly fit for a princess. I can go to the flea market in Montagnola myself!"

Normally she would have responded with something salty like "Better flea markets than pubic lice!" or "Go delouse yourself." Last year, a certain person's habit of cruising the cabanas at midnight had led to an infestation that took three days, two loads of bleach-spiked laundry, and a whole bottle of Kwell to cure. This summer she had little time for his sparring. "I have my own things to worry about."

Her eyes lit up thinking about him: a guy in his mid-thirties with a solid family business, maybe a factory that made something nice like cashmere sweaters or crocodile shoes. She was getting ahead of herself—she knew it, couldn't help it—but already she was dreaming of a black BMW Five-series, a silver Porsche cabrio for weekends. If one actually engaged her fantasy nuptials further, everything came rushing out in torrents of pent-up desire: the winter skiing in Cortina, the occasional vacation to Mauritius, the shopping trips to Milan to view the fall collections, and more. She could forgive her future beau for not having a villa in Riccione *centro*—maybe that was excessive—but a small two-bedroom apartment in Porto Verde in one of the newer high-rises wasn't too much to ask for. "*Was* it?" The man would be tallish, darkish, but definitely *not* southern Italian. With light eyes, slightly bowed legs—a soccer player's build—long tousled hair, a thin gold chain—in a word, figo!

Then, finally, she would be free of Daniele, of the little bedroom they shared with the twin-sized bed and the shopping bags hanging as artwork on the walls, of the unrenovated fifties kitchen with its Kelvinator and smell of leaking gas. She would no longer have to commiserate about the state of Italian men—they were all mamma's boys or *finocchii*—with Carlotta, a single thirty-five-year-old hippie living downstairs. Carlotta smoked pot all day and got her kicks dressing up Davide, the beautiful boyfriend of their partner in the bar, trying on string bikinis and playing with each other's breasts. Both had the same-size A-cup. Carlotta's were natural; Davide's the result of rounds of anabolic steroids.

A bare fluorescent bulb cast light on reality—dust balls in the corners of the kitchen, chipped Formica countertops—illuminating the limitations of a home built for the working class, not a single woman looking to make a splash. It was Nicoletta's seventh year in the house. *Seven years.* She frowned in that particular Italian way: wrinkling her brow, pursing her lips, making her eyes pop for a second, then go blank. She ignored the gaze of little Willie. An American with sloppy bleached hair and artfully ripped Levis, Willie was looking at her, but most likely thinking about someone else—like the kind of girl he really desired—a minute, nut-brown pugliese with huge fake tits and a tight ass. He hadn't gotten laid in months either.

"Don't you meet *anyone* in that bar of yours?" Daniele shouted from the other room, intuiting her longing. "At your age you should be screwing like an sea urchin!" In Italy, *ricci*—sea urchins—apparently got a lot of action. She donned a pair of rubber gloves, squirted alcohol in a pail of water. "Not everyone in Bologna is gay either," he continued, not letting her off the hook, "just most of your friends."

"Daniel!" she screeched, losing her temper. "*You* fuck anything that moves. I know!" She dipped the mop in the liquid and swabbed at the linoleum, sandy from an early sirocco. "But I'm a girl—not a puttana!"

"Fucking is fucking," Daniele said, opening the refrigerator to get some Ferrarelle. He took a swig and passed her the bottle. "It's like drinking water—and you're as thirsty as the rest of us."

Could Nicoletta actually have sex?

"She'd rather suck a cigarette than a guy," Willie insisted.

"Gets drunk, not laid," Daniele winked.

I was more diplomatic: "She's not loose, that's for sure—or even easygoing." On most days she was cutting up salami sandwiches at the bar or cleaning late into the night. Or she was at home, where she lived with her divorced mother in a tiny apartment off the via Ferarrese, baking raviolilike pastries stuffed with pine nuts and mostarda to make extra pocket money. Any free time was spent on a treadmill burning calories or under a sunlamp getting tan. She had little privacy, no time for intimacy. The beach was her one escape valve—and there she had Daniele in her bed at night.

She lived for Friday, when, after emptying the espresso machine of its grinds, wiping down the countertops, and repacking the luncheon meat in clear plastic, she would cadge a ride off me—or one of her other friends—to rush to the beach before midnight to become a different person. It wasn't easy for a girl who dreamed big—who wanted to wear cocktail dresses by Dior—and not just the cologne. But she was still young. She had ambitions. That summer, for example, she was determined to make the step from promoter—she earned free club entrance and drink passes by bringing young Italians to the disco and introducing them to the scene—to hostess. These slinky creatures with shiny hair and sharp cheekbones performed the combined job of supermodel and maitre d'. Only they could seat you at a white-hot table where everything that was fashion happened.

Fashion.

The word was magic across the Riviera. It had little to do with the clothing industry—specific designers or franchised boutiques. It wasn't the Friday night *passeggiata* of yuppies who came to Riccione dressed in striped Etro shirts and Car Shoes. (That wasn't *figo.*) It wasn't hip-to-the-moment, screaming *ragazzini da urlo* who sported John Richmond denim with the words "Pure" or "Rich" printed on the ass. (That was trash, what Italians called *meraglio* in dialect.) Fashion was the moment—that mystical happening in time and space when the fiery cocktail of looks, style, plus a very dark tan came together and combusted. It was the *rayon vert* of summer, our own *Pauline at the Beach*—that much longed-for feeling of transcendence.

Flash! There was "la Perla," the once prominent surgeon turned transsexual, chatting with emerging punk rock designer Andrew MacKenzie at Victor's Pub on via Ceccarini! *Boom!* Here was Platinette, the Italian version of Divine, flirting with a motorcycle racer over mojitos on the public beach, Malindi, along with all of the other *fighetti!* Light as lemon mousse, fresh like the scent of basil, *fashion* created the frisson that made Riccione sparkle.

Before leaving for the beach on a Friday night, I would help Nicoletta and Carlotta close the bar. Carlotta's hair would be tied in a turban, accentuating the sea greenness of dramatic eyes whose brows had been electrolyzed then retattooed in a pencil-thin line. Nicoletta wore low-cut jeans and a shrunken top that made her ever-flattening belly protrude. Carlotta stacked chairs from the terrace, then covered them with a plastic tarpaulin. Nicoletta rang up the day's sales and entered the results in a black ledger. They were entrepreneurs now—no longer just workers—but the toll that work was taking on them could be seen in the hollow of cheeks, in the dark puffiness under eyes. No amount of rubbing with lemons could get the smell of canned tuna fish off their hands on some days. The bar was becoming them.

Now, in the little Misano kitchen, Nicoletta prepared to defend herself. She turned the radio to her favorite station, Radio Sabbia, pumped up the volume, and listened to the lush art noise of Suede.

> *She is strung out on a TV dream*
> *And she's the taste of gasoline*
> *And she's as similar as you can get*
> *To the shape of a cigarette*
>
> *And she's in fashion*
> *Ouh Ouh Ouh*
> *And she's in fashion*
> *Ouh Ouh Ouh*

She closed her eyes and let the pop music purring from the speakers caress her. I wondered: Could she really understand the lyrics? Did the words coalesce into meaning or remain fragments beyond her comprehension? She stopped wiping the cabinets for a moment—Italians have a dirt phobia and routinely disinfect surfaces with alcohol—tossed away her mop, and began pacing the linoleum floors with rhythm, hips thrust out at angles, rising and falling in sync with the synthesizer. She lit a cigarette. She moved around the room, shaking out her curly hair. She mangled the language, but the words came out of her mouth sensually enough.

"Call me a barmaid if you like," she said seductively, "but I have the tits of a trophy wife." And in one fluid move, losing all inhibition, she slipped out of her dress to reveal panties from the La Perla outlet and small apricot breasts squeezed into a push-up bra. Just across the alleyway, in the house next to ours, boys in their teens crawled out on the rooftop to watch. "Now," Nicoletta commanded, "who wants to dance with me?" I was reading a bike magazine in bed. "David! *You!*" I slipped on my flip-flops and came into the kitchen, wearing just boxers. She pulled me into her arms. I pressed tight against her bosom—keeping everything covered—and then, finding my own rhythm and no longer caring, began spinning her round. I twirled the barmaid until she was so dizzy, so loose that she fell down on the floor in a loud thud, laughing.

Nicoletta was a girl of some beauty—yellow cat's eyes, abundant ash blond hair (when not dyed shoe-polish black or eggplant purple). She had a nice smile and a golden tan. Oh, how she longed to be thinner! She talked about her extra five kilograms as if they were individual assassins, lying in wait to shoot down her hopes and dreams one by one: the hot date on a Saturday night, the high-season cruise to Mykonos, the flatter stomach with a diamond piercing measured in carats.

Were those extra kilograms real or figments of her weight-obsessed imagination? I'll try to be objective. Nicoletta had a graceful neck, small breasts with pretty, honey-colored nipples, and a long torso—almost vine-like in nature. Moving down her trunk, okay, I have to say it: she had thighs. There was no cellulite. The skin was not curdled. But there they were—curves of womanly flesh that located a potential admirer, not in San Juan or Rio de Janeiro or someplace Latin American as she would have liked, but right here, closer to home, in voluptuous Rome, or even Naples.

Nicoletta wasn't going to take that bullet lying down. Whenever I traveled to New York, she begged me to bring home industrial-sized containers of ephedrine—it had recently been banned in Italy—and lists of other promising herbs and potions. "You know I wouldn't ask you if it wasn't absolutely necessary." Any treatment with a whiff of viability was tried. She guzzled iced tea brewed with kava root and downed liters of aloe extract—all in an attempt to lose that last vestige of *ciccia* that testified to a life led fully. She was convinced that a bit of baby fat—the smear of butter on toast—was what separated her from club superstardom.

The Suede song trailed off. Dreams of *fashion* sputtered. She was feeling low again. Unconsciously, she started massaging her stomach, pulling the skin flat from the sides. "I am *so* bloated," she said, looking in the mirror. "Look at me! How I am going to go out tonight with this gut?" She slapped it hard, in anger, as if it were guilty of a crime. She went to the bureau and got the strap-on vibrating machine that she had recently purchased from a television ad. She taped the electrodes to her thighs, flipped on the control switch, and commenced jiggling.

"Well, if I drank double martinis all night, bella, smoked two packs a day, and ate only carrots, I'd feel bloated too," said Daniele, coming in from the bathroom. He had just finished posting the house rules, mandates like: "Clean the toilet bowl once a weekend or whenever it's dirty!" and "Americans: wash the floors with a wet mop first, then a second time with detergent!" and could now give us his full attention. He had known Nicoletta since kindergarten and slept with her in the same bed at the beach house for years. He was happy to confirm what most of us knew to be the truth. She hadn't been laid in months, maybe years, maybe ever.

"Daniele, is it time for my period?" she asked. "When was the last time I had it?"

"We haven't had that in at least a week, dear," he said, wrapping a green pareo around his waist and slipping into a pair of Nicoletta's sandals, the new Gucci ones with the house pattern.

"Maybe it's just the sea air," she said closing a window. "I'm just not used to it so early in the season." Then she saw him. "Daniel, no!"

"What?" he grinned. "I'm just going out for a little passeggiata. I have some errands to run . . ."

"Get your feet out of my shoes," she yelled, throwing a sponge at him. "Dai . . . your fat toes will ruin them and I paid two hundred euro—and that was on sale!"

"Bella!" he mocked. "My toes are much slimmer than yours," and he unfolded his long legs on the lounge chair—they were mostly hairless but not waxed—and let one sandal dangle off his foot in an artful act of seduction. "Capisci?"

Daniele was not feminine per se. He belched and farted like a footballer despite a strict summer diet of only white things: steamed fish, potato chips, mascarpone, and ice cream. But put a pair of heels in front of him—anything by Sergio Rossi or Gucci—and he was rushing for the lipstick and eyeliner. He carried around a Dopp kit containing foundation, a blemish correction stick, and plum lip gloss just for such occasions. At the drop of a hat (the arrival of lovely Davide from downstairs, for exam-

ple) and armed with the right props, he could become an umbrella girl at a Superbike race or a starlet in a slip dress and
panties—without any fear of looking truly hideous. If he didn't
have a date on a Saturday night, there was always the blond wig
in the box, beckoning. In Bologna, it was the easiest way to get
laid.

Daniele was an occasional drag queen. He didn't create or
plan elaborate outfits like a Leigh Bowery. He didn't perform an
"act" like the great Divine. His art was improvised *arte povera*,
done right there on the spot with whatever materials he had on
hand. A big flowery towel made for a perfect headdress. *Ecco!* A
soft tangerine dishrag became bikini underwear. *Pronto!* A plastic shower curtain with daisy decals transformed itself into a caf-
tan. *Ciao!* In full drag, Daniele made for a handsome woman,
older than his years, yes, but still desirable.

Now he slipped Nicoletta's nylon seventies dress over his
shoulders, *"Fica!"* clicked on his cell phone—it played an Abba
download—and shimmied toward her singing, "Dance with me. I
want to be a partner can't you see . . ."

"Dai, Daniele . . . not now, I have to get ready."

"If I went out to Michelino like this," he said, referring to
the Isotaki Tange–designed fairgrounds that doubled as cruising
grounds for wife swapping and other forms of lurid *battuage* in
Bologna, "I could lay just about anyone. Ciao!"

"If Giacomo saw you now, he'd kill," she answered. "And I'd
worry about *him* right now," pointing to the headshot of the
boyfriend above the vanity, "because he is going to be here any
minute."

"He can go take a shit for himself! *Passiva!*" Daniele was
rummaging through closets, looking for a floppy hat to finish off
his outfit. Changing the subject, he called out to Willie in a wee
voice, *"Vieni, vieni, vieni,* come here, I want you to see this blond
girl that I met on vacation in Torre del Lago."

Last week, while Giacomo had been taking an engineering

exam (he worked at an ice cream parlor part time and studied the rest of the time), Daniele and his cousin Gianluca had lit out together, secretly "in camper," for an extended sex spree. A dedicated libertine, "la Jelly" (short for *gelataio*) was Daniele's new role model: he never worked in the season, drove a Six-series BMW convertible, and had franchised his ice cream parlors all the way from Sasso Marconi to Sharm al-Sheikh. His claim to fame was a nontraditional approach to flavors. Instead of the classics (*crema, cioccolato*) he had invented new tastes like "Triple Ecstasy," a rich sludge of chocolate chunks, caramel, and peanut butter in a messy marshmallow swirl—held together with a healthy dose of vegetable fats and fillers. Ice cream like this paid for a cook, a masseur, a team of plastic surgeons, and a special wig made by Cesare Ragazzi Company—Jelly was Ping-Pong bald and CRC specialized in undetectable toupees—and the free time to trawl for sex at numerous truckstops and pine barrens across Italy, from Lido di Dante near Ravenna to Taormina.

On their latest romp, Daniele had brought along a third-generation Sony-Ericson cell phone that doubled as a video camera. Now he pulled up a series of ten-second clips to show Willie. "Here is the girl. I found her!" A deeply tanned, pixilated blonde was sashaying and mouthing sweet nothings to the camera. Willie looked at her curiously, cocking his head.

"I guess I'd meet her," he said. "Are the tits real?"

"No, I don't think so."

"Definitely then. Call her!"

Daniele wouldn't look at me. I had spotted the plum lips and foundation straight away. The blond wig was the same one he had in the closet. "Her name is *Lola*," he whispered, broad smile breaking across his face, "*Fav-o-losa!*" The hot song that summer was a Spanish novelty called "Lola," a pop tune about a girl from Barcelona who sang about her dreams: walking the docks of old Barceloneta, night and day, looking to get fucked.

Nicoletta had seen this act too many times before. "As I was saying, ragazzi, I'm determined to lose five kilos. I know that if my stomach were flat, ciao! *I* could have any figo on the beach from here to Porto Verde."

"Lose too much weight and your tits will disappear," Daniele warned. And he darted into the kitchen to grab two cantaloupes to stuff a halter. He came back juggling to Café del Mar. Occasionally a wrinkled penis—Daniele's—peeked out of the folds of his pareo. We screamed when we saw it.

"Put that gherkin away," Willie begged. "I've seen bigger pickles on a drag queen."

"*Brutta vacca,* how dare you criticize the one body part science has found no way of enlarging? I have to live with it."

"Daniel," Nicoletta said seriously, "getting back to my boobs." His gave off a faint smell of decay, of earth and excrement. "You know how sensitive I am . . ."

"You're sensitive about *everything.*"

She flashed a dazzling sweet/sad smile, betraying her lack of anything resembling guile, and pulled on a T-shirt. "Just leave my tits alone," she said giving him a kiss on the forehead. "It's these things I have to worry about," indicating her hips, making her way toward the bathroom to find the Dior anticellulite cream. She reappeared with a brown bikini hanging from her fingertips. "Now ragazzi, how am I going to get into this tomorrow? *That's* a good question!" She crossed her eyes, then focused on me. "There are a lot of kilometers to run, David! We need to set up a program. I'm going to start skipping lunch and run around the Giardini Margherita instead."

"Nico, you're beautiful just the way you are." I always said innocuous things like that.

She waited a beat and then announced: "Actually, I have a date."

Daniele looked at her in shock. "Tonight?" She nodded. He squeezed the cantaloupes so hard that they started dripping juice.

"Well, at least it's a meeting, an appointment . . ."

"Is it someone new or someone who knew you *before* the operation?" Daniele asked.

"Cazzo! Give me those melons, before you ruin everything!"

"When you get new tits, promise me yours won't leak," Daniele said. "I want to be able to play with them."

"That's it!" she shrieked, "I am finished with you." And she stomped downstairs to consult with Carlotta.

44

Nicoletta's last name is Nasini, which, in Italian, means "little noses." Her patronymic is a perfect irony, since she used to have the most beautiful *large* nose, before she had it shortened, narrowed, and turned up at the tip by paying a plastic surgeon approximately one fifth of her annual wages one Christmas. Though she had been saving up for months, we all begged her not to do it. The old nose belonged to an Etruscan queen. It should have been carved on a coin of the realm or printed on a national stamp. I tried to convince her that what she had on her hands was a work of art. "Don't change it. Think of Paloma Picasso," I said. "Big and beautiful—like an inspired character in an Almodóvar film!"

"*Was*, David, *was*. That nose is past tense come January."

And just as she threatened, right after the winter vacation, when I came back from visiting my family in Miami Beach, it was gone. The new nose is pretty innocuous if you ask me, exactly what Nicoletta had hoped for, tired as she was of the nobility of a body part, which while admired by friends, did *not* translate into getting laid on the weekends. Her rationale that the old nose was completely out of proportion with her lifestyle, which consisted mostly of not eating and going to discotheques, had some merit. Still, I missed it. Once, I suggested—rather boldly—that she should have saved it. "I think you'd have gotten used to it as you got older."

"Don't talk like it was Venice, David," she snapped. "It never belonged on my face in the first place."

The new organ was truly a little one (*un nasetto*), though not to the complete satisfaction of Nicoletta. She still saw a bump high on the bridge. Though no one knew what she was talking about, she was convinced of the relocation of some cartilaginous tissue from the old nose northward. "It migrated." Months after the original operation, she was frequently seen reshaping her nose with her fingers, adjusting angles and slopes, crafting the more perfect instrument, the dream nose she really wanted. All summer long she made threats: "That *stronzo* (shit) of a surgeon is going to redo that bump. I'll sue the fucking prick!" And six months later, in winter, he did just that.

Nicoletta's wasn't the only characterful nose I knew to be sacrificed on the altar of contemporary taste. Noses like hers were disappearing up and down the peninsula. The grooved, down-curving proboscis of the weary nurse assisting Judith in Caravaggio's *Judith Beheading Holofernes* is rarely seen in teenage circles. Giuliano de' Medici's sloping instrument with its exquisitely elongated nostrils, captured in Botticelli's portrait, is a rare occurrence today. The proliferation of hooked and honking, red-mottled and bulbous protuberances that populate Michelangelo's *The Martyrdom of St. Peter* are falling victim to the surgeon's scalpel at a frenzied rate, superfluous body parts to be cut away like cancer. A big nose is no longer the beacon of a great culture, a glorious people—the physical representation of God's aesthetic work on earth. Thank Christ for babies and old people—bearers of what was once national treasure!

45

"So who is this new guy?" Daniele asked (this time more gently) when she came up from Carlotta's. "Is it a first date or has he already met 'the Nose'? What will he think about your list of restoration projects? Ears, lips, thighs—does he know that he is dating a work in progress?"

"He knows nothing. And I'm not having anything else done either. I have no money. I have to pay the mortgage on the bar." Daniele looked at her knowingly, raising an unplucked eyebrow.

"Really?"

"Well, maybe I'd just freshen up my lips . . ." she admitted, blushing. (Carlotta had been trying to talk her into a winter surgery trip to Brazil.) She cocked her head to the side, pouted her lips in what must have been her version of a desirous pose, and kissed the air: "Ciao!" Then she licked them. They were a bit thin, but then again, most natural Italian lips were starting to look that way since so many women (and a growing number of men) had taken Donatella Versace as their role model, plumping up their pouts with collagen and/or butt fat that had been extracted, distilled, then whipped in a blender and reinjected.

"When I was in Rome, it felt like another planet," Daniele said, rubbing Lip Zoom all over his mouth. "Besides all of the freaky normal things, like the muscle-bound bodybuilders with plucked eyebrows and waxed assholes—I'm talking about straight guys here, not the fags in the Gay Village—everyone was licking their lips all day long and pouting."

"It must have been distracting," I said, giving him his props. "What were they doing?"

"Bella, they had been watching the last runway shows in Milan." He pushed out his own suspiciously plumped-up pair and minced: "*Hmm!*"

"Ragazzi, the world is just upside down today," Nicoletta said. "You're the American, David. You explain it to me. How can a real man want lips like Monica Bellucci?" But I had been to Rome only a few times, mostly to visit our conservative lawyers in the Piazza di Spagna. I only knew secondhand that Roman truck drivers were auditioning for soap operas at Cinecittà and that *coatti*—slang for grease monkeys—dreamed of nothing else but modeling underwear in Milan. Now, looking more closely at Daniele's own pair, Nicoletta started questioning: "Those are not *naturel!*" she claimed, inspecting the tissue. "What have you been doing behind my back?" He just smiled cryptically. "You realize that your mother is going to kill you when she sees you, the poor woman." The discussion was interrupted by a phone call. Giacomo was coming over in five minutes.

Daniele moved like a fury. He rushed down the marble stairs to slip into Villa's garden and cut branches off his rosemary shrub to create atmosphere. He lit tea candles on the terraces and set out incense in burners. The efforts were purely selfish in nature: he was hoping to coax a blowjob out of the ice cream man before he returned to work the late shift. The doorbell rang earlier than expected. Daniele stashed the shower curtain in the oven and, to Nicoletta's horror, dropped the sandals in the garbage. He popped some herbal Viagra—"bella figura!"—slid into a pair of Levis, laced up a pair of sneakers, and opened the door like a real man, cold beer in his hand. "*Ciao amore,*" he said calmly, as if it was the most ordinary summer evening.

The gelataio had the body of a true *romangolo*, a squat, muscular frame, with huge hands that had grown rough and strong from years of mixing flavors. He said Daniele was his first boyfriend—and his last. He expected that they would be together forever. "Ciao, Dani," he said using a nickname, "I brought your favorite, risotto." He gave Daniele an awkward hug, still unsure how to demonstrate affection.

"Grazie . . ." Daniele kissed him on both cheeks, escorting him to the bedroom where he flopped into bed, exhausted. Daniele then excused himself, retiring to the bedroom as well. "Ragazzi," he said to us before closing the door, "it's time to eat."

It was the first Friday night of the season and Nicoletta needed to get ready. But first she wanted to squeeze in a workout. I met her in the cement garden under our house with its collection of stone statues: frogs, dolphins, and a Padre Pio statue. She wore pink terry-cloth short shorts, a sports bra, and, now that she no longer had any fear of showing off her profile, her hair pulled back in a ponytail. With the smell of pine and salt in the air, we ran down the via della Repubblica toward the water, past the *piadina* stands, then on to Porto Verde and the condominiums built around a marina in the 1960s. We did a few laps and then jogged toward the go-cart track where adolescent boys of all ages spent hours crashing into each other in orgies of recklessness. Forty minutes later, we were following the Adriatic highway back to the house, passing the grim "Sexy Shops" that lined the highway with their imported dildoes and pirated XXX videocassettes.

We came back drenched in sweat. Nicoletta stripped down, put on a white cotton housecoat, and drew a bath. Her bathing habits—like her tanning rituals—were orchestral in their complexity. She would simmer in scalding water for hours, preparing her skin to receive all manner of unguents: creams, moisturizers, highlighting shadows, sparkles, and glitter. She positioned tapers around the tub, lit a stick of incense, and poured tiramisu-scented bubble bath in the water. She soaked. And soaked. No one was allowed to talk to her during this period. She sliced cucumbers for her eyes and did a mud mask enriched with Dead Sea salts. After half an hour, she rinsed down, dried off in another fluffy robe, blew out her kinky hair, and misted her body with Chris 1947 cologne.

During all this time she never once talked on the phone—or spoke with any of us. She just moved around the house in a kind of trance, preparing for an imaginary lover. Finally, she came into the kitchen. She handed me a blue bottle of Nivea—it was understood that I was to rub cream into her shoulders and lower back while she massaged her breasts with breast moisturizer, to give them "bounce." I warmed the cream in my hands and then began touching her body, which was covered with the tiny hairs of girls who don't eat food. It was my most intimate contact with a woman since college. I massaged her back with all of the care and intensity I could manage, hoping to transmit through her skin some spark of real warmth, some human connection. When she came out of her pre-Friday-night coma, she began asking me questions: Was her skirt too tight?

"No."

"Tits too small?"

"Nico, *never!*"

"Oh David! I love talking to you! You always understand." Her last questions: "Legs too chunky?" I preferred to dodge this one. And then, most importantly, because for this she could make adjustments: Was her tan dark enough?

The Bolognese summer *giro* is about rules, inevitabilities, and certain impossibilities. For instance, if you go to the beach, which all Italians do, you must be tan. Or you want to get tan, because the destiny of bolognesi from May to September is the color of bronze. Flaunting a modern fear of the sun is an act of social suicide that no Italian can understand, and what they typically call, derisively, an *americanata* (a stupid thing). When I go to the beach wearing my floppy hat and long-sleeved T-shirt and rub cancer-guard SPF 64 on my face, Italian friends inquire suspiciously about my health. "Do you have food poisoning?" or "Are you sick with the *colpo d'aria*—a draft?"

The other night at Matis, a stadium-sized discotheque near the factory, right before we came to the beach, a draft attacked Nicoletta. At around four in the morning after a long evening of Negroni cocktails and cigarettes, Nicoletta was dancing with us—very confidently—near the bar. She looked great in a Miss Sixty wrap dress with glitter all over her breasts. Her stomach was lovely—tight and moisturized that night—peeking out occasionally to show off tight ridges and gold reflective dust. Suddenly, a draft from the air conditioner (despised creatures throughout the peninsula) found her exposed navel ring and entered. Moments later, her stomach *froze up*—or so everyone said. She couldn't move, couldn't speak, and turned olive green before slumping to the floor. We were forced to stop dancing in the midst of Kylie Minogue's "Can't Get You Out of My Head" to carry her out to the car. No one thought of accusing her of taking bad ecstasy. Classic colpo d'aria.

Drafts are real medical conditions here, perhaps due to the evocative but dangerous fogs and cold mists that wrap the Pianura Padana like an infectious blanket of disease from September till spring. Even in summer the fear lingers: a fresh, rogue wind from the sea that enters the neck during a nap in the shade can land you in bed for days. This is why it can never be hot enough for Italians. When I am at the beach, someone with skin the shade of boiled liver inevitably comes up to me and suggests,

"Maybe you should go home and get some rest," as if my pale form spooks the enjoyment of sunbathing the way a teetotaler ruins the taste of wine.

Sun worship is for connoisseurs and requires the layering of lotions. Lost is the grail of Bolognese singularity—the pure pumpkin of the *tortelloni alla zucca*, the simple porkiness of good prosciutto. Nicoletta slathered haute cuisine on her skin—anti-wrinkle cream for the eyes, sunblock for the nose, and a thick gravy of cocoa butter and baby oil for everywhere else. She smelled of exotic fruits and spices and was also known, on occasion, to attract beach flies. For most of the year her skin was the color of toast, and she was rightly proud of her navel, which had no color at all because it reflected no light—like a deep, black hole in space. But it was early in the season and her tan was not all that it could be. When she asked me, before getting dressed, I could not tell her what she wanted to hear—that she was as dark as a brick and could wear white. So, on that first Friday of the season, she chose something with some color in it: low-rise orange jeans, high-heeled yellow snakeskin boots, and a fluorescent pink top. I thought she looked like a Popsicle.

Daniele was still in the bedroom with the Good Humor man. Willie had gone out to Porto Verde to meet a new girl for an *aperitivo*. It was a rare moment of quiet in the house. Nicoletta and I walked outside to the terrace to have a glass of wine. We stretched out on plastic beach chairs and gazed out over the countryside. "Close your eyes just for a minute," she said, looking at the sky and sipping *trebbiano*. "Wait a second. Open them . . . just, now . . . What do you see?" The carnal sun was about to slip down behind the house and plunge the Riviera into darkness. Everything was bathed in cotton candy pinks fading into soft purples. A warm wind redolent of farmland and orchards, of ripe fruit and earth, of the old agrarian Italy, rolled down the hills to caress the coast. Nicoletta's faced glowed with chiffon color. It was that moment at the beach when masks fell and faces repositioned themselves: when male melted into female, boy became girl, and, if disbelief were suspended, age regained an aspect of its youth.

I said: "Anything could happen in this Italy without monuments, without rules."

"It is going to be a beautiful night at the club," Nicoletta whispered to me. "I can just *feel* it." We looked up the beach toward Gabbice Monte, a rough granite promontory overlooking the sea. The terra-cotta roofs of our neighbors' houses turned coppery. The skies colored cobalt. Neon signs of nearby hotels—the Atlantic, the Ambrosia, and the Majorca—flickered green or midnight blue, lurid enough to catch a carny. From miles around, Italians were on the move—plucking eyebrows, shaving chests, waxing legs, combing hair gel into long bangs—getting ready to come to the sea not for its natural landscape, but for the nature of its transgression. The siren call of Misano, like all Adriatic beach communities, was a discotheque. Across the street, Italian grandmothers were frying fish, making a clam sauce for pasta, feeding their families or just each other, barely dressed in housedresses and slippers. Out to air, like pigeons on a sill, were all manner of shoes—sandals, sneakers, flip-flops, high heels, and brogues on terraces and rooftops, leaving their scent and soul to the warm night air.

46

The club was called L'Echoes—pronounced "LEK-os"—but commonly known as "Liz" after the drag queen/impresario Maurizio Monti, aka "La Liz," who ran it. Liz, when he wasn't in Liz mode, was as bald as a baby and proud of it—much like Sofia Loren, who, when she isn't working, often walks around Miami Beach without any wig and no makeup. *Sofia Loren*—the big sunglasses, the heavy cleavage, and the fluffy hair—is the movie star. When not doing appearances, Naples's most famous septuagenarian is happy being the older woman—wrinkled and worn—that she really is.

Liz was the same. Every day I saw him at a run-down gymnasium in the center of town called Excellence, where he exercised with a macho, five-foot-two personal trainer named Salvatore whose tweezed eyebrows, red-dyed hair, and inflatable muscles made me blink. He was more made up than Liz! The pair would spend hours in pretzel-like positions, stretching, preparing for a workout with weights that lasted less than ten minutes. Liz wanted tone, not muscles. With Salvatore, Liz acted more or less the man—if floppy shorts, a ratty tank top, and an old bandana signified masculinity. The only sign of his profession was his hairlessness. He rigorously waxed his body head to toe. He thought a working performer should be a clean canvas for his art.

Tonight at the club, Liz was in full dress mode. With klieg lights trailing her every move, she arrived in the garden, dazzling, in a Pucci print slip dress and go-go boots. A blond fall cascaded down her shoulders. In a great huff, she swirled over to our table, blowing kisses, patting down her sweaty forehead with a cotton pad. "Liz! Liz!" the crowd hollered. She made sure that her girly hairiness flew all over the place in answer.

"Ciao, ciao! Welcome to Liz! My flight is leaving in just a few minutes," she kept repeating, waving to the crowd. "Mykonos or Ibiza, I can't remember!" Everything was silver, pink, and white. The theme was Liz Airport. There were passports for menus, drink tickets that looked like boarding passes, luggage hanging from trees. She dedicated one dizzy minute to us, stage-whispering to Nicoletta, "The new nose looks great!" and reaching out and actually stroking it with a rose-lacquered nail—like a socialite petting a dog. Then she disappeared.

Nicoletta was radiant. Her yellow eyes flashed like fireflies. The nose had been noticed. It had been noticed! *"Non ci credo, non ci credo!"* she crowed ecstatically, babbling about how everything tonight was going to be "pure fashion!"

"At least you won't have to redo it again," Daniele muttered under his breath, but Nicoletta had heard nothing. She was lost for the evening.

The club was designed like a multilevel, outdoor, 1970s living room. Walls of speakers separated the dance floor from the bar. Boughs of marine pines created a canopy of darkness. Hanging from the branches were big glass balls that lit up the sky. Set out on long white banquets next to the pool and its statuary were roast legs of veal, whole carved turkeys, shrimps in Russian mayonnaise sauce, and platters of mushrooms, grana cheese, and celery sprinkled with balsamic vinegar. There were wedges of melon, slices of pineapple wrapped in *Speck*, and little pots of chocolate crème caramel and panna cotta for dessert.

No one ate a thing.

It was the first time in weeks I had seen Nicoletta relaxed at dinnertime. "I *am* starving," she said as soon as we sat down at our reserved table near the pool, "really ravenous!" She proceeded to dissect two thin strips of prosciutto—cutting away the fat from the meat, skipping the accompanying melon because it was one of those fruits that tended to bloat her. Instead she speared some pineapple off my plate—Italians believe the fruit burns fat and aids digestion—and proclaimed herself quite full and satisfied after five minutes of chewing. "Open the wine, David. I am dying of thirst."

"Was the prosciutto a little salty?" I asked.

"A sponge has no taste buds," Willie answered. "Give the girl some booze."

"At least eat some veal," Carlotta suggested delicately, though her own dinner plate carried little more than two shrimps and a few cherry tomatoes. "Meat puts color on your cheeks."

"Carlotta, if I eat any more, I swear, I will have to go home and take a cold shower to reduce this *buzza* [gut]. I'm bursting out of my dress."

"Maybe you're pregnant?" Willie suggested, crudely.

"Immaculate conception!" Daniele couldn't resist.

"Stop badgering her," Carlotta snapped. "I'm keeping an eye on her at the bar. Lately she has been eating."

I uncorked a pinot grigio and poured for the table. Nicoletta's guests, club kids from the provinces, Pesaro, Cattolica, Forlì, were busy chatting about the usual things: diets, sunlamps, which deejays were playing at the various clubs—Cocorico, Peter Pan, and Byblos—and though it was only the first weekend of the season, where they were planning on going for *ferragosto*, that dead week in August when all of Italy shut down. After the requisite ten minutes of dinner chat and poking at the food—maintaining bella figura—most of the table drifted toward the bathrooms. There, after a few lines of blow, clubbers leaned against the trees and commented on the fashion parade.

"She looks just like a toilet bowl!"

"He has the face of a bidet."

"Drunk as a goose!"

"Out there like a balcony!"

It was a summer of white at the beach—most summers were. White cotton sport jackets for guys with studded T-shirts underneath. White miniskirts for girls and jeweled halter tops. Western had its adherents: there were snakeskin boots (reptile was always popular) and suede cowboy hats with colored feathers. From twenty feet away, it was like walking onto the set of a Jennifer Lopez video. Close-up you realized these were the same tattooed and tanned factory workers, secretaries, gym trainers, part-time catalog models, and shop clerks that you saw every day in Bologna, just dressed to the nines.

After the dinner plates were cleared, Liz Airport went into work mode. Club royalty who, just a few moments ago, had reigned over tables ordaining what was cool and what was, as they disparaged, "yesterday," now became hired help. They were the bartenders, bouncers, *cubisti* (go-go dancers), and coat-check girls who had been hired by Liz to serve the masses of ragazzini, many from Naples, who came to Riccione to lose themselves in the night.

In the hierarchy of *terroni*, the pejorative term for southern Italians, Neapolitans rank near the bottom of the list. Sicilians, with their multilayered culture and gorgeous island, are considered sexy, passionate. Sardinians are a charming lot, rough and provincial. *Calabresi* run hot and cold and have a capacity for violence. Neapolitans are just vulgar. And now these feral children were invading the club in packs. The boys prowled the dance floor, arm in arm, sometimes shirtless, wearing droopy boxer shorts, often without underwear. The girls were dressed almost not at all—just tube tops and teased hair—tottering on impossibly high heels, guarded by insanely jealous boyfriends.

Though officially frowned on, these "almost Africans" were secretly admired by the Bolognese. Their light eyes against dark skin, their finely tooled bodies, and most of all their electric openness were exotic, liberating at the beach. Neapolitans had no problem inviting you, boy or girl it didn't matter, to dance, to drink, or to fuck you hard in the woods behind the club. They screamed at the top of their lungs. They gesticulated wildly. They held nothing back. The boys stank of sweat and Versace Jeans cologne. The girls reeked of baby powder.

The night's energy was rising. Daniele got up from the dinner table. It was time to make the rounds. We went upstairs to see Monia, who was bartending at the suspended lounge that overlooked the smaller dance floor. A girl bartender with perfect fake tits, "Money" was known up and down the beach for "standup" nipples that looked like baby pacifiers. She did no other work but this all year long, mixing drinks—one shot for her, one for the customer's cocktail—scrupulously saving her tips, so that in winter she could do nothing more than sit on the cold beach in Riccione and contemplate the color of sky and water. She had ten tiny silver earrings and her eyes were the most unusual hue, the blue of a stormy sea. Federico, her sweetheart of a boyfriend—a shop clerk on via Ceccarini—was drinking a Negroni. Like so many good men before him, Money's assets had cast a spell on him. Mesmerized, he was now fondling them to the insistent rhythms of drum and bass—deep in stoned delirium.

Money mixed us some Negronis and together we watched the crowd build. It was that electric moment of uncertainty before a night took off. The trip could be "raging" or just slow and boring—beats banging on, repetitions of a synthesized snare drum. It depended on factors outside our control. We were in the hands of deejays and drug dealers now. Everyone hoped for a special night—when the deejay took control of the floor, transporting clubbers to exotic aural places, leafy jungles, hot deserts, and deep canyons of shimmering sound. When the music was rocking, when the beats were real enough, the deejay could suspend time. He'd take you to a deep place where sound, an ocean of ambient noise, felt like pure emotion. He could stop the dance floor dead in its tracks and reveal something that could not be seen or heard, just *felt*. And then, like all club things beautiful and transient, the rhythm would shift . . . The mood would suddenly change and a different vibe would appear, fragments of jazz, a piece of dance hall, more deep house, and the crowd would lurch on—swaying, searching for the next perfect beat, an even deeper groove.

Daniele and I kept moving through the crowd, sifting faces, clocking bodies. This was *fashion* too—moving effortlessly through the sea of clubbers, ignoring the many, greeting an occasional friend, calibrating just how much energy to offer up to the floor—head nod, half a smile, casual embrace. Once in a while we threw out a double kiss. I followed Daniele's lead, occasionally throwing my head back—smiling wide, showing teeth—showing that we were figo too. I was young (younger in Italy than I had ever been in America) and beautiful (sometimes I felt it too). We were here not *just* to drink vodka lemons or Negronis all night. We did not come *just* to dance to Frankie Knuckles (the father of house music) or Ricky Montari (inventor of the local Riviera sound). We walked to the glassed-in dance floor—covering ground, always in motion, in *giro*, creating the fine illusion that we had appointments to make, people to meet.

In the midst of a pack of soccer players, I lost Daniele. Did he dive into an overstuffed couch with a young striker? He did have a weakness for tousled hair on a bowlegged guy. Or maybe he went to get another long drink at the bar with one of his many girlfriends: Stefania, who belched and farted louder than he did, or Anna the Russian, whom he slept with on occasion and who wore fur hats even in summer. Had he run into Carlotta's constant companion, Benedetta, a hawklike lesbian whose halter tops were so loose that every time she moved an arm or a leg, one of her thin tits popped out?

I spied Nicoletta on the other side of the room. She was corralling a group of twenty-year-olds—the kind that collect Nike "Silvers"—across the dance floor. I waded into the sea of bodies, bumping into glitter boys high on ecstasy and their bubbly girlfriends in sequins. The noise was so loud, I could only see her lips move, "Let's go to the *privée*. I want you to meet someone."

"Who?" I shouted over the pounding music and shouts of ragazzini. Nicoletta looked back at me and only smiled.

Matteo.

The *privée* was set up like the business-class lounge, gated off with plastic chains, potted plants. Only high fliers could get in, no economy passengers. Seated at a table in the corner of the room, surrounded by attendants, was Nicoletta's date. For a second it looked like he was wearing nothing but a tennis tan. His form-fitting T-shirt was in a material so gauzy that his nipples were completely defined. Around his waist was a Louis Vuitton belt. "He's from the provinces," Nicoletta reminded me, "everything has to have a logo." To Nicoletta, he was perfection—a cup of creamy mascarpone.

"Matteo," she cooed in a tone of voice that I had not heard before—no scratchiness, no reedy birdlike whine, "*ciaoouuu,*" stretching the greeting into a warm and sexy caress. Matteo smiled a big, lazy grin. He made the gesture to get up from his seat and greet us (but didn't) and then, in a gravelly voice, thick with smoke and liquor, said *"Benvenuti,"* the growl of a sleepy lion. The slurred accent, from deep in the wilds of Le Marche, was almost Roman in its overextended vowels. The kid was maybe twenty-five years old.

"Let me introduce you to my housemate, David," Nicoletta offered. "He's from New York City." Matteo shook my hand like a rapper, in three different positions.

"NYC . . . *Dude!*"

"David works at the factory," Nicoletta said.

"*Vroom-vroom.* Let's hang out sometime," he said in broken English. "I'll teach you some Pesaro Italian. You'll speak like a fisherman."

Nicoletta was smiling. "His parents have a boat down in Le Marche," she explained. "I'm going out with them on Sunday."

"Do they fish," I asked, "your parents?" I had learned how to speak broken English too.

"Actually we own a meat-packaging business," reverting to Italian. "I only fish so that I don't have to eat sausage everyday."

"Let's not talk about food until Monday, ragazzini," Nicoletta said. "I ate so much tonight I feel like a stuffed capon." She began rubbing her stomach. "Madonna, che pancia!" She was already getting restless. "Let's go, M. But first, dear, could you get us another round of drinks?"

"Where did you find him?" I asked her while he went to the bar with the free-drink tickets that she had pressed into his hand.

"Did you see those gray eyes? Like two headlights!"

"He's a cute little *torello*, a stud. That's for sure."

"I have goose bumps I am so excited . . . Can you see that I am sweating?"

I asked her again where they had met—a question Italians never liked to answer. Their circles were as impenetrable as the Vatican. Her answer was so predictable that I felt like a fool for asking: *"In giro."* Around. She smiled nervously and ran off to follow him. He was her find, her treasure, her personal piece of figo and she was not going to let him get away.

Matteo came back with a tray of vodka lemons. Nicoletta was immediately on his arm. "Let's go out to the garden and look at the pool. I think people are skinny-dipping." He said nothing. "What about having a drink with Daniele?"

Daniele was spinning discs in the deejay booth—pop trash like Abba and the Bee Gees—and shouting random words in pidgin English in the microphone. "Josie, you pussycat! Outer space. *Man*, I really dig *that*." A burgundy scarf was tied around his neck to prevent stray disco drafts from throwing his evening off-kilter. In his dead serious, freakish way he was a good deejay, snapping his fingers, tapping his ass, playing the air guitar with pursed purple lips. "People from Ibiza," he sucked on a microphone, "clap your hands!" The crowd roared.

Matteo slow-smoked his cigarette. He let the smoke wander out of his mouth, only to suck it up again with his nostrils. He had been going to clubs since he was sixteen. Nothing was new to him. "Actually, could you tell me where the bathroom is?" he asked innocently.

"David will take you," she said, shooting me a look as if I were not to be trusted. "Then right back!"

It was a long trip. Matteo was greeted by all manner of people. There were giggling girls who just stared at his body. There were older women, "cougars" who had preyed on other Matteos before. They looked him up and down, appraising, starting with the shoes—always with the shoes—then moving up to his head and then back down to stop squarely at his crotch. You could tell that in a heartbeat, if given so much as a chance, they would be down on their knees, blowing him in the stalls. He had passed that test. But they also made clear—in their own cruel, hard way—that while this kid was a *maschietto*, a tasty little morsel, and they would gladly *do* him (and perhaps they already had), he was not a true stud, no Italian stallion.

Matteo sloughed it all off. A club natural—warm, aloof, dazed—he just kept rolling, passing wisecracking drag queens, saying hi to happy gay boys, giving each of them a piece of his energy—a smile, a squeeze of his ass. He joked. He parried. When we got to the black marble-tiled bathroom, he went straight to the sinks. "Take a good long piss," Matteo told me, "I have work to do." He stripped off his filmy shirt to reveal a fine-tuned boy body, hairless except for a medallion of soft blond in the middle of his chest. He bent over the marble counter—it was wet and obviously he didn't want to get himself dirty—and wiped it down with paper towels. Once dry he took out his lighter and ran its flame over the surface just to be sure. Then he chopped out four thick lines of coke with his Bancomat cash card. He snorted two in each nostril, licking his index finger to wipe up the dust. Then he rubbed his gums.

I watched all of this in the mirror while draining the bottle of wine I had drunk earlier. When I was done, I washed up, then dried my hands under the hot-air blower. Matteo sneaked up behind me and put my neck in a vise. He was glowing from the coke. "Don't tell anyone about this or I'll have to kill you!" he threatened. His eyes, wide open and dazzling, were shot with stars.

"Not a soul," I said. "My lips are sealed." I could smell the chemical on his breath.

"Cool," he said and looked at me, helpless in his grip. "You know, I always wanted to have an American friend like you." His smile was huge, the white shining teeth of a rock star. He tugged on my ears playfully and gave me a fast ambiguous kiss on the lips.

"We better go back to Nicoletta," I said nervously, "or she will go absolutely nuts. You know how crazy she is . . ."

"Like a hyena."

"You have to be careful with her."

"Don't worry, I am an angel—a piggy little angel."

The night was wearing on and the music got louder and louder. Secret club doors were opening, new rooms revealed themselves: the *privée* within the *privée*, the subterranean chill-out room under the stairs, the incense corner with palm trees and a coconut smell. The club was a living, breathing thing, a mutating organism, a carnivorous plant that unfolded its leaves under cover of night, consuming partygoers in layers of ravenous pleasure. As raucous as it got, and it was a melée at three in the morning, with Liz directing dueling deejays playing deep house, drum and bass, old disco, and even power pop from the eighties, there was still the rumble of motorcycles, the deep bass line on the soundtrack. Next to the disco was the Misano racetrack. The backbeat of the evening was the thunder of racers, rough men from Germany and the Netherlands who knew nothing of fashion or house music, bikers who had ridden through the night to get to the track as early as possible to test their nerves on one of the fastest courses in Europe.

"Let's go for a ride together sometime," Matteo said as we were walking back to Nicoletta.

"I didn't know that you ride?"

"I'm *Italian*," he said in a deeper tone of voice, underlining his masculinity, "I love anything fast: boats, bikes, pretty girls."

"I should have guessed. Race bike?"

"Actually, a Triumph," he sounded slightly embarrassed, "a Speed Triple, totally tricked out." I nodded. "I'm waiting for your new race bike," he said, lighting the coke-drenched cigarette. "At twenty thousand euro, it's not chicken feed. I have a lot of sausage to sell."

It was high tide at the club. All of the people that Nicoletta had met in Bologna, on the beach, at her cafe, people to whom she had slipped a tiny pink card that read "Nicoletta, sugar, spice, and promotion," were now entering the disco or calling her cell phone. They wanted to be put on a list. If you came to a club like L'Echoes and you weren't on a list, you could wait outside—like an immigrant—on a line that lasted hours. Nicoletta was trying to make a name for herself at the beach. She didn't run her own night like Liz. She couldn't pull an all-A-list crowd. But she could rope in young guys like Matteo who wanted access.

We left him in the *privée* with his friends. When they said goodbye, he kissed Nicoletta hard on the mouth, tapping her ass like a wheel of parmigiano cheese—checking to see if it was ripe.

"So what's his story?" I asked her. "Are you two dating?"

She looked at me with smiling yellow eyes. "No, we're just *friends*."

"It looked like he's really into you."

"You *really* think so?"

I nooded. "He seems a bit young . . ."

She was immediately offended. "Well, he is actually very mature. He is taking a break from his girlfriend this summer. They've been together since they were sixteen. He wants me to show him around town." I didn't say that I thought he had been around, all on his lonesome.

47

The next day around noon, I woke up with a slight hangover, hungry. Willie and I went to the kitchen to fry some piadine for breakfast. I cooked the pancakes in a few drips of olive oil until the edges turned brown, then scrambled some eggs. Nicoletta appeared in her diaphanous baby doll nightie and blackout sleep mask. The cracking of the eggs had woken her up. "Can't you boys keep it quiet?" her voice was rusty. "You know that I'm a light sleeper." Her hair was like a pad of old steel wool, orange in the sunlight, about to come apart.

"I don't know a quiet way to scramble eggs. Is it the cracking or the scrambling that bothers you?"

"*Mah va là*, David. Maybe if you closed the kitchen door and had some respect, I could get some sleep around here."

"It's noon, Nicoletta," Willie risked.

"*Boh?*" she gestured, raising her shoulders and pulling down the corners of her mouth simultaneously. "I got in just a couple of hours ago."

"Well, maybe if you drank less it would be easier to sleep," he said.

"That's not it," she snapped.

"Maybe your room is too hot," I said. "It makes you cranky. Open a window."

She and Daniele closed all of the doors and windows at night, drew the shades, and hid under heavy sheets and blankets, fully dressed in pajamas and socks like mummies. The air in the room was so stifling it burned to breathe. "This is the way we sleep."

It didn't occur to Nicoletta that her irritability might be due to a number of other factors. There were the vodka lemons and endless smoking. Staying out till dawn for days on end. The diet restricted to a few strips of prosciutto, green apples, and coffee with artificial sweetener. It could make anyone edgy. Add a handful of ephedrine tablets to burn thigh fat and liters of water to flush her system and you had a recipe for real crankiness.

"At least eat some eggs," I said to her. "There's no cheese, no butter. I promise."

"No thanks," she said, "I'll just eat some matzoh."

Nicoletta must have been the only non-Jew in Italy who regularly ate matzoh, called *pane azimo* in Italian. It had two ingredients, flour and water. Nicoletta took hers with just one condiment added—an artificial sweetener called Tic. She had developed a new table gesture. With one hand she held the matzoh, with the other she gripped the blue bottle of Tic, dribbling a few drops, then with her pinky spread them across the unleavened bread's nothingness. Then she ate. She would consume sheets and sheets of matzoh at a sitting, repeating the automatic motion with the bottle of Tic. Her guts must have been plugged with this mortar—cement as strong as the stuff that had built the pyramids. No wonder she was always bloated.

Dry of mouth, she had little desire to talk about Matteo. Then she became distracted by her cell phone, which started beeping and buzzing incessantly, like a mosquito. Text messages were coming in fast. I crept up behind her and peered through the thicket of her hair to look at the screen. I thought I'd find secret information about last night. But there were only numbers, complicated like Morse code. "Bagno 22." "Da Nello alle 2." "Club 21."

"Yes, ragazzi, it's number nineteen again," Nicoletta announced. "*Deciso.* Everyone will be there." And in five minutes, without saying another word, she wrapped her hair in a big turban, rubbed baby oil all over her skin, and went off to the beach. We saw her hours later (I always avoided midday sun), burnt, sleeping with her mouth wide open, tongue lolling, and despite the smallest nose in all of Misano Adriatico—snoring like a grandfather.

48

It was one of the hottest summers on record. Forest fires raged in
Spain, destroying tens of thousands of acres from Galicia to An-
dalusia. Waters dropped to historic lows in the Danube, closing
the blue river to shipping. In Italy the heat wave started in mid-
June and never left, like a houseguest who was invited for the
weekend but stayed an entire season. The fruit harvest was at
risk. Cherries from Vignola—the white-and-pink ones kissed by
a girl—came and went in the shortest season in memory. The
prized black cherries served in bowls of icy water—*duroni*—were
as hard and small as marbles. It was so hot that the figs curdled
on the trees. Tomatoes withered in terrace gardens. Vintners in
the hills began to worry about the Sangiovese. Normally the
vines like sun, but the heat had growers talking about the thick-
ening of grape skins and the risk to plants with immature root
systems. Prices for stone fruit rose dramatically. Spirits sank. At
the beach a brown algae bloom covered the Adriatic in an oily
slick—a death warrant for whole species.

It was the hottest, driest summer in 250 years. Rubber wheels
on Eurostar trains melted. Cars overheated. People put their
sheets and pillowcases in the refrigerator and wet down towels to
wear on their heads, drafts be damned! Dogs grew skulky, wandering around the cobblestone streets soundlessly. The only sentient beings unbothered were the pigeons. The heat suited them

just fine. People were too tired, too sun-broken to shoo them off porches or disturb their great revival meetings in the Piazza Maggiore.

Anyone who could escape Bologna did. Elected officials issued proclamations reminding Italians to look after their older neighbors—pensioners dressed in woolen suits, hiding under sheets of newsprint in the gardens of deconsecrated churches trying to stay cool, or drinking lemon water with a teaspoon of salt—old people's Gatorade—so that they wouldn't dehydrate. But these communiqués were issued from summer houses in Sardinia, in Capri, far from the scalding apartments of a generation of poor factory workers who had nothing to do with la dolce vita or *fashion*.

The pope in Rome prayed for rain but it never came. Ambulance drivers bore the brunt of the burden. By the time the bodies were found, it was hard to tell the difference between them—bones poking through parchment—and their bedsheets—corded, knotted, twisted tight by death throes. Italy being Italy, the newspapers focused on the fun—a country laughing, rollicking in the sun, feeding ice cubes to dogs, watering down children, applying sunscreen to the more sensitive animals, like the hairless Chinese dog, at the petting zoo. In the fountains across the country, public discretion was relaxed and girls in g-strings splashed with their boyfriends in the water of summer bliss. At last the statue of Neptune in the center of Bologna, surrounded by sea maidens with liquid crystal squirting from their breasts, fulfilled the intentions of its sculptor.

One Saturday morning I couldn't get out of bed. I shut my eyes, positioned my head right next to the fan and hid under the sweat-drenched linen sheets. At noon I began sending out text messages to my friends. "I'm not coming."

"What?"

"I'm staying home."

"*Ma tu sei matto*. You're really crazy."

Nicoletta wrote: "I'm so sorry about the other week. I wasn't really angry with you. It was just that I caught Matteo fooling around with this dirty whore in the bathroom. She was down on her knees giving him a blowjob. They didn't even notice me. That is why I was so cranky."

"Don't worry about it. I'm just feeling lazy in the heat."

"You spend all this money to have a beach house and then you don't want to go" was the SMS from Daniele. "What is the point?"

"I'm okay in Bologna," I wrote back. "It's actually relaxing here."

"Bella. Vengo a prenderti." Which translates as "I'm coming to get you, you must be so crazy you need professional help."

"Bologna is as relaxing in summer as a pizza oven."

"But there is a cool breeze on the terrace . . ."

"What cool breeze? Someone is blowing smoke up your ass? This is Daniele! You don't even have a *pinguino*," he said, referring to the small portable air conditioner that Italians call a "penguin."

I called my American friends. They came over with provisions: cheap beer, wine, ice cubes, watermelon, sunscreen, and DVDs. We lit up joints and drank *pignoletto*, as insubstantial as cool tap water, but fresh enough in the heat. On my terrace, Willie and Jeremy stripped down to their underwear. Willie wore black briefs. His skin shone with the red, orange, and gold tones of the city itself. Jeremy, paler, wore the white saggy boxers of an old man. Someone had the idea of turning on the garden hose that I use to water the plants. The boys sprayed each other down. The water went into their faces, up their shorts, down their backs. When the flow hit the terra-cotta tiles, it created steam, gathered in rivulets, and started pooling down the drainpipe, clogged by decades of ivy and grapevine. Through gutters and leaders the water made its long way to the ground, through a *no-taio*'s back porch, across someone's scorched rose garden, to splash down in a backyard patio that I could not see, but only hear, the sound of a mountain stream over stone.

"Come out and play, big dog," my friends yelped. I stripped down to boxer briefs, fluffed my dick in the automatic way that one does when changing at the gym, and walked outside. Willie's wet blond hair was in his eyes and he was spinning in circles as Jeremy watered him down. "On the streets of the Bronx . . . is where I want to be . . ." A *Bronx Tale* was on Rai Uno. Calogero was hanging out on a street corner in the Fordham section of the Bronx talking to Sonny about the girl of his dreams and whether she was "one of the great ones." As I watched my friends frolicking in the water, I thought that summer life in New York had been like this for generations. Not much more than an open fire hydrant, a green garden hose, and geraniums the size of snow cones. Sure, the water here smelled a lot like the Reno itself, but if you closed your eyes and shut off your senses, the brackish substance was close enough to pass for the real thing. Willie put the hose to his lips and let it fill his mouth with wetness, the coldest thing in the city. "Don't drink," I told him. "It's sewer." But the water gushed in anyway, filling the cavity of his mouth, spilling over the sides before he spat it out.

The calls kept coming in. "What are you guys doing up there?"

"We are rolling around in the garden like dogs."

"Stop fooling around. Get in the car and come to the beach right now. Tonight at L'Echoes there is a buffet dinner in honor of tomorrow's Superbike race at Misano. Didn't you know? Come."

But we stayed. Willie hung the hose over the grape trellis and attached a colander to its nozzle. He put a wicker chair underneath and turned on the tap whenever he needed a shower. I went to the freezer and took out mint and coconut sprays and misted us down between stints under the hose. We were like seals, slick and lazy on the terra-cotta rocks of a rooftop, howling with pleasure under the improvised rain that Willie called vertical swimming. We cooked a big spaghetti dinner with homemade sauce and ate meatballs the size of planets as the sun went down in a big ball of fire of its own.

While Nicoletta was supposed to be finding her Bolognese *bene* with whom to wed and commence shopping, she was in fact chasing a self-described "coke monster" from Le Marche. His headlamps had her trapped in their silver beam, a deer at the crossing. She was "drinking from his lips," as Italians say, hanging on his every word. On weekends, she would wangle an invitation to sail on his parents' boat off the coast of Pesaro. She came back talking excitedly about Matteo's father, an old sea dog with a snowy captain's beard and skin tanned the color of Connolly leather. "And the mother?" I wanted to know.

"Large!" Nicoletta was shocked that a woman of her station could eat in front of company, grazing freely on chunks of grana cheese, fat olives, peanuts, and tiny gilt-wrapped Fiat truffles. She was still quite handsome, Nicoletta assured me, wrapped artfully in Missoni purples, magentas, and burnt oranges, but "What a size." On the boat, Matteo's parents had talked about how Italy was changing, how the next generation—the children of the great generation of entrepreneurs (their own)—was getting spoiled and lazy. They didn't want to work. They just played hard: drugs and discos, fashion and exotic travel. Matteo said nothing during these discussions, preferring to slip away to the bow to light up a joint of fine Amsterdam hashish, the kind that burns pale blue. "Where was the energy to build?" his parents wanted to know, "the desire to invest in the future?" These were conversations foreign to her, a child of a divorced mother and a disappeared father, and thrilling. Up to now, her life had been just a struggle to survive. "These people have time to *think*," she told me in wonder.

"Matteo is just looking for kicks," I warned her, "nothing heavy."

One night in August, I had been working late at the office and decided to leave for Misano around midnight. It was unusually humid. You could smell sea everywhere. Our house was full of people when I arrived, many undressed or in bathing suits, eating a bit of rice salad with tiny frankfurters, peas, carrots, black olives, and gherkin pickles. On the kitchen table were bottles of red wine and slices of watermelon. Earlier, the group had gone to San Giovanni in Marignano for *Le Notte delle Streghe*—the Night of the Witches. It was the time of year for the *sagra*, a celebration of sorcery. In Italy, everything has its sagra. There is the sagra of the porcini mushroom. There is the sagra of the black cherry. The wild boar has its own sagra and so does the *porchetta*, a steamed, herb-stuffed pig cooked in the Castelli Romani, the hill towns outside Rome.

The Night of the Witches in Romagna celebrates fertility. Its origins stretch back to the Dark Ages when spells and incantations protected the lands deep inside Romagna from evil, allowing them to grow rich and productive, producing the best durum wheat and ripest fruits. Tonight the hills were full of mosquitoes, not just witches, so everyone came back to the beach to continue the party. Matteo was in the spare bedroom, stripped to the waist, chopping lines from a rock of cocaine. He was like a carpenter: sawing, cutting, making lines, saturating cigarettes with cocaine, *alla francese*, preparing big spleefs of rolling tobacco and

Amsterdam pot. He sent his apprentice, Yusef, a spritely Moroccan with yellow teeth, to warm the ceramic plate on the stove. The heat helped pulverize the cocaine more effectively.

Nicoletta was swirling around the room—considering the heat, impossibly elegant in a black cheongsam. Her hair was marcelled, parted on the side, held in place with a white gardenia. She had on black satin sandals with straps that wound all the way up her legs. She came into the room every few minutes to do a key bump, a tiny fleck of cocaine obtained by sticking a key in a bag of powder. She snorted, then disappeared to entertain the other guests—good bolognesi drinking on the terrace. Despite all of her prodding, Matteo would not leave the room. He didn't want to chat with Carlotta or Benedetta on the terrace or exchange repartee with Davide, his boyfriend, and their gay friends. Each time Nicoletta came back, his hands drifted toward her butt, poking, playing. "Dai Matteo," she protested, "come outside." He was doing double lines, two in a nostril. Phone calls came in. Other friends came over, buddies of ill repute, people who didn't pay their bills at Nicoletta's bar or dress nicely. It was not the image she was looking to promote.

"Davide, she wants a fighetto, that's not me," he said when she left the room. He sent Yusef for some more cigarettes, then dipped his fingers in the coke powder to rub over his gums. "I'm just a pig." He took a swig of peach vodka. "What do you say if we get some real girls up here?," letting his tongue hang out, passing me the jug. His pale chest—he never took any sun—was sweaty, luscious, marble cold.

"Nicoletta is an innocent," I said. "She just needs some experience."

"Yeah, but not from *me* . . . Changing the subject, I know a couple of blond girls who would blow us right now, both at the same time. Two pieces in one mouth! You up for that?"

I struggled to remain loyal to my friend: "Nicoletta wants—"

"Yeah, yeah, I know. But that's not me. I'm more like you,

lost in the wide, wide world." He flashed his silver smile and staring eyes, draping his arm around my shoulder. He started stroking my neck, almost unconsciously. He had been partying for three days straight, L'Echoes, Cocorico . . . It was summertime. Ferragosto was upon us. Anything could happen. Matteo's college roommate, Andrew, announced a plan: "Basta with these bolognesi! Let's all go to Pesaro." He started talking about a secret beach, a place farther south, on the way to Ancona, where the girls were all easy—really fine, with big natural tits, dark tans, lots of tattoos and multiple piercings. A place where they knew nothing about brands and designer stylists and fancy haircuts that cost more than two hundred euro. Where the *fanciulle* didn't have best friends who were hairdressers and girls were happy just to sit around in string bikinis and give blowjobs.

"That would be paradise," said Matteo. "All of this talk makes me horny!" He had kicked off his sneakers, unbuckled his belt, and was undoing the buttons on his jeans. He put his hand down his pants to feel his *paccho*. "There is nothing for us here in Riccione. Right, Dave?" Nicoletta appeared again, scowling in my direction, drunker, white wine in hand. Matteo lit up another joint. "Come here, Nico," he said, motioning for her butt. "Sit on my lap and warm me up. I'm cold." But she disappeared without saying a word. All that was left of her was the scent of her cologne.

We didn't see Matteo again that summer. Whether he disappeared to Pesaro or Senigallia or somewhere else along the coast, to a looser beach town, a place where the drugs were stronger and the sex easier to obtain, we couldn't say. The next day we found copies of his magazine *Forbidden Encounters*, left on the stand next to my bed. It was a swingers' rag from Le Marche that advertised singles and couples, all "clean and discreet," real people (not whores!) who wanted to have sex (without limits) in groups, at gas stations. We didn't know if Matteo had left the material on purpose or if the magazines had just slipped out of his backpack when he crashed on the floor.

"That's it," Nicoletta declared when she flipped through a few lurid pages covered with phone numbers. "It's over!" She had been hoping to spend ferragosto on Matteo's boat sailing to the islands off Croatia. "I've had it." She called Luca, her hairdresser friend, and the two made the fastest summer plans ever to spend the rest of August in an all-inclusive African village for less than one thousand euro.

Nicoletta sent us pictures from Kenya. There she was sitting on a dead palm tree, in the overexposed emptiness of a white sand beach in her bubblegum pink bikini. Her smile was as huge as ever, teeth taking up much of the picture frame, but the skin on her face was thin, at risk of bruising. In another shapshot she was pointing at Luca, wearing a flowered sarong. Her finger was so sharp it could slice salami. "She's not eating," I said to Daniele at the kitchen table, both of us drinking orzo in large cups. "It's time to intervene."

Carlotta walked in from downstairs, where Davide and his boyfriend were taking basil baths. We could smell the green astringent steam up here. "Look," she said, unconsciously stroking her own racing form while viewing the images. "I'm certainly no role model, I've been through my own troubles, not to mention my sister's bouts with bulimia. But I've actually seen Nicoletta eating."

"A mouthful isn't a meal," I said, shaking my head.

"She started eating prosciutto. It's a beginning. David, remember last year, when she was only eating apples, carrots, and unseasoned salad?"

"Yeah, she didn't have to go tanning as often," Daniele piped in. "The beta-carotene turned her skin orange bright."

"I think she's allergic to carrots now," Carlotta said, peeling one. "One bite and she turns into a tangerine. Eating meat will hopefully help get her appetite back." The next picture had Nicoletta in a yellow tube top and a green miniskirt dancing with Luca. Her breasts, flattened by the elastic in the band or starved into submission, had effectively disappeared. She was just a tiny nose, that silly grin, but mostly ears, large and shiny as dinner plates. Daniele looked at her legs.

"Yes, it's still my Nicoletta—*proprio lei.* No matter what she does, no matter how skinny she gets, she will always have those big thighs and fat ass." I shot him a dirty look, but he continued, "Don't yell at me for saying it. I think she looks quite beautiful."

"Don't ever tell her that. I'll kill you."

"It hurts me to see, but this is what she has always wanted. To be just like this."

When Nicoletta flew in from Africa late in August, she took two trains, a bus, and a taxicab to the house to see us. She actually screamed when she walked in the door. "*Non ci posso credere!* I can't believe it! I can't believe it!" She was just one large face on a dark rail of a body. "I am so happy to be home." We had a small house dinner to celebrate, and I cooked couscous with raisins, chicken, slivered almonds, and preserved lemon. In deference to Nicoletta, I made a mini portion that had no raisins, no spices, no couscous for her . . . basically just the chicken with a few grains of pasta attached. She ate almost nothing anyway, but was full of joy. She glowed from within, flirting with illness, but still pearl luminous.

After dinner, we went out for drinks at Malindi. Malindi was past the Art Deco Grand Hotel of Riccione, down the beach, past the numbered cabana clubs with their lined-up lounges and color-coded umbrellas, between the harbor of Porto Verde and Cattolica. It was a lonely stretch of bare sand, but alive. The fancy *fighe* with Sergio Rossi sandals and branded bikinis were long gone, but a mechanic who serviced motorcycles and knew the father of Valentino Rossi had told us that the racer would be coming to the beach tonight. The stink of maria was in the air and the sunset made the beach glass and rusted beer cans shine like precious stones. Old tires sparkled like Christmas wreaths. Weathered lifeguard stations became sculpture, backlit and dramatic.

Perched on the roof of a makeshift canteen, a deejay was spinning samba music to the swaying crowd, our summer giro. Daniele went to the bar to procure a jug of white wine with peaches. We sat down on the Indian carpet cushions that covered the sand to drink. It was late summer and tans were velvety like chocolate. Tattoos, a spidery decorated arm or a parrot-colored shoulder, caught the fading light. In this pause, before night fell and the work of mixing drinks or checking coats began, someone—it must have been Monia—murmured, "Che bello stare in Italia." And in that moment, staring at the soft, coral skies straight from Fellini's *Amarcord*, on an industrial beach full of litter and lust in Porto Verde, it was indeed beautiful just to be in Italia.

Valentino Rossi, the winningest rider in Grand Prix history, pulled up on his scooter. The young race royal was wearing a baggy pair of surf shorts, giant sunglasses, and flip-flops, but was otherwise quite naked. "It is strange to be so near an undressed person as famous as he is," I said to Daniele.

"You're right, that scrawny thing should cover himself up, bella. He is as dried up as driftwood!" Rossi's hair was bleached blond, his earrings were big silver hoops, and the trademark sideburns were growing wild. The good Italian scratched his crotch, clowned with his girlfriend of the moment, Martina Stella, the actress from *L'ultimo bacio*, and escorted her to Beach Suite Number One, an improvised assortment of potted palms, lounges, and old railroad ties that created a priveé on otherwise very public sands.

The racetrack at Misano was just a few blocks away and we could hear, even now, the high-pitched wheezing (Japanese) and the Cosmodromic *vrooms* (Italian) of superbikes put through their paces. Go-cart tracks lined the beachfront. Moto Guzzis and Aprilias occupied every local garage. And while the young generation, unlike my *padrone di casa*, avoided talking about the last war, its Futurist motifs—speed and racing—remained ever present. Giacomo Balla's woodcuts of two-wheeled dynamism still fueled the fantasies of boys intent on winning at Monza and Laguna. Umberto Boccioni's fractured combat planes lit up the skies with fireball shells exploding in molten reds and oranges. As Valentino settled into his lounge chair and kissed Martina, word passed instantly on cell phones throughout all of Romagna. Everyone wanted to stop and stare, exchange *due chiacchiere*— two words with him—to ogle his beauty, to be part of his giro. Monia sent a text message to her friend who was still shopping in Riccione, a girl who had slept with him: "*Vieni qua . . .* ," she tapped into her Nokia, "you have to see this!"

Nicoletta grew tired all of a sudden. The trip (and her thinness) had finally caught up with her. "You know what I really want to do, more than anything in the world?" she told me, "is just get into bed and sleep." We went home. I cleaned up the dinner plates, put some Cesaria Evoria on the stereo. Then I lit the Japanese incense that smelled of marine oaks and primrose. The house felt like a dark, mossy ocean. It was hot in the rooms, but before going to bed Nicoletta shut all windows and closed the doors. She drew the blinds and fastened the shutters to avoid any breezes. She put on a pair of satin pajamas and donned her sleeping mask. She got into that hot narrow bed with Daniele and switched off the lights. I didn't need to see what they were doing. I knew. I swear I could hear through the door, "Dani, hold me tight." And in that imagined embrace, that innocent coupling that I had seen so many times before, all of her pain and rejection, all of her eating issues and sexual insecurities slipped away. There was no fear, no sadness. Wrapped in his long legs, smooth and enveloping, but not *waxed*, she fell asleep dreaming. Tomorrow night she would go to the club and wear her whitest dress and the sparkly sandals. Liz had finally agreed to let her hostess.

50

My own moment, as a *rider*, came a few weeks later with another timed trial, this one an endurance race with modern sport bikes. The event was a promotion for a new-generation motorcycle that Jacques had designed and I had project-managed. A cross between a big enduro and a supersport, the Xstrada went wherever there was asphalt. The bike sported an updated version of our air-cooled twin engine, an old warhorse from the 1970s, now boasting ninety horsepower, advanced electronics, and a "twin-spark" fuel injection system borrowed in name and nature from Alfa-Romeo. The radical bike was no great beauty. That was for sure. One journalist described it as a crash between a vacuum cleaner and a humidifier. "Body by *Baywatch*, face by *Crime-watch*," a customer wrote on our Web site. "All that is missing is a clown nose, feathers, and fuzzy feet." And though the company was skeptical about its chances in the marketplace, it immediately became one of our big successes. Out of the box we produced and sold over four thousand units, cementing, if not Jacques's aesthetic genius, at least his savvy at predicting trends.

After Mr. H.'s death on the Motogiro, I vowed to begin the race with a talk about responsible riding. I stood up in front of the assembled riders on the night before our departure and said, "I know that many of you are professional testers, club racers, expert mechanics." The heckling started immediately.

"You got that right, Mr. Big Important Executive," someone hooted. "No need for training wheels here!" and the bikers commenced rounds of high-fives.

"But this is Italy . . . ," I continued.

"*Viva l'Italia!*" the Italian contingent cried, hugging each other in mock patriotism, then returning to the work at hand: sending out text messages to favorite hookers working the circuit around Cortina. "Honey, I'll be home at eleven. Warm up the lubricant." English lads writing for bad boy magazines like *Superbike* and *Fast Bikes* were bored and bleary-eyed before my sermon even got going. They only paid enough attention to jeer: "Aye, mate . . . whatever the toss you say!" I talked about responsibility. They toasted each other with vodka/Red Bull shots and ordered pots of tea spiked with whiskey. It was party time.

"I know you're all great past and future champions," I slogged on.

"Yeah right, mate, fast as Fogarty!"

"But what you are *not*—at least in Italy—are star navigators. You don't know the roads . . ."

"Hotties will help us find the way," brayed the leader of the English brat pack. He poured himself a shot of whiskey, gargled with it, spit it into a tumbler filled with ice water, and downed the properly mixed drink. "Better get my rocks off early. Then I won't have to do all that trick riding to catch up to you nancy-boys."

"The only place you're fast, mate, is in bed," his buddy cracked. "Two pumps and a squirt, it's all over. At least, that's what your Doris tells me . . ."

"The poor unsatisfied slag . . ."

I tried to keep going, ignoring the commotion. "Your riding safety is most important to us."

"Oh, don't get your knickers in a twist, granny," said the drinker. When he paused to take another swig, I seized the opening to wrap things up. It was all spiraling down fast.

"Remember, just be careful. The phone number of the safety sweep and the mechanic's van are printed onto your event tags." Finally, a split second of silence from the crowd. "Call only if you need to."

The itinerary of the race was grueling: from the factory in Bologna to the ski town of Santa Caterina, up to Bolzano, near the border with Austria, a wide loop around the Dolomites, then on to Kranjska Gora in Slovenia, and finally back down again to the rocky mountain spires of Cortina d'Ampezzo. Over three hundred kilometers of riding a day. We left Borgo Panigale in bumper-to-bumper traffic. It was the end of summer vacation and all of Italy was on the road. After two hours in gridlock, our riders got antsy and began dodging and weaving between cars and trucks, desperate to get to the hills and valleys and twisty mountain roads of the Veneto. We made our way toward Lavarone, a town where Freud had first analyzed a work of art, the novel *Gradiva*, by Wilhelm Jensen, in 1906.

The protagonist of Jensen's novel is an archaeologist, Norbert Hanold, obsessed by dreams of a young maiden who lived in Pompeii and whose image he has seen on a bas-relief. In the alabaster sculpture a beautiful girl, head bowed, is lifting her silken robes above her ankles as if she is about to walk on water. The novel was no exceptional work of literature and today is largely forgotten, but Freud invested it with magic, color, and the possibility of hidden fantasy. In Lavarone copies were everywhere.

As we approached the town and its jade green lake, I spied a single swimmer cutting the water's glassy surface, legs and arms moving with grace and precision. I dropped into second gear and rode at an easy pace to the finish line. What errant sunbeam got lost in the eye of one of our riders, who, blinded by the green of the water or the blue of the sky, inexplicably missed the last turn of the day, a simple right-hand bender on a downhill coast into town? Had he been distracted by the swimmer's shimmering crawl? The rider was thrown—he flew over a rocky ledge and crashed hard into decomposed granite—mangling himself and his bike. Another race, another accident. This time the man broke the lower part of his leg and suffered a compound fracture of the thigh and pelvis. Luck in his case was the softness of the gravel and a state of unconsciousness attended to just in time by a team of skilled paramedics. It could have been far worse.

While the injured man waited for emergency care, sweaty bikers were streaming into the parking lot, greeted by girls in traditional dress bearing trays of golden apples and mulled wine. A thundercloud passed overhead. It was a vintage-era Agusta helicopter, blades scrambling the air. Mario, who was addressing the crowd from a band shell, kept up a light banter. "Everything is okay!" he boomed into the megaphone, smiling hard. The helicopter set down, sending ripples across the lake. Its hatch opened and out rushed white-coated men carrying a stretcher. "Don't worry folks! Nothing serious has happened!" Paramedics attached an oxygen mask to the comatose man, wrapped him in a trauma blanket, then disappeared into the copter's bowels. As the helicopter whisked its payload away to a hospital bay in Trent, Mario practically sang out: "Dinner will be served at the Hotel du Lac at 8 p.m. *sharp*! But only after we finish the gymkhana—a test of your riding skills. Bowling pins have been set up on a narrow course. Avoid knocking them over to win points."

My secretary, Luisella, an acerbic girl from Galarate, a town known for not mincing words, said, "Yeah, the victim is real *happy*. He crashed on the first day of the race, destroyed a twelve-thousand-euro motorcycle, and will have to wear a body cast for months. Sounds like a *ball* to me." She took one look at Mario's shit-eating grin and said: "*Che scemo*—what a fool!" loud enough so that everyone in earshot could hear her.

"He's still smiling, folks," Mario repeated, this time in English, and the helicopter disappeared in the darkening sky. I thought that maybe the rider was going to see the maiden walking on the lake after all.

My mentor was a tester named Fabio. He was the first person who helped me understand how riding could unlock hidden parts of the personality. He took me under his wing and helped me to finally let go and fly. Fabio was "a real-world biker"—to quote from our marketing jargon—not a racer, not a stunt man. Instead, he was that rare motorcyclist *not* obsessed with doing burnouts and wheelies. He preferred teaching—actually helping newbies hone their street skills. Strangely, this was a rare commodity at a company that was ostensibly about attracting new bikers. Testers, lean as greyhounds, refused compromises to make our motorcycles more comfortable. (They didn't care about overweight Americans.) Engineers did nothing to soften our infamously hard-to-pull-in clutch. (Women riders were not on their agenda.) The race religion of the testers was so extreme, so rigid, with so little room for flexibility, that my boss called them "communists." I thought they were more like Jews—suspicious of converts, nonproselytizing.

Once, the head of the department, an engineer widely known for his purist approach, took a bike trip across America on the new Xstrada. When he returned, the executive responsible for consumer marketing pounced on him. "Admit it, Carlo," Ronald said, gloating, "didn't your ass burn on those straight highways?" The seat of the bike had blistered the butt of everyone who had ridden it and Ronald had been fighting a decade-long battle to add an extra layer of foam under our saddles.

"It was a wonderfully fine seat," answered Carlo, unruffled, "extremely comfortable." Which was why six-foot-four Fabio now set up all motorcycles for product launches and promotional rideouts. He wasn't thin, he wasn't tiny, his ass could be trusted.

Fabio was the road guide for my team, which included journalists from men's magazines like *GQ* and *Maxim* and *Esquire*. He examined each of our riding abilities straightaway. "Your form isn't bad, *niente male*," he said to me, privately, "but everything is just a little bit rigid. Your legs are clamped around the fuel tank like you're hanging on for dear life. Your hands are too tight on the bars. Ease up." And then we went riding. Fabio called it "waltzing," swinging from side to side, carving up curves that went left, then twisted right, downshifting on the inclines, pulling in the clutch to disengage the gears and letting the bike coast down descents—as quick as gravity and guts would allow.

On the Wednesday morning we rode toward Santa Caterina Valfurva, a storybook town of covered wooden bridges and Alpine lakes. But first there was the Gavia Pass to contend with, at three thousand meters. We rode through forests that went from leaf to pine, rising in altitude, then conifer dwindling to scrub. We made a fast, steep ascent up the mountain on perfect slick roads without guardrails. All of a sudden, crossing the tree line, the landscape went lunar. The smell of turpentine, of old-growth forest disappeared, replaced by the sharp odor of good clean air— but not much oxygen because at this altitude there was little of it.

It was not uncommon for riders to get altitude sickness at these heights and smash, inebriated, into glacial rock, lost in silent dreams. Rock—a turbulent mass of striated mineral and ice—once moving and now eerily still, was still alive, still capable of action. We reached the summit of the glacier. Only lichen lived openly up here in the high heavens, a symphonic sea of muted pigment, color with no substance. Everything was rarefied, shimmering. I breathed hard and felt light. Ordinary things, usually not worthy of notice, like road pylons—half white, half black, tipped by a red reflector—took on vivid importance. Transformed, they became objects of deep contemplation in an environment stripped of reference points. Repeated for miles, marking the edge of the twisting road, the pylons became zebra stripes galloping across a great savannah of sky. They became the hypnotic keys of a jazz piano, rippling in scales and triumphant arpeggios into the infinity of space. The mind played tricks in the clouds. I got lost in the silliness of my metaphors. A sign appeared that warned of curves ahead. Two hours of them.

Roads that had once been slick now deteriorated into dirt and moraine. Fabio guided me through the crystalline landscape, an environmental experiment in rock. He pointed his finger down toward the ground, indicating where I should take the turn—drawing the radius with a silent nod of his helmet. He braked, shifted, dropped the bike, made his turn, exited the curve, and then sped off into the straightaway. I was expected to follow his line. The goal was not to try to close gaps by fast acceleration—with an engine that made ninety horsepower, with lots of low-down grunt that was cheap, amateur stuff. But rather the idea was to stay with him—cleanly executing turns in tandem, at speed, a spectacle of synchronized riding. Downshift, feather the back brake, turn, out of the box, accelerate, streaking across the bowl, letting the ass and legs do all the work, not the hands. "If the ass feels good on the bike, the bike feels good," Fabio told me. After a long day in the saddle, only your thighs and ass should feel tired, "like you've been well fucked." I didn't crack a smile when he said that. I was too tired. That night I asked how my riding had been. "Okay," he said and then went to bed.

The next day was the Stelvio, consisting of one hundred "passes," or turns, one of the most dramatic experiences to be had by motorists on two wheels (or, for that matter, four). Before the Iseran Pass was opened in the French Alps in 1936, Stelvio was the highest motorable pass in Europe.[19] Today it is no longer the highest, but still one of the most dramatic. The road itself is a marvel of engineering with steep rises on each side, made possible by some fifty hairpin bends carved deep into the stone approaches, and with corners so tight that to do them at any speed requires a setup in the opposite lane (where the oncoming traffic is). At the top of the pass is a spectacular southern view of the road folding back on itself, like a box of ribbons. The north face is even more dramatic with its Ortler mountain vistas and snowfields between the summit and Trafoi, just below the tree line, winding down into the Adige Valley below, rich with chamois, marmot, and fox.

I began the day in bright sunshine and with high hopes. We rode up from Bormio, a lush area of rolling foothills and gloomy forest. By midday we could see the peaks of Stelvio, piercing a blinding sky. I felt the intense buzz of challenge, the desire to please Fabio with some skillful riding. The roads were dry, a peculiarity of the Stelvio microclimate, which receives little precipitation, even in winter. I rode toward the first approach. I felt confident. There in front of me was a lineup of trucks and cars, motorcyclists, and heavily sweating cyclists in Lycra, each waiting his chance to tackle this monarch of mountains.

Executing sharp turns at slow speeds on a motorcycle—without crashing—requires real skill. I set up the first hairpin. I was awkward, jerky, but didn't fall. I proceeded through the turns, sweating out one after another: multi-apex, blind turn-in, off camber, tricky left-right-left flickers, all sorts and manner of turn. Other riders, much more experienced than I was, dumped their bikes right away. "Fuck me, mate!" they howled at each other, humiliated.

"Get out of my way," they cursed, "you fucking idiot!"

"Dizzy bitch!"

The excuses multiplied. "I'm used to Brands," a tester yelled out, referring to the perfect tarmac of the English circuit. "The gradient here is all wrong." Race bikes like the Yamaha R1 and Suzuki GSXR didn't have enough steering lock for hairpin turns at such slow speeds. I might have felt proud—I hadn't fallen yet—but I was at the very limits of my skill. There were still dozens of turns ahead of me. My hand was getting tired from working the clutch. My thighs began to tremble. I didn't know if it was muscle fatigue, improper riding position—or just fear. One misstep though, and two hundred kilograms of bike would be on top of me. That kept me focused. I cleared my head of all thoughts and just concentrated on executing switchbacks.

I got better, choosing a smarter line, starting the turn early, flowing through the apex at some speed, steady, righting the bike, shifting up, off again . . . this time in second gear, doing the straights, riding not so much faster as cleaner. I reached the summit of the mountain and parked my bike on its stand, exhausted. I dismounted, took off my body armor—it was warm out now— and crawled down the lip of the glacier into a shallow overhang studded with edelweiss, which thrives above two thousand meters. Laid out before me beyond the escarpment was the most beautiful set of sterling switchbacks in all of the Alps. On the road below were scores of motorcycles, swooping and diving, resurfacing, sometimes falling, carving up mountain curves in a conga line of color that lasted for miles. The sun lit the valley brilliant, a banner of natural wonder. The sky radiated robin's-egg blue. The snowfields of the Gran Zebru were soft as ermine. Below was a lush green valley of flowery meadows and fertile land under cultivation. The ice caps of the Ortler range glittered in front of me above, a king's crown.

I sat in the sun for what seemed like an eternity and just watched. In general, a motorcyclist is not contemplative about nature—he doesn't peer into its grand mysteries. He doesn't ponder rock or river or gorge. Unlike an alpinist, he doesn't attach moral qualities to the majesty of mountains. He rides. He speeds. He passes by. Ravine, wheat field, crevasse scroll by in one continuous filmic loop. Geology interests the biker only to this extent: *If there is debris on the road, I may crash.* A biker's vision is close-eyed, not panoramic. It focuses on the next few feet of pavement, the next bend.

Back on the road ten minutes later, Fabio reproached me like the gentlest of dads, the dream parent we never have: "Loose and effortless, remember?" I had survived the ascent, yes, but my riding was still not elegant. "Where is the grace?" Coming down from the roof of Europe, we set off for the glorious Giovo and Pennes Passes. Here the roads were fine, well paved, allowing my Pirelli Dragons to toast up nice and sticky. Now the rubber was transmitting every imperfection of the road—each bump, each ripple—communicating back to me through the handlebars. My riding became more fluid. I felt more in control.

Deep in the canyon below, a group of boys barely out of their teens were riding up the service road parallel to ours on kit *super-motards*—the latest trend—at blistering speeds. Wearing open-faced helmets, colored running shorts, and sneakers without socks, they had no riding protection and not a care in the world. Their faces were tanned and their legs finely muscled and hair-less. With each curve, each gear shift, the scenery of their bodies changed: a new shade of tan, a variation on tawny muscle. Their facial expressions—angry and reckless or joyous and laughing—changed each time I looked at them. They took one look at the rich parade of expensive sport bikes on display—the high-end BMWs, GSs, the race-bred 999s—and, sneering from half a mile away, decided to put on a show of some trick riding. One after the other, the boys pumped out fat stomping wheelies, riding straight up the slopes, unicycle-style, shouting *"Finocchii!"*

Why couldn't I be free or rowdy or irresponsible like them? I felt the sweat dripping down the crack of my ass—anxiety stir-ring. My face went hot with shame. I had escaped America to take risk, to experiment, to lose myself. It was time to finally let go and *do* it. Homophobic insult aside, seeing those boys in their total freedom, in their utter arrogant beauty, challenged me. I wanted to fly. Fabio was far in front of me. He had missed the spectacle of the supermotards and the gauntlet the boys had thrown down. I picked up the pace and switched gears, opening up the throttle and taking advantage of the Xstrada's massive midrange power. That was the easy part. I looked out through the fly screen, across the clocks, to survey the road before me. There were wide, sweeping turns, easy enough to navigate. I lifted my ass off the seat and felt the cool rush of air under me, slipping in between my legs. It felt pretty good. My body was more limber now, even loose. I let my legs dangle, almost touching the ground with my boots. Warnings came into my brain, to slow down, to stop, not to push myself. I blocked them out. I wanted my chance to let the centaur run free, finally, on his own account.

I picked my line and saw it through the turn, leaning all the way over, looking through the turn out toward the horizon, no longer checking down toward the pavement for reference points or watching the front wheel to see how the bike was doing. "Look down, go down." It still rang in my ears from all those years ago. But now my eyes were up, up high looking toward the heavens on the roof of the world. Fabio's finger was like a metronome, pointing out turns, left, then right, and back again. We rode through gloomy forests and canyons of rock and glacial pebble beaches in vast snowless fields. Temperatures rose and fell. The sun peeked out from a cloud and then got lost again in darkness. Clouds rolled by in great blankets of frozen mist. A pink house in a solitary glacial town, isolated and magnificent, appeared on a crest and then disappeared, setting into the sunlit apricot rock. Time stopped and I was lost in the beautiful blur of emptiness, just riding. So this is what it all came down to—getting lost in the dumb sound of an engine. Letting myself disappear in the flicking of a few hundred pounds of metal side to side as if it was my ten-speed Schwinn, hearing the whoosh of myself, alone on the road, howling against the wind.

And then it happened—well, sort of. We were taking a series

of turns and I really felt great. I didn't need to worry about my choice of lines. I trusted Fabio and just followed his pace. I was perfectly in sync, flying in formation, a swallow soaring, diving from side to side with grace and purpose. I was in third gear and stayed there. I didn't brake. It was a wide banking turn on perfect tarmac—a perfect, fat-elbow U. At the apex, hauled all the way over, looking out into the cloudbank, unable to differentiate between slope and sky, three thousand feet up, grateful that there were no sirens to catch my gaze, I heard the smallest of metallic scratches. It was a joyous sound—a foot peg touching ground. In my mind's eye, I could see the blue spark, a gorgeous explosion of abrasive electricity, billet aluminum scraping asphalt. I positioned the bike just a little bit farther over, accepting the dare, pushing my knee out just a little bit more—in a sort of a wiggle. That was it. The knee slider grazed the road, plastic on pavement. It was cheating, I knew it. But I had to have that nick on my kneepad, the gilt medal on the uniform.

Afternoon became evening. The weather turned. The sky went black and orange. Rain came on. Near the Alpine approaches to Slovenia, the snow began. Then hail, rain, and ice, in varying orders and grades of intensity. Lifelong bikers lost their front ends in the wet, cursing themselves for not having the right raingear, angry that there was no alternative but to soldier on through the slush. I was still in the afterglow of my moment. Riding the motorcycle through these woods, on those roads, across these mountain Dolomites had let me discover nature— not what it looked like, I could hardly see anything in the storm, but how it *felt*.

I thought of the pictorial achievement of Turner's snowstorms—the infinite modulation of whites and grays and blues. He did not merely *depict* the meteorological phenomenon, his brushwork took you right inside the squall. Suddenly, the downpour eased and the skies started to clear. In the pale light of evening, an English rider motioned me to pull over. I rode to him at the side of the road, bordering the riverbank. He had spotted a cow—the friendly face of the barnyard, mother of milk and cheese—floating off in a river of mud. Or so he claimed. I thought that maybe, stupid with altitude sickness, he had begun seeing things. But right there, swirling in pools of turbulent chocolate, was the dun-colored cow herself—a great horned beast—floating downriver, sailing like the silent canoes of my childhood, fast and awesome.

I was amazed by the stillness of it all—the liquidity of the mud, the noiselessness of the cow, and the threatening nature of the sky, the color of a bruise. And then it started. Smell of lightning came on strong—flint on stone. The storm roared back to life. Sheets of rain came sluicing down. Thunder echoed across the river valley. Yellow lightning lit up the sky, casting truth on the terrible nature of nature: a wall of mud was coming down the river in a great wave, sweeping away trees, houses, and the unknowing, unlucky cows caught in its murky path.

Over the objections of my group, many of whom were experienced riders, I made a decision to ride to the nearest village in search of lodging. It took us hours. We finally found a truck stop and negotiated with the owner for the few narrow beds in the loft over the barn. We ordered plates of ham and cheese—there was nothing else to eat—and drank warm cans of Fanta, watching the weather wash out the remaining roads on a black-and-white television set, snowy with interference. Then, grown men—tough veteran bikers all—stripped off their gear and went off to bed, two in a bunk, shivering under old crocheted Afghans, waiting out the storm.

51

After getting my knee down, I returned to Bologna excited for the final races of the season, the trade fairs, and the Motorshow in December that attracts a million screaming teenage boys. I finally had my own war tales to tell. The September cool came quickly, and one day after leaving the factory I parked my car in the lot on San Felice and walked toward Piazza Malpighi and the place that I had been avoiding for all the years I had been in Bologna. During most of my time here, I had been clinging to the artifacts of Americanness, refusing to wear city shoes in town in favor of ninety-nine-cent flip-flops, continuing to drink cappuccino after midday instead of switching to the required espresso. I thought that by maintaining old habits, I could keep certain aspects of myself intact. Now, after the months immersed in Antonio, in Riccione, in biking, I felt free to ditch it all and just go native.

I walked across via del Pratello, past the hippies smoking spleefs and the bums haggling over the price of greasy sticks of hashish in the square in front of San Francesco. I walked past the church, past the Glossatori—medieval jurists entombed in stone sarcophagi—past the Trattoria Fantoni, where well-off Marxist professors from the university and their acolytes ate fresh *papardelle* with rabbit, down the cobbled street toward the tiny store where new wing tips, loafers, and monk straps were gleaming in the window like a litter of puppies.

I walked under the stand of stately linden trees, their leaves turning brown at the edges, now free of any scent, beyond the minimalist designer chair store that sold plastic furniture by Philippe Starck, edging closer to Peron e Peron, *"calzature su misura."* I wanted to look at brogues. In the window were neatly lined-up pairs, warm and slick as if newly born, glowing in the colors of custom leather. Bitter chocolate. Caramel. Spotted cream. Butterscotch.

The shoes were stuffed with cedar trees and lined up on a rough wooden rack, charred by years of use and old polish. A heavy canvas awning protected the contents of the store, and above there was an even thicker curtain of tree so dark and lush that its shade blocked out any threat of sun or sky. A halogen pin light, trained on each model, heightened the drama of the cobbler's trade, making animal hide shine. Across the street, dogs in the run at San Francesco chased overfed pigeons. Barking riotously, the mongrels danced up and down the alley pursuing the fat birds, leaping in the air whenever their jaws got close enough to bite.

When an Italian has shoes handmade by a cobbler, he never buys black. Anything can look good in black: a greasy motorcycle jacket, a well-worn wallet. Black is the color of nylon Prada bags. And the color of the carabinieri's police uniforms. Once, our apparel division made a particularly nice gray T-shirt for the launch of a new sport bike. Everyone thought it looked great—slim and sexy—with red stripe inserts on the shoulders. After many years of trying, our designers had finally achieved something *cool*. At a prototype meeting, I suggested that we expand the line with new colors to increase sales. Heads nodded in agreement. "Black would be a winner," I said. "Tough, ninja-like." Their faces froze. "Jet black," I repeated in case they hadn't heard. Brows furrowed.

"Davide," someone was brave enough to break the ice, "we just can't do it."

"Why not?" I asked. "We do everything else in black. Pants, leather jackets . . ."

"No one *wants* to look like a policeman," mumbled the head of the department.

"Tell that to Miuccia Prada!" I answered. "We'll sell double or triple the number of T-shirts if we do black." People looked down at their sketchpads, as if unwilling to discuss the issue further. Someone busied himself with a cell phone, sensing a confrontation. "At least do a prototype!" I cried, frustrated.

"You may not know this," someone ventured, "but your T-shirt in black will be very confusing."

"To whom? Everyone loves black. Most of you are wearing it right now!" But they wouldn't budge.

"We will not sell a single shirt," the department head said ruefully.

"We are not just selling in Italy," I whined, trying to reason with them. "No one in America knows that Italian carabinieri wear black uniforms with red stripes."

"That may be true," said Ombretta, a beautiful Bolognese with glossy black hair and a leather miniskirt. "But imagine if they found out?" We had come to the crux of the matter: an unpardonable *brutta figura*.

"Would it be better not to run that risk?" I asked gently.

Ombretta nodded her head. "Yes." It would. And in the end, after so many years in Italy, I had to agree. Taking such a fashion risk would be just too much for us.

"You guys are right," I said to everyone's great relief. "We could ruin our image with such a move."

"Exactly!" someone practically shouted. "Now you are thinking like a real Italian, Davide. You understand!" We weren't a fashion company and couldn't play by Milan's rules. We needed to stick to motorcycles.

"Let's get a coffee, as black as you like it!" someone suggested, and we all marched off to the bar to spend the rest of the afternoon drinking *caffè corretto*—black coffee "corrected" with a splash of grappa. Black may be the color of fashion and of coffee, but at least in Bologna it was not the color of T-shirts. You don't sell more motorcycles by making Milanese fashion and you don't get your money's worth by picking black handmade shoes. Black doesn't glow.

I walked inside the store and met its proprietor, Mr. Bruno Peron. A short man, Peron looked exactly as a cobbler should. Whenever he smiled his bristle mustache moved up and down so fast I thought he could polish boots. On his feet were shining cordovan moccasins. "It's a skin," he told me, "not a color. Like crocodile, no two hides are alike." He had an easy manner and a great desire to talk. The man took one look at my sneakers and began shaking his head in horror. "It must be a sauna in there!" It wasn't warm out, but my feet were sweating.

"It may seem counterintuitive," he said, "but even in summer, the foot needs to be protected from the street. Heavier shoes offer more protection, not less. And tennis shoes," he laughed, enjoying himself thoroughly, "they're just lethal!"

"I mostly wear Nikes," I said sheepishly.

"Do you ever wonder why your feet are always lily white and fungal? Sneakers don't breathe. If I were the minister of health, I would outlaw them completely. In twenty-five years' time we are going to have a health problem of enormous proportions. Mark my words: a whole nation of fallen arches and damaged heels. Now, what can I help you with?"

"I want to have a pair of good shoes made."

"Well, that has a lovely sound to it. I only make good shoes."

His store was like a well-appointed closet, everything smelled of cedar and shoe polish. Dominating one wall was a blowup of *The Robb Report*'s cover story that listed Peron e Peron as the fourth most exclusive cobbler in the world, just after J. Lobb. "Whatever you want, I'll make it. Sporty, classic—there is nothing new in the world of shoes, it's all been done before: Tyrolean style, Norwegian mode, English banker . . . It's just a question of tweaking, of taste—elongating the form, squaring up the toe."

He took me into his workshop and started showing off his beauties. "Look at this wonder"—he was showing me a rare style invented by an artisan named di Mauri back in the 1940s. "Do you realize the workmanship it takes to extend the sole like this and attach the upper with stitching so fine? Do you understand the *significance?*"

Half a century ago, cobblers in Bologna developed a technique for making shoes of extraordinary softness and flexibility. The innovation consisted of attaching the sole to its upper by means of a sleeve of the supplest calf. The new form allowed mobility of the toes while maintaining the structural integrity of the weight-bearing heel. The Bolognese sole or *sacchetto Bolognese* was not easy to accomplish—real skill was needed to fabricate shoes of the highest quality. The stitching of the lining had to be absolutely perfect. Otherwise, once put to work on the hard cobblestone streets and terrazzo arcades of the city, the shoes would warp and wrinkle, exposing their wearer not just to embarassment, but to real discomfort.

He began pulling samples: wine reds, burnished coppers, mottled tans. "Bologna was once famous for its shoes!" He showed me varieties of style: cap toes, loafers, monk straps, and collector models in washed orange crocodile, dyed green shagreen. "Try this on, I beg you! Just to see what something real feels like." He was offering me a loafer with an elastic closure and buttons up the vamp. The shoe resembled a custom shirt. He handled the model like a jewel, rotating it so that the blue skin caught the light and sparkled like a sapphire. "I can do any finish you want. We can slick it up. We can age it and create patina. *You* tell me."

He was itching to take my measurements, to make what they call "a shirt," a rough mule of pigskin that is then fitted, repeatedly if necessary, until a shirt becomes a glove, the perfect sheath for a customer's own foot. This prototype was then used to make the actual shoes, in the leather and style of your choice. Prices started at one thousand euro. "Once the first pair is made," I asked him, "can I just call in and order shoes by phone or even Internet?" I too had seen the occasional article about bespoke shoes in *Cigar Aficionado*.

"As many as you like. I have clients who order *dozens* at a time." And he pulled out from his desk a picture of an Aston Martin. "This client of mine owns five thousand apartments in New York City. I just made him a pair of shoes that has the same leather that lines the cabin of his automobile. Can you imagine that?" Though I didn't say so, I very well could.

I walked home face ablaze, a parcel of cedar shoetrees and a horsehair brush slung over my shoulder. I was considering a slick pair of loafers, with squared-off toes, high vamps, and a rather raffish tongue, in patinated parchment leather, which cost two thousand big ones. The sun slanted in from the west, casting warm light on the brick face of San Francesco, built from the red earth of the Pianura Padana, the flat soil of riches. The church is a basilica with three naves, built in a mixture of Gothic and Romanesque styles just ten years after the death of the saint himself. To the left of the church is the rectory where early Franciscan monks lived and worked.

I bought a bottle of good Sangiovese and took it up to my terrace to watch the sky change from blue to pink to orange and back to blue again and wondered how long the nights would stay clear and fresh like this. I opened the bottle, looked up at the setting sun on the horizon, a big ball of smoke and fire, and saw birds circling in the skies high above the sacristy and campanile of San Francesco. They made no sound, no cry, just patterns of dark and light in a purple Italian sky. They were *rondini*, tiny swallows, and since it was late in the season soon they would be returning to their winter grounds in Africa. But tonight they had taken to flight in these skies as if it were March.

I poured myself a glass of wine. Sangiovese is a rather ordinary varietal wine, tasting of berries and minerals, oak and earth. The same grape, watered by the rains of Tuscany and warmed by a Tuscan sun, becomes Chianti. But Chianti is part of another Italian story. It is rarely drunk in Bologna.

Normally I don't like birds. Beaks make me nervous. But these swallows, still far away in the distant sky with the promise of leaving soon, suited me fine. Italians like birds—on their dinner plates. The closer a bird is to being in shooting range, the better. If birds are near, you never know when a shotgun will go off. I am afraid of the rustling of feathers. To Italians, fluttering wings means papa is about to bag a roast. Jacques told me many times that whole species of birds had changed their migratory patterns, choosing Yugoslavia instead of Italy, because Italians shoot and eat anything that crosses their air space. A plate of *uccellini con polenta* is a delicacy across Emilia-Romagna all the way to the Veneto.

Tonight, the birds billowed like clouds and the neighbors came out to watch. A young girl stopped cooking her *tortelloni* with peas, cream, and prosciutto and delayed her date to have a look. An elderly man climbed up to his flat rooftop and got out binoculars. The young couple that staged nightly sexploits in a picture window that overlooked my garden (while I watched the evening news, stealing occasional glances) got dressed and came outside. The rondini had long ago given up the big Italian cities like Bologna for smaller places like Faenza, Ferrara, and Castel San Pietro. They were rare now. But tonight they swarmed in numbers. As the dark came on, the sky went indigo and the lights of San Francesco bathed the towers in amber light. The birds sailed across the sky in great arcs, making dramatic dips and bows and ribbons across the sky.

I saw a man, alpine hunter hat in hand, gun at the ready, watching in disbelief from his rooftop campanile. I expected him to shoot at any moment. He kept one hand on his Berretta, fingering the trigger, and with the other stroked the red feather on the brow of his cap. The spectacle of the darkening sky, thick with birds throbbing and pulsing to a silent percussive beat, was enough to still the crowd.

In 1913 Giacomo Balla painted two major works: *Speed of the Automobile* and *The Flight of Swallows*. Though his treatment of subject matter was abstract, he remained true to the representation of motion. He depicted the specific gesture, its repetition, and its evolution into new gesture. For Balla, birds were not nostalgic. They were futuristic. Each flap of wing was a single frame of modern action, an image captured. Birds broken up into their constituent parts, landing, taking flight, merging, beating wings, soaring like flickering images on film in an endless loop of motion, spooling toward infinity. In the flapping of wings, Balla captured the rhythm and rhyme of movement, the poetry of the individual and the brute power of the mass, the solitary swallow, the flock of thousands. He applied paint across the canvas, from left to right, in rolling browns and grays and greens, strong and clear brushstrokes like tightly packed feathers, preened and glossy. The birds appear and disappear in the chiaroscuro of dramatic flight, passing across time and space and covering great distances. This energy is captured, but not controlled, like beads of quicksilver on glass.

At last the constellations came out and the swallows receded into darkness. Altair—one of the brightest stars in the firmament and one of the closest to earth—lit the night sky as it had since antiquity, as it did when the Bolognese were still religious and this part of the world was famous for higher learning and the world's first surgeries and not just mortadella and fast cars. The Swan appeared. Visible to the naked eye, made of stars forming a Latin cross, the Swan represented Zeus to the ancient Greeks, transformed into a bird so he could fly to his lover, Leda of Sparta. Their offspring were, from one egg, the twins Castor and Pollux, and, from the other, Helen of Troy. Now the skies went deep black. The only thing to distract you from dreams of an ancient but perhaps not so remote Italian evening was my neighbor, the middle-aged widow who usually fried sausages in a big black pan, who just then turned on a television: "*che stronza*," what a jerk! Her room was now bathed in the blue neon glow of *Friends*, taking the scene from the twelfth century and fast-forwarding it to the twenty-first.

EPILOGUE

We never sold the company to the Chinese. Though their advisers had fanned out across Europe trying to seduce struggling manufacturers with promises to cut the cost of their goods, we escaped the snare. Agents of Asia came to see us every so often with a steel frame or an aluminum swing-arm in hand that looked familiar. "See this part?" they would say, waving our metal around. "In China it costs 60 or even 70 percent less to make! And the beautiful thing is the quality. Not just the same as European, even better!" But we held on. Calls came in from investment bankers claiming they had the cash to buy us outright. "What about due diligence?" the boss asked each new group as it made its way through the plant. "Wall Street lawyers? Accountants? A deal memo?"

"Not necessary. We'd prefer to just write you a check." The latest rumor was that the Chinese didn't care about factories or technologies or even the state of ongoing businesses. They just wanted to buy European brands so that they could learn more about marketing. We went through at least a dozen fishing expeditions. A concrete offer was never made. Maybe the Chinese couldn't purchase a public company that traded on two stock exchanges. Maybe the Italian government wouldn't allow one of the jewels of its industry to fall into Asian hands. Maybe the

Mafia, from its secret mountain redoubts, decided to get involved. I never heard a convincing explanation.

We suffered through years of slowdown. The euro's rising value priced our bikes at ever higher premiums to the Japanese. Sales in the United States declined. By the time we found a buyer for the share of the company that our American owners had refused to sell at the height of the boom, our enterprise value had shrunk dramatically. The value of the company—once so lofty, so brandlike—had slid right back to the multiple of an industrial manufacturer—in fact, to the very same value at which we had purchased it. Of course, the brand was stronger than ever. We were making sexy T-shirts. We had opened a chain of themed "Moto-hotels" in Dubai. But not as many people seemed to want to buy our expensive sport motorcycles.

The new story, penned by none other than the boss himself, was that we had to become smaller to survive, to make fewer but more profitable motorcycles. It was time for another turnaround. An Italian family with billions in profits from the sale of its salami-processing business rather liked the sound of the new tale. It hired the lead investment banker who had put together our original deal, one of the few moneymen who actually had made a profit on the company. He had gotten out just before the Internet bubble burst, never trusting that brand growth would lead to real profits. Now he thought the cycle was once again turning favorable—and at these multiples there wasn't much lower we could go.

The news of the impending sale was celebrated in Italy as a true triumph. The company would become Italian again! The engineers were victorious. Designers, brand managers, and marketers—necessary evils during American management—were nothing permanent. Nothing lasting like the output of engineers who toiled, not with paper or photographs or PowerPoint presentation slides, but with real things: like metal and advanced materials such as ceramic and titanium. The vicissitudes of our adventure on Wall Street had never touched the engineers anyway. Their dreams were entirely intact. To win at Monza! To rule the straightaway! To dominate the chicane at Laguna! To ride faster, getting that knee puck down, racing on to the checkered flag, beating all comers.

Antonio visited me during the final negotiations for the sale of the control stake of the company with his own news. I walked downstairs to the guardhouse to pick him up. At first I almost didn't recognize the man wearing a corduroy jacket with thick ribbed naps and a gray turtleneck sweater. His hair had grown in and was now curly. He looked like an Ivy League professor, complete with wire-rimmed glasses—not unlike my cousin who taught physics at Columbia. I kissed his cheeks and he froze. "Not appropriate office behavior," he whispered in my ear, keeping his body at a rigid distance. "You don't kiss a businessman. It's just not done."

I said, "I'm a manager here. I do what I want."

After all the years together, it was still hard for him to accept the simple fact that we were a couple. Though he wasn't from the south, I thought of that region still in the thrall of Magna Grecia. For centuries, maybe millennia, it was normal in places like Lecce, Brindisi, and Bari for an older Italian man (married, of course, with children) to take on a boy as his lover. Much more than just his sexual companion, the boy was his personal charge. The man cared for him, guided him, and protected him from the wide world. No one would have used terminology like "gay" or "bisexual" or "closeted" to describe these relationships. Such social constructs did not exist in antiquity.

Though I was not a married man, I thought of them every time Antonio resisted a modern word like "boyfriend" and called

me his "brother." As much as I wanted to believe in the commitment we had for one another, a reflection of the heroic love of
Achilles and Patroclus, as much as I mused that our ancient
bond would endure for the ages, the real world had begun to intrude. As each year passed, fewer boys walked arm in arm down
Bologna's arcades, bound in friendship, as they had when I first
arrived in Italy. What was once an utterly innocent gesture of
affection—an expression of camaraderie—was becoming imbued
with homoerotic significance.

Young men didn't hold hands as Alessandro and I did when
we saw each other in the morning for coffee, or sit with their
arms draped around each other's waists during lunch in the park.
Male images like these weren't available on MTV. And as Antonio's recoil from my lips had just proven, even the double kiss itself, the most Italian form of greeting, was fading from easy
usage.

"I have great news for you," his black eyes flashed. "I just got
elected to the city council in a small town near Padua . . ."

"As a member of the Nazi Party?"

"Very clever. No, left-center coalition."

"I had no idea you were interested in politics," I said, surprised. "But what does that have to do with your hair?" Despite
his youth—he was in his late twenties by now—it was receding.

"I couldn't get elected looking like a Fascist skinhead. So I
had to make some adjustments."

"Your mother must be thrilled."

"Actually she hates the attention."

I could fill in the blanks easily enough, the threats to "out"
him, the sexually detailed blackmail from ex-lovers. "Don't you
realize that you ought to be an openly gay politician?" I started to
say, but my voice trailed off.

"I think you are forgetting the power of the church, bro. You
still don't know Italy well enough. It could destroy me." As

much as I wanted to see Antonio in a heroic light, gilded by myth, I was starting to feel a distinct lack of courage, a refusal to fight. He asked to see the plant. And as I had done for so many bankers and lawyers and investors who had passed through our doors over the years, I took him on a tour.

What were they looking for, these legions of people who came to visit us? What did they see in the heavy machinery and the warehouses of spare parts and the sweating workers of our old factory? An idea that place was still important in a world that was ever more convinced that everything was movable, entirely interchangeable, as duplicable as Venice in Vegas? Dino kept reminding me of the magic—something in the brick and mortar—that made Borgo Panigale special. "Keep looking," he urged me. "One day I'm sure you will see it."

I doubt he had ever seen what we saw now. The afternoon shift was ending and line workers were finishing their daily lot of motorcycles. Rays of light came streaming through the clerestory windows, gilding the bodies of ordinary men, makers of beautiful things. And now these sunlit gods were heading off in groups of twos and threes to the showers to wash off the grime of production. "I understand now, bro," Antonio said, eyeing the muscled workers as they raced to strip off their greasy work overalls and rank T-shirts, take lightning fast showers, and then rush home to their wives or girlfriends. "It's not the bikes you're interested in. It's their builders." He begged me to let him wander the locker room for just a minute, to watch the hunks and the hotties showering down. "The factory is a paradise of *boni*!" he cried. "Take me to see some muscle!" And though it hurt me to witness his desire, I took him to the threshold of the changing room and directed his wanton gaze toward the stalls. He looked at the wet bodies, quite plainly in hunger and awe.

NOTES

1. Hugo Wilson, *The Ultimate Motorcycle Book* (Dorling Kindersley, London, 1993), p. 170.
2. Piotr "Polish Pete" Surowiec, "S2R Launch," *Fast Bikes*, February 2005 (Highbury Leisure, Kent), p. 53.
3. Tony Thorn, *The Dictionary of Contemporary Slang* (Pantheon, New York, 1990), p. 500.
4. Athos Vianelli, *Le piazze di Bologna* (Newton & Compton Editori, Rome, 1979), pp. 39–40.
5. Anna Kavan, "World of Heroes," in *Julia and the Bazooka* (Knopf, New York, 1975). "The race track justifies tendencies and behavior which would otherwise be condemned as antisocial in other circumstances."
6. Michele Lupi, introduction by Valentino Rossi, *Racers* (Feltrinelli Traveller, Milan, 2003), p. 19.
7. Ariberto Segala, *I muri del Duce* (Edizioni Arca, Gardolo, 2000), pp. 181–83.
8. Segala, *I muri del Duce*, pp. 264–65.
9. Julian Rothenstein and Mel Gooding, *ABZ: More Alphabets and Other Signs* (Redstone Press, London, 2003), p. 10.
10. Segala, *I muri del Duce*, p. 213.
11. The Allied objective was to take Bologna by Christmas.
12. It was not liberated until almost six months later, on April 21, 1945, at the close of the war in Europe, by Polish, American, and Canadian troops.
13. The icon is of Byzantine workmanship from the twelfth century.
14. Dante Alighieri, *Inferno*, canto 12, versi 55–57.
15. Wilson, *The Ultimate Motorcycle Book*, p. 111.
16. Ibid.

17. Ibid, p. 105.
18. Claudio Marcello Costa, *Dottorcosta: Vita e racconti di un medico e della sua clinica mobile* (Fucina, Milan, 2002), p. 37.
19. Hugh Merrick, *The Great Motor Highways of the Alps* (Robert Hale Ltd., London, 1958).

ACKNOWLEDGMENTS

Fred Seidel saw the possibilities before anyone else. What started as a heated debate about contemporary motorcycle design became a dare to write about my adventures in the Land of Engines. No one challenged or corrected, provoked or prodded, more than Fred, helping a first-time writer avoid bad poetry. I am so appreciative of his mentoring and friendship.

I am grateful to Jonathan Galassi, who nurtured the book from its beginnings, nudging me toward the best of the material. The hours spent with him when each chapter was finished were among the most satisfying educational experiences of my career. Annie Wedekind shaped the sections and polished the sentences, coaxing narrative out of memory. My agents, Andrew Wylie and Jeff Posternak, protected and goaded me on, providing more inspiration than they know.

I would especially like to thank Daniel Lehrer-Graiwer and Brian Albert, my first readers, for their sensitive and insightful responses to the pages. Simon Hammerson is my motorcycle muse. To my Bologna family, Andy Eichler, Michael Paratore, Kristin Schelter-MacDonald, Christopher Spira, and Julia Vitarello, *grazie mille!*

And to my boss, a deeply creative and talented man: I am forever in your debt.